A Practical Guide to

WORKING
WITH
DIVERSITY

A Practical Guide to
WORKING
WITH
DIVERSITY

THE PROCESS
THE TOOLS
THE RESOURCES

JOY LEACH
with

BETTE GEORGE   **TINA JACKSON**
and
ARLEEN LaBELLA

American Management Association

New York • Atlanta • Boston • Chicago • Kansas City • San Francisco • Washington, D.C.
Brussels • Mexico City • Tokyo • Toronto

This book is available at a special
discount when ordered in bulk quantities.
For information, contact Special Sales Department,
AMACOM, a division of American Management Association,
135 West 50th Street, New York, NY 10020.

This publication is designed to provide accurate and authoritative
information in regard to the subject matter covered. It is sold with
the understanding that the publisher is not engaged in rendering legal, accounting, or other professional service. If legal advice or other
expert assistance is required, the services of a competent professional
person should be sought.

Library of Congress Cataloging-in-Publication Data

Leach, Joy, 1948–
    A practical guide to working with diversity : the process, the
tools, the resources / Joy Leach with Bette George . . . [et al.].
        p.   cm.
    Includes bibliographical references and index.
    ISBN 0-8144-0244-5
    1. Diversity in the workplace—Planning.   2. Organizational
change.   3. Communication in organizations.   4. Organizational
effectiveness.   I. Title.
HF5549.5.M5L43   1995
658.3'1244—dc20   94-44293
                                                                 CIP

© 1995 AMACOM, a division of
American Management Association, New York.
All rights reserved.
Printed in the United States of America.

This publication may not be reproduced,
stored in a retrieval system,
or transmitted in whole or in part,
in any form or by any means, electronic,
mechanical, photocopying, recording, or otherwise,
without the prior written permission of AMACOM,
a division of American Management Association,
135 West 50th Street, New York, NY 10020.

Printing number

10 9 8 7 6 5 4 3 2 1

Contents

Acknowledgments

Professional Resources, Inc. (PRI), is an organization development and training company specializing in promoting collaboration and empowerment in the workplace. Since the early 1970s, PRI has helped organizations meet the challenges of a changing workforce and a quality-conscious business world by maximizing their most valuable asset, their people.

PRI's work is built on the pioneering efforts of many theorists and practitioners in organization development and related fields. We express our gratitude to such professionals as Peter Block, Emilie Conrad-Da'oud, William Cross, Carol Gilligan, Betty Harrigan, Natasha Josephowitz, Kurt Lewin, Marilyn Loden, Ann Morrison, Charles and Edith Seashore, Deborah Tannen, R. Roosevelt Thomas, Jr., and Marvin Weisbord.

The book reflects the contribution of our talented colleagues with whom we have worked over the years: Rita Andrews, Dorien Bietz, Brian Booth, Carol Emmett, Kari Fisher-Uman, Bobbi Harada, Terri Harrell, Joya Jimenez, Mike Kostrezewa, Gail Lehmann, Carolyn Lichtenstein, Peg Long, Tony Moore, Dorothy Nelms, Lynne Revo-Cohen, Craig Storti, Shirley Thomas, Penny Thomas-Kezar, and Sandy Wood.

We would like to acknowledge Karetta Hubbard for her vision, insight, and willingness to mentor and collaborate with us.

We give special appreciation to Jo Ann Morris-Scott, Lynn Myhal, Joel Ramich, and Dick Ronollo for sharing their valuable insights and giving us feedback on each chapter of the book as it evolved.

We give special thanks to Robert Tennyson Stevens and Rae Thompson of Mastery Systems Corp. and cofounders of Organizational Mastery for sharing their conceptual framework of outcome technology and their permission to weave this powerful technique into the book.

This book is enlivened and enriched by the people with whom we have worked at all levels of organizational life. We express our deepest appreciation to our clients.

We appreciate the patience and caring support of our families: Maris, Ian, and Rich Goodstein; Paige, Ben, and Matt Eldridge and Vern George; Dave, Julie, and Joanna Jackson and Barbara Henrie; Colin, Alison, and Dennis O'Brien.

Introduction

For more than two decades, Professional Resources, Inc., has consulted with organizations and guided them through the process of creating environments in which all employees can be more productive. We have listened to people in organizations tell us what does and does not support the creation of the kind of environment that fully includes them as individuals and employees. In recent years we have consulted with organization leaders, created and facilitated workshops, and conducted organization studies that help people understand diversity issues.

It is the people inside an organization who hold the keys to the unique and specific changes their organizations can make. In the same way that a person eventually takes charge of his or her own growth and development, so does an organization. Diversity as an organizational concept has matured to the point where organizations can look within and supplement this with outside advice and guidance. This book is offered as a support to organizations of all kinds. It enables organizations to self-explore, reflect, grow, and change as they face the challenges of working effectively with a diverse workforce.

The metaphor for working with diversity is a conversation—a simple and rich concept. It is primarily through conversation that powerful cultural change can take place. People in conversation create connection, develop understanding, discover creativity, and form commitment to action. Through meaningful conversation, people in organizations create a vision of a diverse workforce. The vision then paves the way for new organizational structures, policies, practices, and norms that serve the organization as a whole and also serve its members.

The essential first steps are to allow the organizational conversation to begin and to create the opportunity for individuals to speak of their experience in safety. These tasks are not necessarily easy. For many employees this may be the first time they have been asked to examine and speak the truth of their day-to-day experience. For others, this may be the first time they feel that they are being heard. To work with diversity effectively, we must listen to what is being spoken, really hearing what is being said. Open, honest, and sometimes difficult dialogue becomes the catalyst for positive change.

This book empowers individuals within organizations to work with their own diversity issues, intelligently and purposefully, by engaging all aspects of their organizations in the diversity conversation. Through gathering information from its own rich resources—its people—an organization can create environments that dismantle barriers and foster full inclusion. It is precisely these environments that enable employees to anticipate, listen, and respond to the concerns and requirements of a diverse marketplace in ways that are highly profitable to the organization.

This book is designed to enable an organization to undertake a diversity initiative independent of outside consultants. It will also help organizations to discern when hiring outside consultants might prove useful. The approach guides the reader through the initiative necessary to open a field of inquiry and then take action based on the information gathered. We call this initiative "working with diversity."

This book is about how to create structures and processes that maximize and fully utilize the contribution of all the people within the organization. In order for full contribution to occur, each individual worker must fully participate. To fully participate, individuals must first be fully included. Therefore, inclusion happens first, then participation. Full employee contribution will be the result. In sum:

Inclusion + Participation = Contribution

The concept of inclusion is at the heart of this work. It expresses the shift from striving for superiority over others to the desire to collaborate whenever possible. Inclusion implies that we are all part of a whole, so that we begin to see "others" as a part of "self." To be fully inclusive, we consciously choose words that support and encourage people. To that end, we have carefully selected the terms used in this book. The following section describes the rationale behind the phrases and words we have chosen.

Choosing the Terms

Working with Diversity vs. Managing Diversity

The choice to describe our approach as *working with* rather than *managing* diversity indicates the importance we have placed on the careful selection of words to send a particular message. We cannot use old words to describe new things. If we are going to act in new ways, we can begin by using language in a new and creative way.

Our emphasis is on working with diversity rather than managing diversity because we believe that *managing* implies exercising control and direction. In contrast, working with diversity calls forth the challenge to be curious, inquire, interact, reflect, and experiment. In most organizations, "managing diversity" is applied prematurely, which limits the progress and obscures the shift in focus to be made.

By selecting *working with* rather than *managing* diversity, we communicate another message. Working with the infinite diversity among us requires us to be respectful, curious, patient, and willing to learn. The words we have chosen to describe the diversity initiative influence the very essence of the work itself.

Diversity

The term *diversity* refers to differences in race, gender, ethnic or cultural background, age, sexual orientation, religion, and physical or mental capability. It also refers to the myriad ways we are different in other respects, such as personality, job function, class, educational level, marital status, whether or not one has children, where one lives, the region in which one was raised, and how one was raised.

Given the number of ways people are different from each other, the conversation about diversity can get cumbersome and complex if we mention every possible difference each time the diversity issue is addressed. Throughout the book, when we mention ways in which diversity may occur, we have kept our descriptions simple and clear to avoid a "laundry list" approach. These brief descriptions are not meant to be exhaustive; instead, they suggest the multitude of ways in which diversity appears.

Diversity Issues

Diversity issues cover a broad spectrum. The most obvious issues include racism, sexism, classism, ageism, and hetero-sexism. Beyond these are many other issues that do not immediately occur to people as diversity issues. Work/family policies, performance appraisal practices, career development policies, and benefits packages are diversity issues in many organizations. In fact, all major organizational practices, policies, and processes that impact the lives of employees are potentially diversity issues. The very structure of an organization itself is often an unintentional barrier in a diverse workforce. As such, the organization itself can be a diversity issue.

When an organization announces its intention to work with diversity, it must first clarify to its membership what the terms mean. There is an all too common misperception that working with diversity is another term for affirmative action and quotas. The distinction should be made at the onset between these terms.

Group Labels

In selecting terms to describe diverse groups, we consulted with our clients, colleagues, and friends who are members of these groups. We have become more fully aware that there are common labels that some people in those racial/ethnic groups often find insulting or offensive. We have recognized our own discomfort with choosing one name for a group of people, knowing it is important that groups retain the right to name themselves.

However, using a combination of the names to describe each group may confuse readers. As a result, throughout the book, we consistently use the following terms: African

American, white, Latino or Latina, Asian American, Native American, and people with disabilities.

We recommend that in organizations working with diversity, people candidly discuss how to describe groups in their organization. Organizations can begin by asking people what they wish to be called. Differences of opinion should be accommodated to the extent possible.

Dominant Culture/Majority Culture

The *dominant culture* is the culture to which the people in power in an organization belong. In most organizations, the dominant culture is white male. Often it is difficult for people in the dominant culture to recognize the unique characteristics of that culture or the privilege that comes with being a member of that group. The *majority culture* is the culture of the largest group in the organization. There are instances when the majority culture is not the dominant culture, as when the majority of employees are people of color and the power structure is held by whites.

How This Book Will Serve Readers

This book is a simple and practical guide to an open-ended initiative to work with diversity in organizations. It presents an integrative approach based on our twenty years of consulting and training in organizations of all kinds. Our work is grounded in the stories of both the majority and minority members of these organizations. We offer support, suggestions, and creative ideas that we have developed in collaboration with our clients. Our experience has taught us that there is not one right way to do this work. The book guides the reader through the steps of opening the field of inquiry with all members of the organization, taking the information gathered, and turning it into a set of "action experiments" to address diversity issues.

The information in this book will be helpful to many types of people, including human resources directors, professionals in human resources and in training and development, organization development practitioners, federal women's program managers, total quality managers and facilitators, people responsible for reengineering their organizations to function more effectively, owners and managers of small companies who must respond to changing demographics, and pioneering spirits who desire to further diversity work in their organizations and are interested in suggestions and guidance on how to proceed.

The short-term impact of the book is that a reader can easily begin to address diversity issues in-house by following the step-by-step, how-to approach. The long-term impact is that the organization can create a more fluid, inclusive, and interactive environment that improves its standing in the local or global marketplace.

In sum, the book:

- Is user-friendly, written for professionals in the field and people interested in working with diversity in their organizations
- Offers a comprehensive, sequential approach to the diversity conversation, including assessing when and how to begin, gathering perceptions about how people feel about the inclusion/exclusion factors in their organization, analyzing the meaning of the information gathered, and implementing solutions
- Uses an integrated approach that combines a philosophical perspective and general concepts with step-by-step practices and procedures
- Includes a complete set of tools that can be duplicated, such as an interview guide, focus group guide, and survey

Structure of the Book

The first two chapters of the book—Part 1—serve as a backdrop to diversity work in general. Chapter 1 describes the historical perspective of working with diversity. Chapter 2 provides a framework for working with diversity.

In Part 2, Chapters 3 through 11 provide step-by-step instructions for organizations that are interested in conducting a diversity initiative. Chapter 3 describes an approach to determine whether a diversity initiative is the right course of action for the organization and offers guiding principles to increase the effectiveness and success of the initiative. Chapters 4 (Commitment) and 5 (Education and Awareness Building) are appropriate for all readers, including those organizations that elect to focus only on education and awareness building. Chapters 6 through 11 are devoted to the six phases of the organizational assessment. Each chapter covers a specific step of the diversity initiative: Planning and Communication, Involvement, Data Analysis, Feedback, Experimentation and Implementation, and Evaluation. Chapter 12 provides case studies from three organizations that have effectively worked with diversity.

Part 3 offers tools and resources that include data collection methods (a focus group guide, an interview guide, and a survey), brief descriptions of relevant training programs (e.g., Introduction to Task Force Management, Building Cross-Gender Communication, Supervising in a Diverse Workplace, Developing Your People), and a Selected Bibliography.

Part 1
The Foundation

1

Building the Foundation for Working with Diversity

A major cultural transition has taken place in organizations as people from diverse groups have entered and dramatically changed America's workforce. Our past represents a work culture that required people to fit into a business model that was based to a large extent on the traits and characteristics of white men. This business model, developed over several decades, has served the economic, political, and social growth of the country very well. However, the United States and the world are rapidly changing. What was once a desire on the part of groups to assimilate and be assimilated is now being replaced by the need to differentiate on the basis of gender, race, ethnic background, age, physical and mental ability, sexual orientation, and many other distinctions.

For many years, the task for individuals of diverse backgrounds has been to conform to a model of behavior in American organizations that has separated them from their individuality and their creativity. Sometimes those who looked different, as well as those who did not look different but in essence were different, found it difficult to survive in organizations. All too often, a monolithic experience in organizational life was created, where people tried to mold themselves in a way that would ensure some success, while leaving the richness of their diversity well hidden.

Some talented and persistent people made it through the cultural maze and made great contributions. However, given the realities of the demographic shift occurring in America today, we can no longer thrive in a global marketplace by utilizing only a few superstars who have become adept at doing business in ways that were once successful and are now too limited. We can no longer tell people who they must be and how they must fit in and expect them to bring us their whole, skillful, creative, and participative selves. We must abandon once and for all the concept of "let's fix them so they can fit in better and we can get back to the task of doing the real work."

What This Chapter Does

This chapter provides a backdrop and historical perspective for organizations undertaking a diversity initiative. It addresses four factors that affect working with diversity: (1) the history of the diversity movement, (2) changes in the business world, (3) the business imperative brought about by changes in workforce demographics, and (4) the accompanying shift in values that organizations are currently experiencing. This chapter discusses these four factors.

A Historical Perspective: Four Decades of Change

A paradigm shift that began in the civil rights work of the 1950s took solid form in the 1960s. During the 1960s, social and moral issues moved to the forefront. Groups of people who felt disenfranchised, particularly African Americans and women, began to publicly state their objections. Mistrust and anger were expressed in our educational institutions, homes, and organizations and in the streets. Minorities and women began a search for their own identities in rejection of the identities imposed on them by the dominant culture.

As a result of the passage of the 1964 Civil Rights Act, organizations began to hire more minorities and women. Equal employment opportunity (EEO) was emphasized, and organizations grew more aware of and concerned about fairness and equity. In an attempt to avoid more discontent and rebellion, "equal" treatment was interpreted to mean treating people "the same."

The 1970s was the era of affirmative action. Equal opportunity was emerging as a proactive business issue, not solely a personnel issue. Issues of racial and sexual discrimination, as well as "reverse discrimination," were taken into the courts. Organizations began to feel at risk about past and current inequities. Many workers felt caught between a desire for more equitable treatment and a fear of reprisal. Polarization characterized organizational life as the courts continued to define what could and could not be done in the workplace. Many people felt the need to be extremely cautious in their interactions with people in "other" groups.

During the 1980s, women and minorities sought to be included in corporations and organizations. Since the American business culture was traditionally developed and shaped by white men, many women and people from diverse groups attempted to assimilate and fit into this culture when they entered the marketplace. Many took steps to adopt the white male corporate image and values, perceiving that there was a narrow band of acceptable behavior and dress. By trying to fit those expectations, women and minorities reinforced the white male business model.

Between the 1960s and 1980s, managers were taught to see people as similar and to be gender-, race-, and culture-blind. Managers who wore these "blinders" saw themselves as successful and were rewarded by their organizations for treating people the same.

Now, in the 1990s, there is a clear emphasis on acknowledging and appreciating all differences. In response, organizations are expanding managers' roles and responsibilities, modifying the work environment to create a place where all employees can function well, and assessing the impact of the changing workforce on organizational systems. Managers and employees are being told to take off the blinders, acknowledge and discuss differences, and capitalize on the benefits diversity brings.

Critical Changes in the Business World

As we move through the 1990s to the next century, it is important to be aware of some of the significant changes that are shaping the world at large and therefore the world of work.

Working with diversity is inextricably intertwined with

Figure 1-1. Critical ways the business world is changing.

- Turbulent change is demanding that business respond quickly, creatively, and strategically in order to compete on a global scale.
- Demographic shifts are changing the face of the American workforce and customer base.
- Political changes are removing trade barriers around the globe.
- Advancements in communication, transportation, and other technologies are creating opportunities for expansion into markets worldwide.
- Training employees is becoming increasingly important as innovative technologies demand new sets of skills.
- Organizations are redesigning systems, practices, and structures to meet the demands of a changing workforce and global competition in order to build a committed and productive workforce.
- The information superhighway is providing almost universal access to a wide range of data. To provide optimum utilization, the data must be managed effectively.

success in the global marketplace and is shaped by the critical changes shown in Figure 1-1. Advanced technologies make global communication simple, and easy access to transportation has joined us to potential partners and customers worldwide. Businesses in the United States have the unprecedented opportunity to capitalize on the richness of diversity and lead the world community toward a new way of doing business together.

The Business Imperative

The business imperative for working with diversity is driven by demographic changes that are requiring organizations to learn to capitalize on differences rather than stifle them. The imperative is further fueled by a number of factors, including: the changing marketplace; the creation of new technologies; the entry of new competitors in the global arena; the influence of the women's movement; the strong voices of African Americans, Latinos/Latinas, Asians, people with disabilities, and other emerging groups; the influx of a new wave of immigrants; and, according to some, the evolution of the human spirit.

Figure 1-2. Trends from *Workforce 2000.*

- Women, minorities, and immigrants will account for over 80 percent of new entrants to the workforce.
- The pool of young workers entering the job market is shrinking.
- The averge age of a worker in America will rise significantly to age 39 by the year 2000.
- As much as 90 percent of new jobs will be service-oriented, and fewer than 10 percent will be in manufacturing.

The business imperative stems from several important demographic trends and shifts first identified by the Department of Labor's Hudson Report, entitled *Workforce 2000*[1] and issued in 1987. Figure 1-2 shows some of the prominent trends documented in the report. The business imperative driving diversity initiatives in leading-edge organizations across the country has its roots in three facts.

1. Our workplace is already diverse in myriad ways and is becoming more so. Attracting and retaining the most talented employees available is a crucial component of the strategic business plan of any organization that hopes to be successful as we move into the next century. It behooves us to work with this diversity in a way that unites a talented, committed group of people, supported by commonly held organizational values, around a common purpose.

2. Our workplace is growing more diverse faster than we can address the concomitant issues. It has become clear to forward-thinking leaders that the United States could face an economic crisis of major proportions if the issues that accompany our changing demographics are not addressed. It is critical that businesses learn to strengthen and fully utilize internal human resources, which mandates working with diversity.

3. The new global marketplace calls for cross-cultural understanding and partnerships. We are moving toward a multicultural perspective that encourages better understanding of other cultures and alternative ways of doing

business. The world seems to be getting smaller with each passing day. The multicultural marketplace presents many new challenges, including the necessity to build partnerships with businesspeople worldwide. Building commitment to valuing diversity becomes essential to the future competitiveness of companies across the nation.

The Shift in Values

A major shifting of values accompanies the critical changes in the way we do business and the business imperative. The challenge to North American businesses is to hold on to the best from the past while embracing new values that will lead us into a prosperous future.

As organizations make the shift from the old paradigm to the new ways of doing business, they are reflecting a new set of values. The task for executives and business owners in the 1990s is to create practices and principles that promote equitable situations and create a level playing field on which all people have an opportunity to succeed.

A new definition of equality that honors difference while assuring equity is evolving. Organizational leaders are taking action to develop employees to their full potential, increase workforce diversity, create environments based upon trust, and utilize teams of people with diverse backgrounds, talents, skills, and viewpoints to better meet client needs. Organizations recognize the importance of emphasizing collaboration, inclusion, teamwork, involvement, and interaction, both because these are the "right things" to do and because they make good business sense. In a global economy, organizations that have learned to capture the richness of their own diverse resources will flourish. They will be able to meet the needs of their clients and customers.

The organization of the future will be shaped by the values of the new paradigm, shown in Figure 1-3. The organization will consist of a community of people that have gathered for a common purpose and in which individuals add value by their contributions, skills, and creativity. In this fluid system, the organization continuously interacts with its internal and external

Figure 1-3. Emerging values for a diverse workplace.

Old Paradigm	New Paradigm
• Hierarchy	• Community
• Exclusive	• Inclusive/fully participative
• Assimilate	• Value diversity
• Give and take orders	• Build consensus
• Control	• Shared power/teams
• Compete	• Collaborate

environment, fully aware of the forces that impact its health, growth, and viability.

The level of inclusion called for in the 1990s and beyond is one in which all individuals in the organization can express their different gifts through full participation. If we can allow this level of inclusion to occur, it will lead us to a level of collaboration and creativity not yet experienced in organizational life. In this inclusive environment, everyone is in, everyone plays, and everyone wins.

In generating the vision of a fully inclusive, diverse workforce, changes in the organizational structure will be necessary. Through an assessment of the systems that are now in place, decisions can be made to retain those policies and practices that promote inclusiveness and replace those that do not. The scope of evaluation of an organization will be broad, investigating and evaluating ways people advance, how assignments are made, what behaviors receive recognition, what constitutes high-quality performance, and which policies are enforced in regard to work/family issues, part-time employment, flexible working hours, etc. In some instances the hierarchical structure itself will be replaced with new and innovative ways of organizing people to get the job done. This requires looking at the ways in which we conduct business to ensure that the best structures, practices, and processes are in place to support the organization to become enriched by its diversity.

In a diversity workshop that was being conducted in a large private corporation, an African-American man who had earned his law degree at Harvard spoke about doing all the right things to be successful in his career. He said that he was not sure if he would achieve the level of success for which he had worked his whole life. He commented that "even after doing all the right things to bring oneself to the door, someone still has to open that door and invite you in."

The focus on diversity is about inviting people in, actively and consciously doing things that bring people forward. For many, this invitation to participate will be a first. Many people of diverse backgrounds believe they have to fight to get what they want and fight even to be heard. Others speak and act in ways different from their natural style in an attempt to meet the expectations and desires of those with whom they interact. If people are required to submerge essential parts of themselves in order to succeed or even survive, they submerge the wellspring of creativity every American organization depends on.

When people fully understand the business imperative, they are more likely to initiate and sustain a diversity initiative in their organization. Many who have championed diversity efforts in their own organizations have found that getting a diversity initiative under way is a bit like walking a tightrope. One must move quickly and powerfully ahead, speaking truthfully about diversity to gain support from women, minorities, and members of other diverse groups. At the same time, one must be cautious about moving too fast since this can alienate white men in the organization, causing backlash that can sabotage the diversity initiative. The best way to counteract backlash is to continually communicate that diversity means *everyone*—including white men.

Conclusion

In working with diversity, a major challenge is to build consensus and sustain commitment. The questions become: How can we move from a mode of competition that destroys teamwork and creativity to a mode of inclusion and collaboration that enables us to become more efficient and competitive in the global marketplace? How do we determine which business structures and practices to hold on to and which to let go of? How do we create a community of employees united around a common purpose and empowered to add value by their contributions, skills, and experience?

The organization of the future will thrive because it has learned to transform itself into an inclusive community where diversity is valued and power is shared. Organizations must trust that now that the challenge is on their doorstep, they are ready and able to take it on.

Note

1. William B. Johnston and Arnold H. Packer, *Workforce 2000: Work and Workers for the Twenty-First Century* (Indianapolis: Hudson Institute, 1987).

2

A Framework for Working with Diversity

The framework for working with diversity—shown in Figure 2-1—is an ideal structure that in reality is often more fluid. Diversity initiatives can begin in a number of different places within an organization and can unfold in a number of ways. However, the framework serves as a guide for organizations to bring a helpful order to their efforts and be mindful of components that are necessary for success.

The framework begins with determining the organization's readiness for a diversity initiative. Based on the level of readiness, the organization makes a commitment to move ahead or not. Some level of diversity education and awareness building is an important next step. Commitment may stop here or may move beyond education and awareness building to a full organizational assessment and change effort.

Six sequential phases make up the model for organizational assessment and change. Once established, the phases are ongoing, interactive, and interdependent. They overlap and may be revisited at any point.

The framework is influenced by external factors, such as mergers, development of new technologies, and changes in the global marketplace. It is also influenced by internal factors, such as the organization's demographic profile and the type of service or product it provides.

What This Chapter Does

This chapter depicts and describes the critical steps of any diversity initiative. The framework presents a suggested sequenc-

Figure 2-1. A framework for working with diversity.

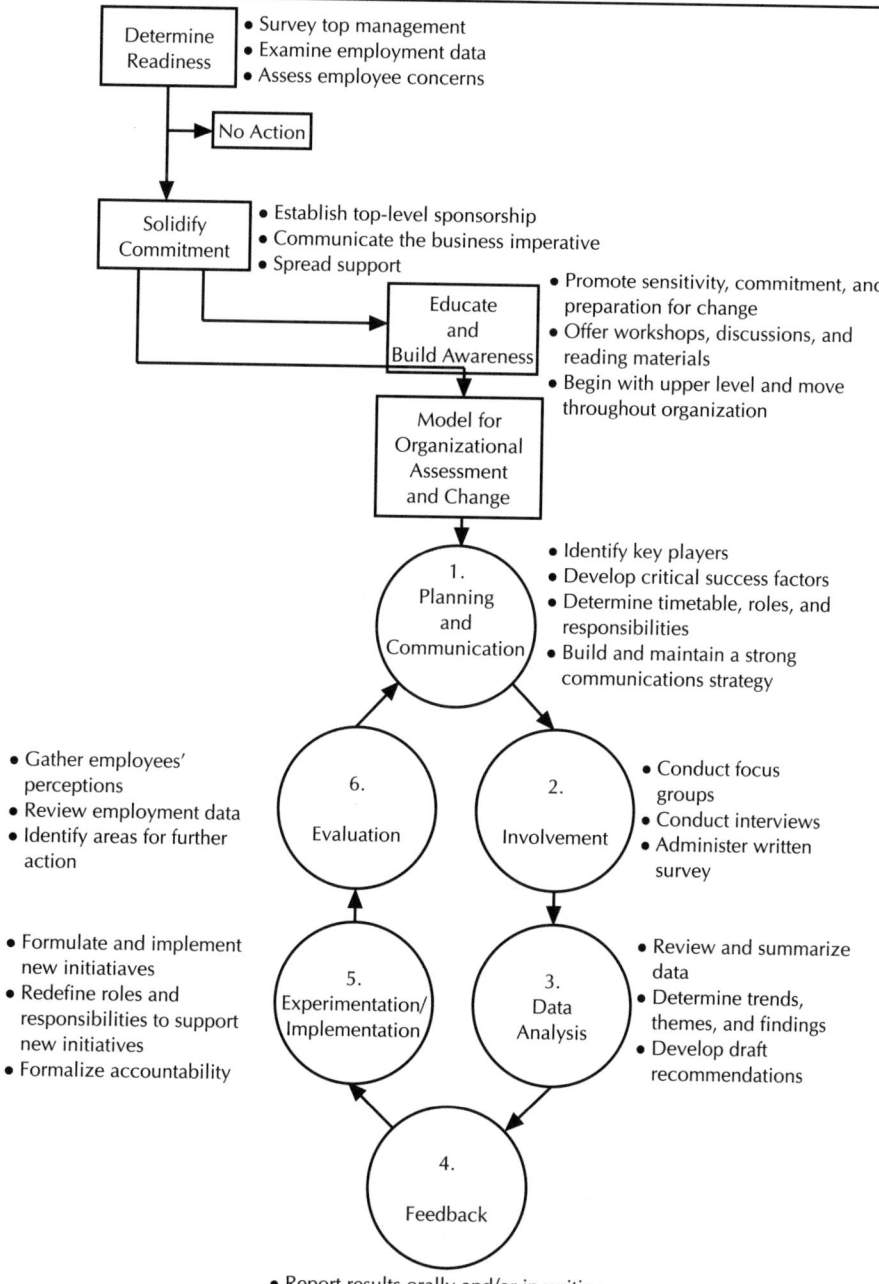

ing of these steps and identifies the key components of each step. Each step of the framework is briefly described. In-depth examinations of each step, along with examples and helpful hints, are provided in subsequent chapters.

Determining Readiness

The primary step of any diversity initiative is to determine if the organization has the need, willingness, and resources to embark on an initiative. The degree to which there are needs, willingness, and resources tells the organization how extensive its initiative can and should be.

There are three key components to determine readiness. First, there is a survey by and of the organization's management to help leadership clarify its own personal goals and perceptions about the organization's current state with regard to diversity. The leadership of the organization examines such aspects as the impact of diversity on the business, emerging concerns of the workers, general practices, and availability of resources. Second, management reviews employment data on facts such as workforce composition, job placement, promotion and attrition rates, and salary level equity in order to obtain a true picture of how diverse groups are faring in the organization. Third, employees are asked to bring forth their feelings, thoughts, and reactions about the topic of diversity, so that leadership and the organization as a whole can begin to assess the general interest and need to address diversity issues.

Solidifying Commitment

Commitment is a pledge to do something in the future by taking a solid stand in the present. The overall goal of this step is to secure and sustain an agreement throughout the organization that working with diversity is important to future success.

A vision of an organization that values and supports the contribution of each member is created by the leadership, and that vision is spread throughout the organization. A course of action is decided upon, and support begins to be gathered at all levels. The course of action may go as far as education and awareness building or may move beyond to a fuller assessment and change effort. Regardless of how far an organization decides to proceed, it is important that employees understand what the course of action is, why it is important, how they can be involved, and who is sponsoring the effort. This last factor is fundamental to the success of any diversity initiative. The leaders of the organization must accept and widely broadcast its sponsorship of both the vision and the ensuing course of action.

Education and Awareness Building

Education and awareness building are appropriate next steps in most diversity initiatives. They are most critical at the upper levels of the organization but are important at all levels. Education and awareness building increase commitment, sensitize people to more effective working relationships, and prepare them for organizational change.

Education and awareness building can take many forms. The most in-depth form is the workshop setting. Other options include discussions during staff meetings, presentations by or for managers, brown-bag lunch programs, and newsletter articles.

Moving Ahead to Organizational Assessment and Change

If the organization determines it is ready for a full exploration of its diversity issues and is committed to formulating and implementing new policies, practices, roles, and responsibilities, then what follows are the six phases of the model for organizational assessment and change. The decision to move ahead should be made with an understanding that assessment and change involve a significant commitment of resources, time, money, and staff hours.

The model is a "big picture" perspective of the entire procedure for conducting an organizational assessment and instituting change initiatives. The phases can be varied to respond to the needs of your organization by changing the order of certain actions, shortening or lengthening the time frame, or adding or deleting tasks as appropriate.

We recommend that organizations develop their own master plan, using this model as a guide.

Phase 1: Planning and Communication

The planning phase typically lasts one to three months. This phase includes two primary tasks: planning the entire organizational assessment (which includes planning the communications strategy) and beginning to implement this communications strategy. Specific tasks within this phase include identifying the key players—including a task force and a project coordinator—charging them with their responsibilities, and developing the critical success factors that will guide the initiative.

Key players are people within the organization who begin and maintain the diversity initiative. Typically these people include the CEO/executive, executive team, task force, human resources professionals, and project coordinator. In the planning phase, these individuals identify the desired outcomes of the diversity initiative in clear, specific, understandable language. They determine the critical success factors that will be used to measure progress throughout the initiative. They outline a specific plan of action, including timetables and roles and responsibilities to be assigned.

Communication is a central and continual theme throughout the organizational assessment and change effort. A specific communications strategy begins during this phase, which publicizes the business rationale and benefits to the organization of moving in this direction. The focus of the communications strategy is to ensure that frequent information is spread to all employees, so that they understand the commitment from leadership, what will be achieved at each phase, and the importance of their involvement. A typical communications strategy utilizes newsletters, E-mail, memos, regular meetings, management retreats, and staff meetings.

Phase 2: Involvement

To involve is to include, connect, draw in, and bring about participation and interaction. Involvement means that everyone in the organization is invited into the diversity conversation.

People can become involved by being asked to participate in an assessment of their organization. They might be invited to be interviewed, participate in focus groups, and respond to a survey. This is the inquiry phase of the diversity initiative, a period of time devoted to asking questions, investigating, and seeking information. Typically, answers are sought to questions such as:

- Who are we as an organization?
- Who are we as differentiated groups within it?
- What relationship do we have with one another, the organizational structure, and the mission?
- How are we treated?
- Are we fully included?
- Are we able to fully participate and contribute? If so, what supports this? If not, what is in the way?

This phase ranges from one to six months. During this phase the leaders of the diversity initiative first discuss how to collect data from employees (i.e., which approaches to use, how to select participants, how to select facilitators, and how to communicate to employees). They fine-tune the focus group guide, interview guide, and survey; decide whether to conduct walk-throughs (site visits); send letters to line managers announcing data collection efforts and requesting their support; and send letters to selected employees requesting their participation. Data collection efforts can overlap or be conducted sequentially. The key players then conduct walk-throughs, if appropriate, and request employment data. The most labor-intensive part of this phase is conducting focus groups and interviews and administering the written survey.

Phase 3: Data Analysis

Data Analysis, or what we sometimes call reflection, means giving careful consideration to some idea or information. It implies time spent thinking before deciding on a plan for purposeful action. This is the period in which the data collected are analyzed for significant findings and woven into a story for the whole organization to hear. This phase allows for time to analyze, consider, absorb, and reflect upon the data collected in order to develop a set of recommendations. The recommendations will in turn be offered for review, input, and revision by others in the organization. A delicate balance must be struck between allowing a period of time for reflection and seeing that the diversity initiative continues to progress in a timely manner.

In this phase, which lasts one to two months, the key players summarize the data collected from focus groups and interviews and tabulate numerical data from the survey. They determine the themes that emerge, looking for commonalities and points of difference across groups. From the themes, they develop preliminary findings and recommendations. To conclude this phase, they write a draft report, share it with selected readers, and then finalize the report and prepare it for distribution.

Phase 4: Feedback

Feedback means reporting the data collected back to those who provided the information in the first place. This is the time to share the organization's story as it has been told by its members. The goal is to communicate to the members in oral and/or written form what has been said and what it means when viewed in total. Feedback sessions offer people the opportunity to begin to talk with each other to determine to what extent the data applies to their department, work group, or team. This phase can be a time of revelation for some, justification for others, and discomfort for quite a few. Whatever the reaction, the feedback is seldom taken lightly. People wait for these results and are very curious to hear the way the information comes together.

Many possibilities can occur when feedback is delivered in an honest and kind way. People are usually willing to hear difficult things, and as they listen and absorb the feedback, many begin to do something about it. As the organizational conversation deepens, the diversity initiative begins to take hold.

This phase typically takes two weeks to four months, depending on the size of the organization and how employees are gathered to hear the feedback.

Phase 5: Experimentation/Implementation

Experimentation means testing solutions and trying different approaches to create a plan of action from the recommendations. There is no single strategy or implementation process that will work best for every organization. In this phase, the organization experiments with solutions to determine what will work and what will not. A tolerance for ambiguity and the willingness to change course when necessary increases the chances of success.

During this phase, which can last one year or more, the task force and other champions develop a diversity implementation plan complete with action steps, assignments, and timetables. The organization's leadership designates a director of diversity to coordinate the implementation initiatives and/or creates an implementation team consisting of employees and managers interested in participating. Members of this implementation team volunteer to research specific recommendations and identify possible action steps. Roles and responsibilities are then strategically assigned, once implementation initiatives are approved. A vision statement and diversity goals and objectives are communicated by management throughout the organization. An accountability statement is devised to track and measure success.

Phase 6: Evaluation

In the evaluation phase, the organization assesses its progress through a number of different qualitative and quantitative approaches. At a minimum, the organization compares its progress to the desired outcomes and goals stated in the diversity implementation plan.

In addition, organizations gather specific information from employees, managers, and customers through focus groups and interviews about how they perceive the organization now that diversity implementation initiatives are under way. The organization collects suggestions from these individuals about further desired changes in formal and informal policies and procedures. Performance evaluation standards are revised to reflect the valuing of diversity. The organization may also track employment data and compare it to the data at the start of the diversity initiative to assess patterns in productivity, profit, market expansion, and use of sick leave and turnover.

Evaluation is an ongoing process and is critical to the success of any diversity initiative. Baseline evaluations are recommended every two years, with comprehensive evaluations every five years.

Guiding Principles for Working with Diversity

Underlying the model for working with diversity are five guiding principles: (1) be curious, (2) be creative, (3) be committed, (4) come from outcome, and (5) speak truthfully and passionately. By following these guiding principles, organizations can open, encourage, and facilitate a continuing dialogue about diversity. Further, they will be better equipped to handle any challenges that arise and move the diversity conversation forward in such a way that commitment is built and a diversity initiative can take hold.

Be Curious

Working with diversity is a formal and informal initiative to explore people's experience in the organization. Engaging in an organizational conversation to conduct this exploration requires you to be curious. Being curious means calling forth the parts of ourselves as people and as organizations that do not know the answers. Being curious rather than judgmental is a challenge for some and a relief for others. The initiative is shaped by consistently asking for more information, by wanting to learn about people's experience of living in the organization, and by being willing to listen with a nonjudgmental attitude to others and ourselves.

As previously stated, the metaphor for working with diversity is having a conversation, with continuing honest dialogue. Think of conversations you have had. Who learns more? The one who is talking or the one who is listening? The critical information needed is gained by listening and learning before experimenting and acting. The goal is to be curious about the people in the organization, their perspectives, and the ways in which they see the work being done. The quality movement has shown us that the people doing the job have the best information on how to do that job most efficiently and effectively. The organization can benefit by taking this approach.

Be Creative

Strive to create an opening and make room in the conversation for meaningful dialogue to develop. Excellent conversationalists know how to keep a conversation going, especially during a difficult or uncomfortable time. The curiosity that you bring to the conversation will give you the creativity necessary to move the conversation along, especially when someone seems to be resistant or wants to shut it down.

Creativity is essential in keeping the conversation going throughout the initiative. When people begin the conversation, most are initially hopeful. However, during the conversation, if they perceive that nothing is happening in response to the information given, people may experience deep disappointment. Creativity enables the organization to keep these people engaged without responding inappropriately to the pressure to act on the information received. At this point, the facilitators of the diversity initiative must be committed to creating openings to keep the diversity conversation alive and to take creative action to achieve this result. This might involve communicating the leadership's strong commitment to address diversity issues, celebrating good news that has emerged during the involvement phase, or taking some measures to correct particularly troublesome situations that have come to light.

Be Committed

Working with diversity to bring about lasting organizational change is a long-term initiative. There will be immediate payoffs, yet these should not be mistaken for the overall results being sought. It is important to do what is required to stay current and to work the process on a daily basis. The result of being current, coupled with paying attention to what is and is not working, will reflect the integrity and the flexibility of the facilitators and the initiative itself. Hold on to what works, discover what is missing, experiment, learn quickly, and trust that if you pay attention, the process itself will teach you what you need to know.

Come from Outcome

The phrases *focus on outcome* and *come from outcome* have two distinct meanings. Focusing on outcome implies standing in the present and focusing on future outcomes. Coming from outcome requires changing places, stepping into the future (as if it were here now), and imagining from that new perspective. We use the process of coming from outcome because it is powerful and allows the participants to actually experience success.

The process of coming from outcome asks employees and managers to imagine what success looks like, feels like, and is like when the organization is fully inclusive and diversity issues are healed. Organizations can enhance and support the effectiveness of their diversity initiative by having clear and vivid images, words, and feelings that are associated with already having achieved their desired outcomes.

Using a licensed technology called Outcome Facilitation®, organizations can create their future by identifying first what the future is and then fully experiencing what their organization is like from the desired future and beyond.[1] For some people this may be the first time they can imagine that their desired outcomes are truly attainable and believe that they can participate in cocreating and enjoying a fully inclusive organization.

Speak Truthfully and Passionately

Words are keys for unlocking our thoughts, emotions, and belief systems. Employees at all levels can use the diversity initiative as an opportunity to learn how to identify dysfunctional behavior through language, end self-sabotaging communication, and consciously speak with passion. Clear, truthful communication is essential in bringing about desired changes in our organizations. As individuals speak their truths, people begin to live their truths. People influence and excite others who feel the passion and, in turn, find their own courage to speak truthfully and passionately.

Conclusion

With an understanding of the framework for working with diversity and the five guiding principles, organizations are well equipped to work successfully with diversity in a comprehensive way.

Part 2 describes the nine specific stages within the process of working with diversity. The final chapter offers case studies from three corporations that are experiencing success with their diversity initiatives.

Note

1. For purposes of this book, we refer to only a small percentage of the Outcome Facilitation® technology. Organizations interested in learning and applying the full technology (which includes using conscious language when describing desired outcomes) can refer to the audiotapes listed in the Bibliography.

Part 2
The Process

3

Embarking upon a Diversity Initiative:
Is It Time to Proceed and How Far Do We Go?

Diversity initiatives get started in a variety of ways in organizations. Often there is an event, experience, person, or group of people that trigger the initiative. An awareness may develop about the need to look at practices hindering the progress of certain groups. Attention to diversity issues may be driven directly by the marketplace, as in the case of an American company recently acquired by a Japanese industrial giant. Suddenly, cultural differences have to be acknowledged and understood in order to build productive working relationships across cultures.

Corning Incorporated's highly successful diversity initiative was triggered when management noticed the high rate of attrition of women and minorities. The CEO understood that Corning's future depended upon the recruitment and retention of the best talent available, and because of demographic shifts, that talent needed to be drawn from an expanded labor pool including white women, African Americans, and other racial/ ethnic minorities. As a result, in 1987, Corning began a comprehensive diversity initiative that continues today. In fact, many cite the diversity initiative as an important element in improving the company's efficiency so that it operates at a profit. Working with diversity has become an integral part of every aspect of Corning's business operation.

Unfortunately, some companies receive their diversity "wake-up call" by means of a costly lawsuit. One large utility

company was ordered by the court to pay out millions of dollars to current and former employees who were discriminated
against because of race or gender. This painful lesson will likely
lead that company into a period of self-examination to determine what changes must be made to avoid repeating past mistakes. Along the way, the concept of valuing differences may be
grasped, and the connection can be recognized between finding effective ways to work with diversity and achieving bottom-
line results.

A significant loss of revenue in inner-city markets was a
trigger for Avon. The company was able to turn things around
by placing Latinas and African-American women in key sales
and management positions. Avon altered its hiring and promotion policies when it realized the change in the composition of
the customer base in cities required a comparable change in
company staffing. Customers demonstrated they were more
likely to buy products from people like themselves, who knew
them and understood their needs and desires.

For one federal agency, a major shift in thinking began
when a group of senior-level women joined together to make
the organization's leadership aware of the glass ceiling that
seemed to prevent women and persons from different racial
and ethnic groups from reaching upper-management levels in
any significant numbers. With strong and highly visible support from the organization's leaders and a commitment to discover the barriers to these groups, this organization conducted
a comprehensive diversity initiative several years ago. The organization is now building on the recommendations from that
initiative with visible success in addressing issues of performance evaluation, career development, adverse work environment, and work/family issues.

What This Chapter Does

The goals of this chapter are to examine the ways diversity initiatives are triggered in the organization, assess when and how
to begin, examine different routes to begin the initiative of
working with diversity, and determine how far you are able to
go. As a result of completing the exercises in this chapter, you

will understand alternative ways to begin a diversity initiative in your organization and will identify the important signals indicating the appropriate approach.

The chapter begins with an example of how a diversity initiative began and developed in one large organization. It then provides a readiness assessment to determine whether to begin a diversity initiative. This is followed by a description of advantages and disadvantages of education and training or conducting a full organizational assessment. The final portion of the chapter includes guidelines for handling the concerns that typically arise when organizations begin to address issues of diversity.

How One Diversity Initiative Began

Barbara was an engineer for a large company. She went to Mark, the vice president in her division, to talk about her perception that women and minorities in their company did not have the chance for advancement that white men did. Mark was surprised at Barbara's perception and told her that he felt that the low representation of women and minorities in the organization was directly related to the relatively low percentage of women and minorities in their field. Although she agreed that this might be a factor, she felt that it did not explain why the women and minorities in the company were not advancing as rapidly as white men and in some instances had not advanced at all. Barbara went on to explain further that she was concerned about herself. She wanted to have a successful career with the company, yet was not convinced that this could be attained, even with her hard work and dedication. She sensed that there were other barriers to the advancement of women and minorities that might not be apparent to the managers and leaders in the organization that were having a great impact on the careers of the women and minority employees.

Mark was open to listening to the conversation. He sent Barbara to talk with Peggy, a woman director that he admired. He made the call to Peggy, set up the appointment, and requested that Peggy speak frankly with Barbara. When the two women got together, they had many similar perceptions, and

Peggy had even more dramatic observations than Barbara about possible barriers to women and minorities in the organization.

After meeting together, Barbara and Peggy shared their common perceptions with Mark and together they decided to work on solving the problem. They invited other interested parties in the organization to meet with them and become the core of a task force to explore diversity. Once the task force was fully formed, its purpose was to bring diversity issues to the attention of leadership so they could be formally assessed and addressed. The team got the support and involvement of human resources and together they reviewed the employment data. They found that women and minorities were leaving the organization when they reached a certain grade level and that the organization was having difficulty attracting and recruiting women and minorities. These facts indicated a need to look more closely at these issues. The diversity task force decided that its initial focus would be to develop a plan of action for hiring and retaining more women and minorities.

It is inspiring when an entire organizational change effort can be tracked to one individual, like Barbara, who took a stand and was then able to gather the necessary support to move forward.

Determining Whether to Begin a Diversity Initiative: The Readiness Assessment

The primary step in determining whether to begin a diversity initiative is an internal assessment of and by management. Through a readiness survey, executives determine if there is an apparent need for a diversity initiative. This decision can be made most accurately when executives gather data from their own ranks and from other sources, including available employment data. Based on the data, the executives can decide whether to proceed and which approach to take.

The readiness survey is a much more simple and streamlined initiative than the full organizational assessment described in Chapter 7. The readiness survey includes a set of questions for management. Managers can ask these questions of themselves, or the readiness survey can be administered by a facilitator from human resources, the organization development department, or the diversity task force, if there is one. The task force is usually a collection of individuals who are brought together because of their specific expertise and their representation of the diverse workforce. Their primary tasks are to gather information and make recommendations regarding a specific topic—in this case, effectively working with diversity within the organization.

If the leadership intuitively knows it is appropriate to proceed with a full initiative, the readiness survey can be skipped. However, we encourage organizations to conduct this mini-assessment because it provides the opportunity to get management's support of a more comprehensive diversity initiative. Further, it gives executives the opportunity to better understand managers' and employees' perspectives on the issues.

If the energy to conduct a diversity initiative is bubbling up from somewhere else in the organization besides senior management, the survey for executives can be used by the facilitator(s) to introduce the concepts to the leaders. The questions can raise management awareness of the need for diversity initiatives. Chapter 4 includes more-detailed information for employees interested in starting a grass-roots initiative.

The readiness assessment includes three components: (1) completing the survey provided in Figure 3-1, (2) asking employees to identify their concerns, and (3) examining appropriate employment data. Conducting a diversity initiative requires a willingness to look at one's strengths and weaknesses and to solicit perceptions from the organization's own employees.

Completing the Survey

The first step in the readiness assessment is to complete the survey. Based on the responses to the questions, executives will be able to identify both the extent of concern and the degree to which senior management's perceptions differ from that of other employees within the organization. They will also be aware of the organization's readiness to address the issues as well as of the possible existence of supports and barriers to full participation.

Figure 3-1. A readiness assessment of and by executives.

The organization's executives should answer the following questions as a starting point to determine if this is the right time for the organization to begin a diversity initiative:

- Would you recommend this as a good place for women, minorities, and people with disabilities to work?
- Do you perceive any advantages to any groups of people?
- Are there perceptions/stereotypes of any groups that might create barriers to success?
- Do people from diverse groups participate in policy decisions?
- Has the organization adopted a mission statement and action plan to implement diversity?
- Does the organization experience problems resulting from having a diverse group of employees?
- Are there any departments or position levels where there is little diversity?
- Does the organization employ people with disabilities?
- Are there jobs where people of one gender predominate?
- Are there jobs where people of one racial/ethnic group predominate?
- Are there perceptions of salary inequities related to gender, race, or disability?
- Are promotion rates higher for certain groups (e.g., men as compared to women)?
- Are attrition rates higher for certain groups (e.g., minorities as compared to whites)?
- Are ethnic, racial, or sexist jokes told and tolerated?
- Do channels exist to report harassment? Do people use these channels?
- Has your company been acquired by a company from another country?
- Have you acquired or established a business outside the United States?
- Is your client base diverse?
- Do you believe that your organization's future competitiveness has any link to its ability to build and effectively utilize a more diverse population?

For each question above, ask yourself:

- Are you or others currently concerned about this issue?
- Do you need more data about this issue?
- Is the organization ready to address this issue?
- What are you willing or able to do about this issue, i.e., in terms of committing resources, staff, time, and money?

Executives may find that they need additional information to get a well-rounded picture of where the organization is and to answer such questions as:

- What are people thinking?
- What are their concerns?
- What issues are emerging that need attention?

The questions provided in Figure 3-1 can also be used as the starting point for interviews of the top layer of the organization.

Getting Employee Input

In the second step of the readiness assessment, access the information needed from employees in various ways. For example, ask managers to talk with people in their departments and on their teams. Ask the organization to brainstorm about groups that they can talk with that already exist within the organization, such as groups for women, African Americans, secretaries, night-shift employees, overseas workers, gays and lesbians, parents without partners, and people with disabilities. Hold a town meeting to discuss the topic of diversity and ask for people's thoughts. Use an employee suggestion box.

Analyzing Employment Data

In the third step of the readiness assessment, examine employment data—the quantitative information collected by an organization, usually by the human resources or EEO department. The data can be used to view trends by different variables including gender, race, ethnic background, age, and disability. Areas to examine include workforce composition, job placement upon hiring, promotion rates, attrition rates, salary levels, and salary equity.

The employment data provide vital information about the current state of the organization regarding employment practices, equity issues, the existence of a glass ceiling, etc., and provide a baseline and a point of comparison later on. The information allows the organization to identify potential trouble spots. Also, there are some people within an organization who consider the quantitative data the only proof that a diversity initiative is warranted.

Look at employment data fully and comprehensively to determine what is going on in the organization. A superficial look at the data may result in things looking better than they truly are. For example, some organizations look at the one African-American man or white woman at the executive level as a sign that they are succeeding in efforts to promote women and minorities. However, upon closer investigation, a glass ceiling may exist—a point beyond which most women or people of any minority group do not advance because of institutional barriers that inhibit their advancement.

For example, in an organization where two African-American women had recently been promoted to upper management, the managers felt the organization was doing well in relation to diversity. From the executive director's perspective, this was a major step in the diversity effort. However, there was a great deal of disappointment among employees at lower levels of the organization. People noted that they were frustrated with the career development and upward mobility programs. Further, employees perceived that the executive director was viewing diversity goals too narrowly by viewing these two promotions as a mark of success. There was concern that the organization's leaders would not give diversity issues the level of attention the employees believed was warranted.

To determine whether a glass ceiling exists and if it does, where it is located, look for patterns. Where are people clustered? For example, are Asian Americans typically clustered in technical positions with few opportunities to supervise or manage others? In one organization, African-American women were employed primarily in support roles. Upon further review, the organization identified a glass ceiling within the support functions. The African-American women overall were holding jobs at lower levels than white women in the support functions.

In some organizations, women and people from minority groups are employed at the upper levels but only in jobs such as personnel or EEO. For example, one organization was pleased that sixteen minorities had been recommended for director-level positions. However, upon closer scrutiny, eight of the sixteen had been recommended for the EEO slot, a position traditionally held in this organization by a minority.

Making the Decision

Upon completion of the three steps (readiness survey, discussion with employees, and review of employment data), it is time to make the decision whether to proceed. There must be clear commitment on the part of the leadership to create an environment where all employees can be fully included, productive, and committed to business objectives.

The organization's leaders must understand the business imperative of effectively working with diversity before it is time to proceed. This decision should not be taken lightly. The ultimate success of an initiative to work with diversity is highly dependent on strong commitment from the leaders. However, if this is initially absent or tentative, people can build support at the grass-roots level in order to influence upward. With enough of a critical mass reinforcing the business imperative for working with diversity, management may eventually be convinced.

There are ways to proceed to at least get the conversation started when the leaders have yet to commit. In many organizations, a lengthy period of time may need to be devoted to advocacy and education in order to bring key people on board. The initial phase may involve a strategy to expand awareness about the issue and build commitment to a long-term initiative. Additional approaches include brown-bag lunches to discuss the business imperative; creating a link to an in-house quality initiative; scheduling a workshop in the area of sexual harassment, gender sensitivity, or cultural awareness; and featuring several speakers over a period of time for cultural events or around significant dates (e.g., for Women's History Month, Black History Month, or in honor of Martin Luther King).

The organization can also look to its colleagues and competitors in the marketplace to determine what these organizations are doing with respect to diversity. One company's top management was convinced of the importance of working with diversity when a group of its midlevel managers mentioned that one of the company's primary competitors had recently embarked on a diversity initiative.

Figure 3-2. Advantages and disadvantages of education and awareness building.

Advantages

• Underscores the value of diversity to the organization
• Increases interpersonal sensitivity
• Spreads a new language and set of values
• Can prepare people for the change initiative

Disadvantages

• Raises expectations for action that might not be met
• Does not surface and address organizational issues
• Does not offer future steps or opportunities for involvement
• Does not lead to deep or long-lasting organizational change

---

Choosing the Best Way to Begin: Education or Assessment?

The actual approach to working with diversity may take several forms. Typically, it involves conducting educational programs and/or conducting a full organizational assessment by gathering information directly from employees. Some organizations focus first on education and awareness building before undertaking an organizational assessment. Many organizations do both steps simultaneously. Under either approach, the readiness assessment provides the organization with important information about how to begin.

It is possible that after assessing readiness, some organizations will decide they lack the need, resources, and commitment to take any action. However, most organizations will ask themselves whether to focus only on education and awareness building or to make a commitment to a full organizational assessment. Knowing the advantages and disadvantages of each approach helps in deciding which step to take. These advantages and disadvantages are indicated in Figures 3-2 and 3-3.

An organization may decide that long-lasting change is desirable, and therefore the model for organizational assessment is the best route. Before embarking on this, check to see that the following necessary requirements exist: a perceived need

Figure 3-3. Advantages and disadvantages of organizational assessment.

Advantages

- Leads to long-lasting organizational change
- Effects change at all levels
- Identifies the most appropriate new policies, procedures, practices, and structures
- Builds organizational unity and morale

Disadvantages

- Requires significant staff hours
- Requires more financial resources
- Spans a longer time frame
- Can cause organizational discomfort by surfacing unspoken concerns and problems

---

to address diversity issues, clear commitment from the leadership, financial resources, staff availability, willingness to change the organization, and willingness to sustain a long-term effort.

The other route is education and awareness building. There are a number of reasons for this approach. First, if the necessary requirements for organizational assessment do not exist, an organization may decide to focus on education and awareness instead. For example, if commitment from top leadership is lacking, education and awareness building can often prove effective in building it. Second, some organizations use the education and awareness building phase as a way to gather support for a fuller change initiative in the future. Third, many organizations that know they intend to conduct an assessment and change initiative begin with education and awareness building as a way to prepare employees.

Guidelines for Handling Organizational Concerns

Organizations must be equipped to handle and move through the concerns and resistance that may arise at the onset of any diversity initiative. The four concerns most frequently exhibited by people participating in a diversity initiative are:

1. Concern of exposure and subsequent legal action
2. Concern that people will expect too much, too quickly
3. Concern that the focus on diversity will negatively affect groups who have succeeded in the past by fitting in
4. Concern that the diversity initiative will be divisive

It is helpful to understand these concerns so that they can be readily identified in your organization. The people responsible for guiding this initiative are in a position to help employees and the organization as a whole deal constructively with their concerns.

Exposure and Legal Action

Some organizations believe that "if people knew the truth around here, we'd be in trouble." They may feel vulnerable with respect to EEO compliance or other legal matters. Others may be concerned that employees' perceptions of their treatment in the workplace—how they really feel about working here—will be shared among employees or leaked to outside people or the news media, which might make the organization look less attractive to possible recruits. Some organizations resist finding out what employees think because they recognize that the "reality" expressed by employees may contradict their own positive image of the organization.

During the course of the diversity initiative, particularly when invited to participate in focus groups, employees may be concerned about exposure and reprisal for raising their concerns in a formal group setting. Therefore, it is important that the organization offer assurance that the information will be used wisely, anonymously, and in context. The organization leaders can explain that the information will be used as a starting point, not an ending point. For instance, if women in focus groups reveal a perception that they are paid less than their white male counterparts for comparable work, the organization can demonstrate a willingness to examine the facts and correct inequities that may be present. When upper management openly addresses a commonly held perception such as this in a timely way, it restores faith in the system and builds commitment to the diversity effort.

The organization can explain that no employee will be singled out in any way. In fact, it is a composite picture from the group that is desired. By collecting the data, the organization will be able to answer questions such as: "What is the common experience of African Americans within the organization?" and "How do white men feel about the focus on diversity?"

Organizations that have concerns about legal compliance can check with their legal counsel. Remember that organizations that are actively working to correct any problematic employment issues are perceived more favorably internally and externally.

People's Expectations

The organization can shape realistic expectations by framing this as a long-term initiative. Gaining a comprehensive understanding of people's perspectives takes time. The challenge here is to manage those who want things fixed immediately. The "fix its," who focus on fixing the problems rather than including people in the conversation, need help listening to people in new ways. When people are not included in arriving at the solutions to problems, they are unlikely to be satisfied or grateful when others make decisions that affect their lives.

People who are really committed to change but believe they will not be able to change things fast enough also need help to manage their concerns. For example, a midsize corporation reacted quite defensively when it received feedback from its organizational assessment. Top management did not expect the amount of anger and frustration expressed by African-American men and women about the lack of career development opportunities. These groups felt they suffered from a lack of vital information, feedback, and career guidance. For a period of time, nothing was done with the information. This inactivity added to the disappointment of many who thought this was a chance to move forward on these issues and confirmed the views of those who "knew nothing would change." In reality, the leaders were simply in an initial state of shock upon hearing the feedback and needed time to integrate their feelings and reactions before moving forward. After a period of reflection, priority was given to career development concerns. One year later, some important changes were under way, guided by a task force of employees, managers, and a representative from an internal organization development department.

If people are included and work on problems, they are part of the initiative. If not included, they often sit back and wait for someone else to change the system for them and complain when it does not work. This is where working with diversity is different from managing diversity. Everyone plays when you work with diversity.

In one organization, a decision was made by management that everyone in the organization would take a mandatory cultural diversity training workshop. People were not given a rationale for the mandate. It was not connected to any overall organizational objective that was visible to the employees. The mandate created a great deal of negativity and resistance on the part of the employees attending the classes. Many of the workshops were divisive and conflict-ridden. People felt coerced into attending something that only furthered their discomfort and resistance to working with diversity. In many instances, people who would have been supportive of diversity training were also turned off. Using this approach, the organization alienated its members and did not promote an atmosphere of valuing diversity.

Another organization that was interested in promoting diversity and valuing differences used a different approach. It conducted a number of focus groups with employees to see what were possible areas of interest for employees to explore. The organization discovered that employees were interested in some form of training in regard to differences. The employees recommended that the goals of diversity education would be better met if people took the classes in intact work groups. This approach would enable the work groups to explore the diversity issues (i.e., job function, gender, personality, job experience, and personal/professional balance issues) relevant to their own group. The organization followed the suggestions and had a successful diversity training experience.

A Negative Effect on Some Groups

There may be a concern that the focus on diversity will negatively affect groups who have succeeded in the past by fitting in. Sometimes the greatest resistance to starting the diversity conversation comes from women and members of other groups who have achieved some measure of success by assimilating and fitting in.

For example, several white women who had made their way up the management ranks and into the inner circle of leadership of a large high-tech company were very reluctant to take an active role in a diversity initiative at their company. In interviews these women made it clear that they were not going to do anything to jeopardize themselves or to make their male colleagues uncomfortable. Even when they acknowledged that sexual harassment was a problem in the company, they indicated that any focus on that particular issue would be divisive. "I've worked too hard to become part of this group," said one woman. "The last thing I want is for these guys to think they have to change their behavior because I am around. That excludes me and does me more harm than the joke telling and locker-room talk that goes on." These women have a legitimate concern. It is difficult to want to question one's own methods for surviving and succeeding inside corporations where the majority of people in positions of leadership and power are white men. It is risky business indeed to describe the reality of one's experience of sexism and racism or other barriers that may exist.

One way to address this problem is to have active sponsorship from the top of the organization throughout the management ranks. When this support for the diversity initiative is visible, women and people from diverse groups often speak more openly and honestly about their experiences. As the organization demonstrates its commitment to diversity, people of all groups begin to feel safer in bringing forward issues that would have been previously kept in silence.

A Divisive Effect

Change is challenging for all of us, and a fundamental change of this magnitude can be particularly threatening and difficult. It causes people to question strongly held beliefs about what works in organizational life and what does not. For many the focus on differences may be perceived as a threat to their job security. You may hear comments such as, "If we focus on differences, we polarize people. What we want here is for people to fit in, to be team players." Translated, that means, "Why can't they be like us?" For many, being around people who are quite different from themselves creates a great deal of discomfort.

White men feel particularly vulnerable as the old ways of doing business are questioned. They are confused by what they see as a shifting of the ground rules for making business decisions as well as for interacting with others in the workplace. Often for the first time, white men find themselves competing with white women, African Americans, Asian Americans, Latinos/Latinas, and people from other diverse groups. (Of course, people from those diverse groups have always had to compete with each other and especially with white men.)

When a diversity effort is begun, it is imperative that the organization and those sponsoring the effort understand the concern about divisiveness that people will express. Some people will worry that focusing on diversity issues will polarize people on the basis of race, gender, ethnic background, physical capability, and sexual orientation. It will help if these people realize that our culture is shifting in some dramatic ways. One shift is from the model of blending together to one of differentiating. The old concept of America as the great "melting pot" does not work for many groups of people who have discovered that melting actually meant assimilating into the dominant culture. The metaphor of a "salad bowl" rather than a melting pot has gained popularity with people eager to retain their cultural distinctions.

As people from different racial, ethnic, and other minority groups come together to share their experiences and to express their concerns and frustrations, some members of the majority culture become anxious. Their concern is that something negative might come from this differentiation and that further divisiveness will be the result. In fact, many think that if people identify with their own distinct groups, we will lose all we have worked for during the past fifty years to bring people together. Yet this differentiation is a stage in a natural and often necessary developmental process that provides the foundation for people to come together in equal and collaborative relationships.

Many people have written extensively about the evolution

of social identity as having four stages that individuals and groups move through as they grow and develop. The stages are:

- Stage I: Acceptance
- Stage II: Resistance
- Stage III: Redefinition
- Stage IV: Reintegration

Stage I: Acceptance

The acceptance stage is characterized by a strong identification with the values and beliefs of the dominant or majority culture. Individuals play out the roles they were socialized to learn and are not aware of any type of sexism, racism, or discrimination. If during this stage they are confronted with any type of unfair treatment, they see it as an exception and dismiss it.

Stage II: Resistance

Something usually happens that either gradually or abruptly jolts people out of the acceptance phase and into the resistance stage. Here, individuals begin to question, examine, and reevaluate some of the values they held in Stage I. Significant and powerful changes take place. Everything is in question. This is a stage characterized by much confusion and clarity, joy and anger, frustration and exhilaration.

The most common types of behavior during this stage are reacting to and against the dominant or majority culture. For example, jokes that people used to laugh at no longer seem funny. Individuals they once trusted seem to have given them incorrect or incomplete information. They react and overreact to the experience of sexism, racism, classism, heterosexism, etc. They begin to express rage, anger, and hurt, and they actively and passively question and confront the practices around them.

As people proceed through this stage, a cleansing takes place, a releasing of old information and beliefs. In both Stages I and II, the dominant or majority culture is perceived as important: In Stage I, the dominant culture was supported and accepted, and in Stage II, it is rejected. The individual is still dependent on being in relationship to the dominant culture.

People do not yet know who they are, but they clearly know who they are not.

Stage III: Redefinition

In the redefinition stage, individuals do not deal with the system but purposely separate themselves from the mainstream. They need and want to spend time with other people who are similar to themselves. They now begin to define for themselves who they are and what it means to be an individual and member of a specific group within our society. They begin to clarify their own values and have a new appreciation of the strengths and qualities of their own group.

This stage is often characterized by the naming process: Who am I? What do I choose to call myself? What do I choose to be called? Naming oneself is a powerful symbol. Historically, this has been seen at the beginning of the women's movement, with many women preferring to be called "Ms." rather than "Miss" or "Mrs." and to be called "woman" instead of "girl." This has also been seen in racial/ethnic groups, as they have moved from terms such as "colored" to "black" and from "Hispanic" to "Latino/Latina." Groups rename themselves as a way to assert their independence and remain self-defining. Choosing our name is one part of defining our role in the culture.

Stage IV: Reintegration

In the reintegration stage, people have a well-developed sense of security in their own identity. Individuals look at their own strengths and weaknesses more realistically and can appreciate the diversity of qualities in all groups. They can interact with all kinds of people without the fear of losing their values or identity. They can constructively confront issues that need to be confronted in organizations and are able to work with people at different levels of awareness because they have gone through several levels themselves. They are apt to see the world in many levels of reality. Because of this orientation, they can confront injustices without alienating other people. They are able to commit to working within the organizational system to make things work better for all.

The proponents of a diversity initiative need to be able to

help all people, particularly white people, understand the above stages. White people have been the dominant culture at work and often do not see their behavior as unusual or problematic. For example, when whites socialize with other whites, this is seen as normal. However, if black employees socialize together, this is perceived as exclusionary.

An organizational consultant was brought into a company by Jerry, its president, because he was concerned about what he perceived as troublesome behavior. Jerry took the consultant to the cafeteria to show her a symptom of the problem. He pointed out that African-American employees were at one table and Latinos/Latinas at another. He talked of his discomfort about these people not mixing with other groups. When the consultant asked Jerry if he noticed any other group eating with people of their own racial/ethnic background, he said he did not. The consultant then pointed out that whites were also eating together. Because the white employees are of the majority culture, their behavior had gone unnoticed.

Whites have been the ones who defined the culture in North American business and have had the power to include or exclude. Now the fear of divisiveness is based in part on the fear that others will gather together in their own groups and set forth standards, norms, and practices that will then define their own group.

In one organization, a white man said:

> We have been the definers of the culture and it was our group that everyone wanted to be a member of. Now we are seeing other groups form in the work arena, and this threatens us. In addition, these other groups are putting us into a "white group," and we don't want to be labeled as "white men." We do not want to be defined by someone else, and we don't want to be labeled as having characteristics that are now perceived as undesirable.

This man's statement is an indication of his developing awareness about diversity issues. By expressing concern about being labeled and stereotyped, he can better comprehend the experience of minority groups. No one wants to be negatively labeled because he or she is a member of a certain group. By gaining a deeper understanding of the costs of stereotyping people, all groups can take steps to stop it.

As an organization begins to address its own diversity issues, it may take years to handle the concerns that are raised. Although the experience may not be comfortable, it is healthy. It is better to work consciously with diversity than to move through these significant times unaware of what is happening.

The diversity movement is intended to be inclusive and representative of all people. It is not meant to include women and people from diverse groups on the one hand and exclude whites and particularly white men on the other. People must be assured and reassured from the beginning in words and in actions that working with diversity means working with everyone.

Generally, when there is demonstrated support for diversity at the leadership level in the organization and that support is seen and felt by the rest of the organization, these types of concerns begin to disappear. Just as these employees have worked to fit into the old culture, so too will they adapt to a culture with changing norms around diversity issues.

The most effective way to address these concerns is through a strong commitment to diversity, coupled with in-depth education and awareness building regarding the business imperative and rationale for embarking on a diversity effort.

Conclusion

As you move through the diversity initiative, remember that organizations that are most successful:

- Adopt an attitude of curiosity and view working with diversity as a long-term initiative, not a "quick fix"
- Have a strong commitment from executives to ensure that the initiative maintains momentum and that employees consistently receive the message that these issues are important to management
- Recognize the bottom-line connection and that by effectively handling diversity, organizations are better

equipped to remain competitive and often better equipped to respond to their customers

- Link working with diversity to other initiatives such as quality improvement, employee empowerment, and customer service
- Have an overall plan for the initiative and allocate the resources required (staff, money, time, etc.) to ensure the initiative's success.

4

Commitment:
How Do We Secure and Sustain Support?

The ultimate success of any diversity initiative depends on securing strong commitment particularly from executives, the board of directors, and other stakeholders in the organization. Part of the initial work is helping these people define their commitment to the diversity initiative and, in so doing, better articulate the commitment to support one another and the rest of the organization.

In turn, this commitment should be clearly communicated and reinforced at all levels of the organization. For this commitment to be built, organizational leaders must understand the business imperative, articulate this understanding clearly, and demonstrate their own commitment to effectively working with diversity. They will then be successful in building commitment on the part of the entire organization.

We hear many opinions about the diversity issues emerging today. Some say, "People will never manage diversity unless they have to, and you've got to pay them to do it well." They believe change must be motivated and rewarded through a person's paycheck. For others, the issue is a moral one and is driven by the "right" thing to do. These people believe, "It's got to be in your heart. You have to want to do the right thing. You have to have passion or zeal around these issues, or you cannot build the required commitment to make a diversity initiative take root in ways that will have lasting change."

Ultimately, it is both the business imperative and the moral imperative that become the driving force toward organizational change in support of effective diversity work. Again, we must emphasize the role of leadership. The leaders must come to terms with what diversity means to them, what they are willing to do about it, and what role they will play in working with diversity in their organizations. They should ask themselves questions such as:

- What motivates me?
- What do I think and feel about working with diversity?
- Am I willing to look at my own personal biases that may stand in the way of my being more inclusive?
- What am I willing or not willing to commit to on behalf of this organization?

In sum, leaders must weigh the competitive, business, and moral implications, learn what diversity is about, and make a personal commitment to make it work.

What This Chapter Does

The goal of this chapter is to help you get the program off on the right foot by building and sustaining strong commitment from the organization's leaders. This commitment from organizational leaders, funneled through a comprehensive communications strategy, will support a successful diversity initiative. The likelihood of a successful organizational change effort is increased when the reasons for undertaking the effort are clear, management is visibly in support, and employees are informed and involved every step of the way.

Guidelines to Build Commitment

Three critical guidelines for the leaders enable an organization to build commitment:

1. Take a stand.
2. Model the behavior.
3. Advocate and educate.

Each of these is described below.

Take a Stand

For a diversity effort to take hold in an organization, someone has to be committed and publicly take a solid stand. Because commitment grows from one person to the next, someone has to have the initial fire that can ignite commitment for other people.

Lew Platt, chairman of Hewlett-Packard (HP), made the issue of working effectively with diversity one of the company's three top business objectives worldwide, as part of reasserting HP as the best place to work for all people. The recognition of this issue by the CEO indicated that diversity would be approached as a critical business issue with worldwide implications. In addition, because diversity was one of the three top objectives, it became one of the cornerstones of the business plan. Therefore, at all levels, from vice president and general manager down through the remainder of the organization, diversity objectives were addressed in the annual business plans.

When James R. Houghton, chairman of Corning, realized back in 1986 that the attrition of women and African Americans was costing the company $3.5 million a year, he wanted to know why this was happening and what could be done to change the pattern. He created a vision for the Corning workplace in which diverse people worked creatively and productively together regardless of gender, color, creed, ethnic origin, lifestyle, or age. He committed his company to a comprehensive effort to value diversity, and he has repeatedly affirmed that commitment through words and actions. Today, working with diversity is a part of every aspect of the business, and Corning is in the vanguard of corporations in the United States, leading the way toward redefining the workplace. *Fortune* now places Corning thirteenth in its list of most-admired companies. There are numerous stories of organizations where the effort succeeded through the commitment of the organization's members after it was initiated by someone other than the CEO. Alicia, a woman who is vice president for human resources for a large corporation in the United States, recognized the critical importance of creating and valuing diversity at her company. She was recruited from another corporation that had been working with diversity issues for many years and was surprised to find a firmly entrenched ex-military culture at her new company. She said:

> I felt as if I had reentered the 1970s. The attitudes and behaviors of top management, all of whom were white male until my arrival, indicated a lack of awareness about the exclusionary culture they had created. For instance, military jargon was the norm. People had to attend all hands meetings, and unwanted reports were deep-sixed. A man who worked for me indicated his willingness to support an initiative I was about to begin by saying, Just tell me where to drop the bombs. In one location, if women did not answer the telephones, the phones went unanswered because the ex-military officers who worked there did not believe it was in their job description to answer the telephone.

Alicia attempted to demonstrate the ways that the company culture excluded people based on gender, race, and whether or not they had been officers in the military. She argued and debated with her colleagues on the executive team about the company's future competitiveness being dependent on hiring and retaining the most talented individuals available; she reminded them the individuals would have to be drawn from a much more diverse labor pool. She mentioned on numerous occasions the lack of diversity at the professional levels of the organization. When she realized she had become quite frustrated with their unwillingness to see the need to change the organizational culture, she decided to use a different strategy. Rather than take an adversarial stance against the group, she chose to quietly and discretely educate and build awareness with Sam, the young man she believed was destined to be the future CEO. Her primary goal was to show this very bright and well-intentioned man the benefits of building a more diverse workforce and to demonstrate to him the ways the existing corporate culture excluded people.

Over time, Sam began to trust Alicia and to seek her out for advice and counsel. He became interested in Alicia's point of view and wanted to know more about her former company's diversity initiative. Alicia provided him with reading material to broaden his perspective. She brought to his attention the concerns and experiences of people in the organization who felt their talents were not being fully utilized or their contributions were being ignored because they were not ex-military. She used herself as an example, expressing her feelings and experiences of exclusion by the leadership. Sam listened and learned from Alicia, who had until this time been the sole champion for diversity among the organization's leaders.

Eventually, Alicia was able to recommend several important changes in recruiting practices and in the way performance evaluations were handled—changes that were adopted with the help of her new ally. Alicia is confident that other changes are forthcoming.

Model the Behavior

The leader must "walk the talk." The leader sets the formal and informal tone in an organization, and these messages need to be congruent in order for the organization to take the effort seriously. For example, it is incongruent to espouse valuing differences while continuing to support job performance evaluations that judge people on style and not substance. This kind of incongruence is immediately visible to employees. It increases skepticism that meaningful change is possible within the organization.

In an organization where Martin, the CEO, had come forth as a strong advocate for diversity, he continued to work in an autocratic, hierarchical manner with the vice presidents one layer beneath him. Martin received feedback from some of these vice presidents that he was advocating diversity yet was not fully including the diversity in his own executive team. The vice presidents challenged him on continuing to work in the old way while advocating a more inclusive environment that valued and appreciated differences. They suggested that he model this new behavior by working more inclusively with his own layers of upper management, and they suggested that whenever feasible he "not conclude until he included." Martin took this advice and altered the way he worked with his vice presidents. Ultimately, this led Martin to working differently and more inclusively with general managers and others throughout the organization.

To the degree the leader is in support, other key people

will line up behind the effort. Some of the people who are major resisters may fall in line at least temporarily and allow the effort to get off to a strong start.

The support and commitment of other leaders in the organization, such as the vice presidents, general managers, and other members of the executive team, are important because they have the authority to commit resources. Furthermore, managers and supervisors at all levels will look to the leadership for support and guidance during the implementation of diversity initiatives.

The actual ongoing, day-to-day attitudes and behaviors of employees and supervisors will be most greatly influenced by these leaders. Although leaders can create the vision and be role models, the managers and supervisors create the support and maintain the actual changes in everyday organizational life. The strength and clarity of the commitment of the leadership will filter down to these people in a variety of ways and will be critical in creating buy-in. There will be multiple opportunities for supervisors and managers to practice the behavioral changes that a true diversity effort requires. Behavioral modeling may involve being more inclusive in decision making, becoming aware of and facilitating differences on a diverse team, helping people build on their individual strengths, and pointing out and eliminating bias and stereotyping that may be present in the work group.

Advocate and Educate

Organizational leaders that are well educated in the benefits of diversity are the strongest advocates. Everyone else in the organization will look to the leaders to see where they are on this issue, and the leaders can most effectively create the vision of an inclusive organization.

The benefits of building a diverse organization should be clearly identified and tied to the comprehensive business strategy so people can see how a diverse organization will pay off. Members of the board of directors can also do a great deal to promote the diversity initiative by carrying the message to the external community.

What if the driving force to work with diversity is not initiated by the leadership? Then champions can emerge anywhere in the organization. When they do, their first task will be to educate and build awareness at the highest levels. Awareness building from senior management is needed to create owner-ship of working with diversity and to build the kind of strong commitment to support it over the long term.

For example, a group of concerned people at a high-tech company became the advocates for their organization's diver-sity initiatives. They came together to form a task force because they believed that working with diversity issues was crucial to the future success of the corporation. This particular group was a mix of people whose experience in the existing corporate cul-ture (predominately white men) had alerted them to the need to address diversity issues. Five women, one of whom was Asian American, and three men, one of whom was a young African American, joined forces to develop a plan they could present to the CEO. The group also included two vice presi-dents (white men) and the highest-level woman in the com-pany, a general manager. The level and position of authority of these individuals had significant influence with the CEO. As a result of this group's willingness to address diversity as a con-cern and to recognize effective management of diversity as a priority, the CEO gave them his full backing, and a long-term implementation plan was put in place.

The CEO's memo to the organization's executives asking them to agree to be interviewed by the consulting firm working with the task force is shown in Figure 4-1. All the guidelines to build commitment are demonstrated in this memo, which clearly expresses the leader's support for the effort, models through his own behavior the kind of participation he wants from his management, and offers an article to begin to educate the managers.

At a not-for-profit organization, a grant to support and ex-pand internal diversity was the driving factor to begin an orga-nizational assessment. The grant was awarded based on the idea that when the internal diversity of the organization more accurately reflected the diversity in the community, support and interaction with citizens would be encouraged and the or-ganization could provide better services and programs to meet community needs. The grant included funds for the formation of a task force to study the issues and required an organiza-tional culture audit to ascertain people's perceptions about diversity issues, as well as their personal experiences in that

Figure 4-1. Sample memo to senior management on diversity interviews.

Date:

To: Senior Management

From: Head of the Organization

Subject: Interviews with Senior Management on Diversity

As I mentioned in the staff meeting last week, we have retained XYZ consulting firm to work with our diversity task force. One of the firm's tasks will be to interview members of our senior management to gather ideas, impressions, and insights on the general subject of diversity in this organization. Feedback from the interviews will be helpful in preparing a diversity implementation plan to manage new and greater diversity in our organization.

I encourage you to find time in your schedule as soon as possible for this important one-hour interview. (Mine is already scheduled.)

As background, I have attached an excerpt from the book *Beyond Race and Gender* by R. Roosevelt Thomas, Jr. The excerpt discusses the significance of this important development as the composition of our country's workforce changes.

I thought the final point in the excerpt was particularly compelling: "In a country seeking competitive advantage in a global economy, the goal of managing diversity is to develop our talents of the most diverse nation on earth. It's our reality. We need to make it our strength."

_____ will be calling your office to make the necessary arrangements. Thank you in advance for your cooperation. We will be talking more about this subject in the near future.

---

organizational culture. The task force became a rich resource of information as it mirrored the problems and challenges facing this organization. The greatest challenge was to solicit full support from the director of the organization in working with diversity. The director took very personally the news that people did not have entirely positive perceptions about life in the organization. Eventually, he became an ally because the task force

Figure 4-2. Ways the CEO and executives can build commitment at the beginning of a diversity initiative.

- Model involvement by participating in the initiative.
- Make a public statement of the organization's vision and philosophy of working with diversity.
- Make diversity one of the top business objectives for the entire organization.
- Have an education and awareness session for all executives.
- Officially appoint a diversity task force to study diversity throughout the entire organization.
- Provide appropriate funding for beginning the diversity initiative (for education and training, organizational assessment, etc.).

---

paid careful attention to internal politics, seeking out potential champions who had his trust.

Conclusion

In his book *Beyond Race and Gender,*[1] R. Roosevelt Thomas, Jr., speaks of a period of time in an organization that is devoted to advocacy. He emphasizes that organizational leaders must approach working with diversity as a business imperative that requires major changes in the work environment to support the full inclusion of every worker. When this understanding is firmly established in the minds of leadership and publicized throughout the membership of the organization, the organization will be able to successfully launch its diversity initiative.

Six ways for the CEO and executives to build commitment at the beginning of a diversity initiative are provided in Figure 4-2.

Note

1. R. Roosevelt Thomas, Jr., *Beyond Race and Gender: Unleashing the Power of Your Total Work Force by Managing Diversity* (New York: AMACOM, 1991).

5

Education and Awareness Building:
How Do We Develop a Common Understanding?

In this chapter we describe the purpose and positioning of both education and training in the organization's overall approach to working with diversity. We distinguish between education and training in our suggested approach. Education imparts knowledge and awareness, while training develops skills and instructs in order to improve proficiency. In the context of an organizational diversity initiative, education is also used to advocate. It is important to think of education and training as more than workshops or video presentations. Organizations can and should use every available vehicle to educate, advocate, and build awareness regarding the rationale for focusing on diversity and the specific ways in which it will be addressed. These approaches are addressed in detail in Chapters 4 and 6.

What This Chapter Does

The goals of this chapter are to examine the use of educational programs that advocate and create awareness, identify critical decisions that must be made before educational programs are initiated, and explore guidelines for developing and delivering the programs. As a result of considering the issues described in this chapter, organizational leaders can determine how to use education and training to support the organization's diversity initiative.

The Uses of Education

Education, advocacy, and awareness building are vital components of any organizational approach to working with diversity. Many companies have found educational programs to be essential in the beginning phase of a diversity initiative. These programs are used in three ways:

1. To advocate an organizational strategy to work with diversity
2. To begin the diversity initiative in an inclusive, supportive way
3. To provide the sole opportunity to work with diversity

Advocating an Organizational Strategy

Educational programs can be used to build awareness and gain commitment from the organizational leadership on whom the ultimate success of the diversity initiative depends. Buy-in is critical from this group of people, who will be responsible for allocating resources and carrying out the initiatives developed in the implementation plan.

A midsize company that provides services to the federal government spent several months educating the top echelon on diversity before taking action to make the predominantly white, male, ex-military workforce more diverse. The president, Tom, realized that his company's continued success depended on its ability to move into new markets in addition to the defense contracting on which the business was based. Tom recognized that the company's future success depended on its ability to market to a new set of nonmilitary customers and to hire and retain additional workers with the skills to meet these customers' requirements. He knew that his leadership team must have a firm grasp of the rationale for expanding its labor pool before commitment to diversity could be built. He also knew that he needed the support of the leadership team to change the composition of the workforce and ultimately to shift the organizational culture from being very exclusionary to one that was inclusive of a more diverse group of workers.

Tom took several steps. He brought in the author of a bestselling book on diversity to speak to the leadership team. He invited the CEO of a company that had been aggressively working with diversity issues for seven years to talk about the value of conducting such an initiative. He also invited a panel of public-sector customers to the company's annual leadership retreat to talk about their future needs. This particular meeting was eye-opening because the panel consisted of a man in a wheelchair and three women, one of whom was Latina. The audience was almost entirely white men. Another time, an external consultant guided an experience to help members of the executive team work with diversity issues at an individual level, viewing their own biases, preconceived notions, and stereotypes. At the end of four months, the leadership team was prepared to support the diversity effort.

Beginning the Initiative in an Inclusive Way

Educational programs can be delivered throughout the organization as a way of including all employees in a comprehensive diversity initiative, communicating the organization's reasons for addressing diversity issues, and enlisting employee support and involvement.

A department within the county government began its diversity initiative by taking all 200 employees through an education and awareness program. Diverse teams of facilitators guided intact work groups in a two-day experiential workshop that enabled participants to see the benefits of the diversity within their own group. Participants explored their own cultural heritage, looking at what they appreciated and disliked about being a member of a particular group. Diversity issues were viewed within a meaningful context both organizationally and personally. Participants generated case studies based upon their own experiences and worked on solutions to the challenges of diversity presented. By working with the diversity that existed in the work groups, diversity was made real.

Providing the Sole Opportunity to Work with Diversity

The educational programs may constitute the organization's entire approach to working with diversity. This decision may be based on the fact that education and awareness is a cost-effective way to show that the organization values diversity. This option may still lead to a more comprehensive diversity effort down the road.

For example, one large government organization began working with diversity by implementing a comprehensive, mandated multicultural program for all employees. Over a four-year period, the educational program significantly raised employees' awareness and resulted in many positive changes in the work environment. As greater numbers of people attended the mandated program sessions, attention was called to the fact that there were few women and minorities in management positions. This commonly held perception triggered the decision to conduct a glass ceiling study that would focus on multiple diversity issues in addition to advancement and promotion of women and minority employees. Because the organization was already sensitized by the training effort, it was ready to look more deeply into the issues that had surfaced as barriers in the organization.

Educational programs can sensitize and prepare people to deal more effectively with one another and with significant organizational issues. They can provide specific information about such things as the laws related to sexual harassment and the Americans with Disabilities Act (ADA). In addition, they can serve as another vehicle for gathering information about the perceptions people have about working in the organization.

Training, on the other hand, implies the development of specific skills that will enhance a person's ability to work, supervise, manage, or lead in an organizational setting that values diversity. Training can also provide teams or work groups with the techniques and skills to handle group issues such as handling conflict in order to increase productivity and overall effectiveness. The training initiatives are referred to in Chapter 10, and sample outlines of training programs relevant to diversity are provided in Chapter 16.

Education and training programs serve important and different purposes in the context of an organizational approach to working with diversity. However, neither education nor training alone can be expected to create lasting change in the organization's values or norms, result in revisions to policies and practices that will create a level playing field for all workers, or be a safe or appropriate channel to surface concerns and problems.

Critical Decisions about Educational Programs

There are seven critical decisions to be made before educational programs begin:

1. What do you hope to accomplish by presenting the educational program? What is the purpose of presenting the program? What organizational objectives will this decision support?
2. When will the educational programs be presented within the organization's overall plan for working with diversity?
3. Who will participate?
4. Will the sessions be mandatory?
5. How long will the sessions be?
6. What will be the makeup of the sessions?
7. Who will conduct the programs?

Each of these considerations is discussed in detail below.

What You Hope to Accomplish

The first decision involves what you hope to accomplish by presenting the educational program, what the purpose of presenting the program is, and what organizational objectives this decision will support. In most organizations, the purpose of educational programs is to increase awareness of diversity issues and the business imperative. The program can also provide the organization with a way to put the diversity effort in context, clarify terms, and explain how the organization intends to move forward to address emerging diversity issues. Another purpose is to give people an experience of exploring diversity issues in a trusting and supportive way that promotes ongoing conversation.

When to Present the Programs

The second decision involves when the educational programs will be presented within the organization's overall plan for working with diversity. The time frame used to conduct educational programs depends upon the organization's goals. Many organizations provide some basic information to everyone early in the initiative. Others wait until after the results of an organizational assessment are known to begin educating people about diversity issues and building greater awareness. When programs are conducted later in the initiative, they can be structured to include feedback from the assessment if desired. This enables the organization to focus specifically on certain problems revealed by the assessment. For example, if gender issues have emerged as a primary concern, the programs might contain a module to explore men and women working together. If racial harassment is occurring in a particular part of the organization, a priority may be to provide education and training to address the topic.

Who Will Participate

The organization can decide whether educational programs will be provided to all employees, to the leadership, or both. If the organization's leadership must be brought on board before anything else can happen, then the first programs should be given to that group.

Developing and conducting an educational program for everyone in the early phases of the initiative is most desirable. With this approach, people feel informed and included. Many elect to become actively involved in the diversity initiative by serving on task forces, forming advocacy groups, or becoming involved in company-sponsored community activities, such as speaking in high schools about their careers or tutoring in inner-city schools. The programs can also provide a safe place to bring forth concerns and perceptions that need to be addressed.

A significant problem arises when leadership is to participate in an awareness building session about diversity issues and a large portion of the leadership is white men. Some organizations have had to go through several layers in the organizational hierarchies to find women, people of color, and people with disabilities to participate. Without representation of diverse groups in the room, it is difficult to make diversity issues real.

On the other hand, the people from diverse groups who are asked to participate in these sessions must be very willing and well prepared to do so. This is especially true if the few people from diverse groups are asked to "recycle" their participation in more than one session in order to ensure that diverse perspectives are raised and understood. Frequently, minority group members have had the experience of informing and educating the majority group many times. Some are tired of having to educate, especially if no significant change has come from their efforts in the past. Some are willing but need to know that speaking honestly about their experiences will not jeopardize their jobs. In addition, members of minority groups should understand that these sessions are not a place to blame or castigate those in power for past inequities. Instead, they are a place for dialogue to begin. Hopefully, conversations will be initiated that will continue long after the sessions.

Cheryl, a high-ranking African-American woman who works for a large chemical manufacturing company, refused to take part in the diversity awareness building sessions for her company's leadership. "I am plain tired of teaching them about me," she stated. "I have been doing that my whole career. When are they going to figure out that this is about them, not about me?"

In another organization where women also felt that they had frequently communicated their concerns with no positive result, an awareness building session focusing on gender sensitivity was scheduled. In this workshop, the technique of the "fishbowl" was used to promote understanding between men and women. The men formed a circle to discuss their responses to the phrase, "What I hope people never think, do, or say about my gender again is . . ." The women observed and listened as they sat outside the circle. The process was then repeated, this time with women inside the circle and men outside. The exercise focused on encouraging the outside group to listen for understanding and on having them describe to the inside group what they heard. Many months later, men and women continued to reflect on that exercise, indicating that they had gained a clearer understanding about the experience of the "other" group. The head of the organization made several significant changes in reporting relationships and policies as a direct result of what he had learned. Powerful learning can be gained when people of both genders hold equal responsibility to communicate and listen to each other's communication.

Whether the Sessions Will Be Mandatory

Many organizations decide to make the sessions mandatory to ensure that everyone is provided the opportunity to hear the organization's message about valuing diversity and the reasons for conducting the program. In addition, everyone is included in at least one learning experience in which the diversity conversation can take place. Unless the sessions are mandatory, the employees most resistant or uninterested in diversity issues may not attend, and the opportunity to include as many people as possible is lost.

If the sessions are mandated, then it is important to have a strong statement from the head of the organization. This can be done in a number of ways. For example, at the beginning of the session, a memo or letter from the organization's leader can be read, a video from the president/CEO/director can be presented, or a high-level person can share a statement, describing the organization's intent and commitment to the effort.

The Length of the Sessions

Educational programs vary in length from a half-day presentation that focuses on the business imperative to a two-to-four-day experience that provides opportunities to explore perceptions and experiences in some depth. Organizations frequently choose a combination of programs that vary in length. Modules can be added to existing management training programs that advocate and educate the need for organizational change. There is no attempt made in these settings to explore issues in depth.

Longer sessions afford the opportunity for people to address concerns in depth, examine their own behavior, and envision a fully inclusive organization at some point in the future. These sessions require more than one day. Again, careful consideration must be given to the purpose of the workshop. It is important to allow enough time for in-depth discussion if participants are to explore personal experiences or discuss sensitive topics.

The Makeup of the Sessions

Will there be separate sessions for managers and employees, or will there be a mix of people from all levels? Will the groups be intact work groups/teams, or be drawn from different parts of the organization?

There are costs and benefits to each of these arrangements. There are definite advantages in mixing employees and managers in awareness building sessions. First, it sends a clear message that diversity awareness is important to everyone and that managers support diversity efforts. Second, much diversity will be missed if managers and other employees are kept separate. Managers and nonmanagers have much to teach and to learn from each other.

On the other hand, employees are not always willing to speak forthrightly about their experience in the organization. They have learned the hard lesson that speaking up about concerns can lead to subtle exclusion or even reprisal. If diversity education and training are to be provided to mixed groups of managers and employees, participants must be assured that they can speak without fear of retaliation.

Who Will Conduct the Programs

For a successful learning experience, carefully consider who will deliver the programs. Use experienced facilitators who are comfortable working with the depth of the issues that may arise. Ideally, the facilitators will have participated in similar learning experiences in order to begin to explore in a very personal way their own biases about other people. If people within the organization are selected to run the programs, have them prepare for their roles by going through a "train-the-trainer" program with several sessions. Part of this program can include a cotraining arrangement with professionals experienced in conducting diversity programs.

We strongly recommended using teams to facilitate the sessions. Use diverse teams of two to four people to most effectively model collaboration and teamwork.

Guidelines for Developing and Delivering Educational Programs

Here are eight guidelines for designing and conducting educational programs:

1. Create a safe learning environment.
2. Seek balance in the composition of the groups.
3. Work with the diversity in the room.
4. Make sessions experiential.
5. Model inclusion.
6. Know the purpose and objectives for the program.
7. Define and clarify ground rules and behavioral expectations for the workshop.
8. Prepare to deal with resistance and negativity.

Each guideline is described below.

Creating a Safe Learning Environment

Program facilitators are responsible for creating a safe environment in which people feel free to share their experiences. They also must be able to sense when people need processing time to work with issues that emerge. Great skill is required to achieve a balance between the content of educational programs, such as a lecture on the changing demographics, and discussion of actual experiences that enable people to get in touch with their own perceptions and feelings about sensitive issues of personal identity.

Charles, a young employee, approached one of the facilitators at the end of a one-day diversity training session in a government agency. He commented:

> You know, it was really hard for me to talk about some of the painful experiences I had in elementary school. Because my mother was Japanese and my father African American, I never belonged to either culture. The kids in my school were tough on me. I've learned to deal with that, but I've never talked about it much at work until today. Now don't get me wrong. I shared

my story willingly, because I think it is important for people to learn from my experiences, but I felt nothing was done with what I said.

It is critical that people be acknowledged by the facilitator for having taken a risk. Ideally, the facilitator would acknowledge Charles for sharing his story with the group and perhaps ask him after the session how he was feeling. Participants need to know that if they share a painful event from their childhood or divulge discrimination they have experienced, confidentiality will be maintained and nothing they say will be repeated by anyone after the session. Further, facilitators can support full participation by explaining to the entire group that individuals who take risks and share their experiences enhance the learning experience for everyone.

Seeking Balance in the Groups' Composition

When assembling groups for educational purposes, try to achieve as much diversity as possible in the groups. Think beyond race and gender to all kinds of diversity: ethnic, physical ability, sexual orientation, education, type of job, level of job, personality, etc. The intent is for people to realize the wide variety of the diversity that exists in their organization. In addition, by assembling groups of diverse people meaningful conversations can occur between people who may not usually interact with each other.

Working with the Diversity in the Room

Learning will be most meaningful to participants if they focus on understanding and valuing the differences of the people in the room. For example, if participants are a mixture of men and women, African Americans and whites, and Ph.D. and non-Ph.D. employees, the facilitators can structure specific activities to help participants discuss those particular differences. Initially, it is useful to urge participants to consider all aspects of diversity when defining the term. However, there is far more to be gained from an exploration of the depth of diversity. The facilitators can accomplish this by encouraging meaningful dialogue between participants who are willing to discuss their own unique experiences and differences.

In an awareness building workshop dealing with differences in personality type, the owner of a small company was in a subgroup with her secretary and several midlevel employees. It was of great interest to them that they could be so similar in their personality preferences, yet choose to express themselves in such different ways in terms of their careers. One member commented that other than social functions, which were awkward for him, this was the first conversation he had ever had with other employees that looked at who they were outside of job roles. He stressed the value of applying the information to the individual members on the team rather than just discussing the issues in general terms.

Making Sessions Experiential

Providing opportunities to learn from experiences helps people connect what they are hearing with their own experience, history, and worldview. This is more effective than only talking to participants about different cultures or providing them with theoretical models for viewing diversity.

Modeling Inclusion

Everyone should learn about their own culture as well as other cultures. For example, when the focus is placed on learning about "the other" culture or those "other" people, a dynamic is created that allows us to remain distant and apart from "the other." We might learn a great deal about a particular culture or group, but we remain separate from that group. When we look at our own culture, we begin to recognize how important it is to us and can better understand why other people value their own.

For example, a successful workshop on intercultural awareness that prepares employees to work outside the United States can begin with looking at the North American culture (specifically, U.S. culture). This helps people see how they are viewed when they travel and work in other countries. Then, when they explore other cultures, they can more readily see the similarities to and differences from their own.

In diversity workshops where the primary focus is on issues of race, there needs to be a sensitivity to balancing the participation of all group members. When only one group—for example, people of color—is asked to talk about its culture, this can set up the troublesome dynamic of the nondominant group teaching and disclosing for the dominant group. White participants also need to be asked to look at their cultural roots. For some whites this can be a struggle, since they have not identified with a particular ethnic or cultural heritage beyond being "American."

It is also important for there to be a balance of participation so another stressful dynamic can be avoided. If the minority groups in an organization are identified as the only ones who have experienced inequity, then those in the majority or dominant culture who have also experienced inequity often get frustrated and angry. All people should be allowed to express experiences they have had in the face of injustice or inequity.

Rich learning takes place when all participants are encouraged to think about their cultural heritage. Did they live on a farm in the Midwest, in a small Southern town, or in large Eastern city? Did they have extended family in the household? Was another language spoken at home? Was the church central to life in the community? These kinds of questions will lead people to connect to cultural roots. You can ask participants what they appreciated or valued about their cultural heritage. In this way, everyone present has the opportunity to recognize and appreciate their own cultural heritage, as well as others.

Knowing the Program's Purpose and Objectives

A department in a county government organization did a good job in setting an overall objective that was clear and precise for its two-day workshop on diversity. The workshop was designed to enable teams and team members to recognize the benefits of diversity in the workplace and to develop an action plan to minimize or eliminate personal and institutional barriers to diversity. The program served as a vehicle for people to raise concerns about institutional barriers and suggest how to remove the barriers. The program focused on increasing personal awareness and thereby improving productivity.

The specific objectives established for the two-day program were to clarify racial, cultural, and gender assumptions and stereotypes; recognize changes in the workplace and identify benefits of diversity; articulate how these differences can be used positively in the workplace; and identify personal and institutional barriers to workplace diversity and develop action plans to address them.

When designing educational programs, ensure that the organization is prepared to develop strategies to address issues raised by participants. When people are asked to speak openly in this way, they need to know that something will be done to address their concerns. Otherwise, negativity can result and move the diversity initiative backward rather than forward.

Defining and Clarifying Ground Rules and Behavioral Norms

During the workshops, it is important that everyone present understand the ground rules and is given an opportunity to participate in setting or modifying them. A typical set of norms and agreements established for a diversity program is provided in Figure 5-1.

Even with the establishment of clear ground rules, participants and facilitators may experience hurt feelings when discussing emotionally charged issues. Sometimes diversity training can impact personal relationships.

Help workshop participants understand and accept that for people to learn, they need to be able to explore, take risks, make mistakes, voice current beliefs, and try new ways of thinking and acting. Remind them that learning implies movement and growth; as such, no learner stays fixed in one mindset for long. A statement or belief that is shared at 10:00 A.M. may have changed significantly by 3:00 P.M. or may at least be more open to modifications in the future.

Preparing to Deal with Resistance and Negativity

People have many varied reactions to diversity training and awareness building workshops. Some find it scary to be in an environment where the beliefs they have held for a long time might be open to change. Some people feel anxious about examining values and perhaps discovering that their behaviors are not perfectly aligned with the values espoused. Others feel

Figure 5-1. Workshop norms.

• View this as a learning process, not an event.	• Actively listen to and acknowledge others.
• Take responsibility for your own learning.	• Pay attention to how you manage and support your learning.
• Stay aware of your thoughts and feelings and share them.	• Be honest about your own biases and recognize your choices.
• Be authentic.	• It is OK to disagree—not to attack.
• Take risks.	• Maintain confidentiality.

vulnerable to be in the midst of a new kind of conversation where the "rules" are new and the interchanges unpredictable. Resistance and negativity are natural responses to these situations. When education and awareness building are conducted sensitively and skillfully, people's fears and anxiety are quelled and their resistance and negativity dissipate.

Conclusion

The education, advocacy, and awareness building accomplished in this stage will provide a strong framework as the organization proceeds with a full assessment. The next six chapters describe the six phases of the organizational assessment, beginning with planning and communication.

6

Planning and Communication: How Do We Organize and Spread the Word?

An organizational assessment includes three major tasks: (1) collecting data from employees and managers through a combination of focus groups, interviews, and a written survey; (2) analyzing the data to determine common themes and trends across the organization; and (3) presenting the findings back to the workforce in oral and/or written form. Chapters 7 through 9 describe the steps in an organizational assessment.

This chapter focuses on two critical aspects of the organizational assessment: planning at the outset and communicating with the workforce throughout the assessment. Initial planning enables the organization to have a clear picture of the direction in which it is heading, including roles and responsibilities for the organization's members. Communication ensures that people are aware of the purpose, objectives, and timeline of the initiative; informed about their role; regularly updated on the initiative's progress; aware of next steps; and able to celebrate successes as they occur.

What This Chapter Does

The goal of this chapter is to plan the organizational assessment in an organized way; establish clear roles and responsibilities for the task force, managers, and employees; and design and begin using a communications strategy. As a result of following the suggestions in this chapter, the organization will be able to organize and set the stage for the organizational assessment and change initiative. Specifically, the organization will identify the key people, describe the role of each, list the desired outcomes of the assessment, formulate a timetable for action, and design an ongoing communications strategy to keep the organization informed.

The chapter includes three sections:

1. Planning the assessment: Initial steps
2. Roles and responsibilities
3. Developing a communications strategy

Planning the Assessment: Initial Steps

Planning the organizational assessment begins by assembling the task force and other key players and assigning a project coordinator. (Detailed descriptions of these functions are provided in the next section of this chapter.)

Initial Meetings of the Key Players

When the key players come together for initial meetings, they develop a plan for the initiative. Planning involves several tasks:

- Defining diversity for the organization
- Developing goals and identifying desired outcomes in clear, specific language
- Determining what information needs to be gathered and analyzed
- Determining critical success factors that can be used to measure the organization's progress as it conducts the initiative
- Developing a specific plan of action with timetables

The group may, for example, determine that its primary goal is to have a blueprint for the CEO within one year of its initial meeting. At a minimum, the task force, the person lead-

ing the task force, and a member of the executive team participate in the planning.

The group interacts with the leadership on a fairly regular
basis throughout the early stages of the initiative. After the
group members have developed their initial plan, they present
it to the leadership for input and sanctioning. This step ensures
that the leader is involved, supportive, and aware and can commit the necessary resources to the initiative.

Outcome Facilitation

There is a technique called Outcome Facilitation that can
assist the key players in creating agreed-upon outcomes for the
organization. The group can begin the discussion by creatively imagining what the organization is like when the
diversity initiative has been successfully implemented and
when employees and managers are feeling the effects of working in an inclusive community. As the group members begin to
share their individual experiences, a common outcome is developed.

Outcome Facilitation is powerful because it focuses on the
destination rather than the journey. It asks people to first know
what their destination is and then describe it in detail from the
position of already being *there*, as if it were here now. The approach is based on the premise that when we are in our current
reality and looking toward our desired outcomes, we keep ourselves from having our outcomes. When we feel removed from
our outcomes, we are often absorbed by what is not working
("Things are bad here," "This diversity issue sure is dragging
us down"). We talk about the resolution in the future tense
("Someday we will have this diversity problem solved"). We
see our outcomes as a vision or future goal that may or may
not be attainable. We give ourselves considerable advantage by
assuming success, believing in our outcomes, and acting as if
our outcomes are a fait accompli. People more readily and easily achieve their desired results when they step into them and
talk about them in the present tense.

The job of the task force and other key players who are
participating in this exercise is to define real and vivid outcomes, employing as many sensory descriptions as possible
(sound, images, feelings, etc.). The group specifies what people
are saying, how people are feeling, what kinds of programs are

in place, what the turnover rate is, how satisfied customers are, etc. Individuals also define and describe their personal outcomes. They specify what they are experiencing, what is happening around them, what they are hearing, saying, and feeling. These specifics become critical success factors that can be used as the basis for evaluating goals and objectives.

When the group members speak from their outcome, they say things such as, "An employee commented to me that for the first time in years, he feels supported and accepted by his peers for who he is"; "I noticed that in the cafeteria, people of all backgrounds, colors, and abilities are sitting together"; and "I feel comfortable being myself, my whole self, at work."

According to Organizational Mastery principles, the Outcome Facilitation® process supports and enhances organizational transformation by channeling an organization's desire for change through a systematic process into successful outcomes and beyond. The success is in direct proportion to the extent of the organization's identification of the need to change, its strong desire to make changes, its willingness to take responsibility for making those changes, and its understanding of and commitment to the tasks required for success.

Once the group has a solid and mutual understanding of the results of the initiative, with established critical success factors, they can create an overall timetable for the initiative, design a communications strategy, and begin communicating with people about roles and responsibilities.

Roles and Responsibilities

Diversity initiatives include the CEO/executive, executive team, task force, project coordinator, human resources department, and all employees. In many initiatives, it is also helpful to use external consultants to supplement the expertise of the organization's members. Descriptions of each role are given below.

CEO/Executive

This person is the sponsor of the diversity initiative. Ideally, the leader is able to articulate the vision for the future that becomes the driving force of the diversity initiative. He or she strongly and continually demonstrates commitment to this initiative. The CEO:

- Commits the organizational resources and staff time necessary to support the initiative
- Selects the task force leader
- Sanctions the entire task force with the authority to accomplish its objectives
- Clearly communicates to line managers and supervisors that he/she has authorized task force members to commit the time required to the diversity initiative, and requests the managers' support in letting these individuals attend task force meetings
- Remains involved to meet with the task force members, as appropriate

Executive Team

This team consists of two to four senior people, such as the head of personnel or human resources, the chief administrative officer, and other important decision makers. The executive team:

- Helps design the overall plan for working with diversity
- Clarifies objectives
- Provides the "big picture," the broad organizational perspective
- Explains the organizational culture
- Allocates resources/budget
- Discusses issues such as how to support employees for their time invested
- Reinforces the communications strategy at meetings and key events
- Discusses accountability measures

Task Force

The task force is a group of between ten and twelve individuals who have volunteered or been assigned to work together to gather information, identify problem areas, develop recommendations, and write a report regarding how the organization can work more effectively with diversity. The task force works together for a limited duration and disbands when it has completed its charge. Ideal candidates to participate on the task force are people of action with sensitivity to various types of diversity, foresight to understand the importance of this initiative, and willingness to make a significant commitment of time and energy, and/or people who may already be involved in advocacy or support groups within the organization. This task force is essential to the ultimate success of the diversity initiative and particularly to ongoing communication with the organization's members.

The task force may be appointed, emerge on its own, or be assembled in response to a call for volunteers. The most positive aspect of volunteerism is that volunteers often bring a passion and investment to the work. This creates enthusiasm and adds momentum to the task force function.

Volunteers need to have solid support from the leadership in order to make sure they can be released for task force meetings and perform duties related to the task force. At times the direct supervisors and managers of task force members can be resistant to the idea of losing their employees for the time required for task force involvement. In this case, communication from leaders to supervisors and managers is necessary to reinforce the value of the task force.

Whether members volunteer or are appointed, it is important to be sure there is representation of diversity. The task force members represent diverse groups within the organization and have an explicit responsibility to represent their constituency. They represent a diagonal cross section of the organization in terms of gender, race, ethnic background, age, disability, sexual orientation, tenure, function, grade, and geographical location (e.g., including representation of out-of-state and overseas workers). In representing their constituents, the task force members can bring information and possible insight into organizational supports (those forces in the organization that facilitate the diversity initiative) and resisters (those forces in the organization that present barriers to the diversity initiative).

It is powerful to include employees at all levels on the task force. Employee involvement leads to greater investment. When employees are given new responsibilities and opportunities to interact with people across the organization, and when they are supported in these roles, they become empowered. This helps to build and maintain commitment throughout the initiative and results in a win-win situation, where the employees and the organization benefit.

Task force members make the commitment to be a working member of the team (both during and in between meetings), complete their assignments on time, and test their assumptions and conclusions with their constituents. Each task force member should have an alternate to ensure representation at each meeting.

The task force includes various roles, such as a leader (typically the project coordinator), recorder (to take notes), and support staff (to handle meeting logistics, copying, scheduling, and room arrangements). In addition, the task force may appoint a facilitator to guide the group discussion. This person may be the same as or different from the project coordinator.

The task force members:

- Maintain communication with their constituents to provide the opportunity for the organizational conversation to occur
- Facilitate the dialogue, which must be a continuing flow of information from the task force up to the executive team and the leader and out to employees
- Serve as the eyes and ears of the organization
- Develop and facilitate the communications strategy
- Provide special insight about supports and resisters to the diversity initiative
- Review data collection instruments (survey, focus group guide, interview guide)
- Receive project updates/feedback on how the project is going, and share success stories as they occur
- Gather support for the project
- Participate in compiling the report on the organizational assessment and recommendations
- Provide feedback and suggestions about how best to present the report to the rest of the organization

Project Coordinator

This person is the administrator, manager, and facilitator of all aspects of the organizational assessment. The project coordinator is often seen as a champion of the diversity effort and is critical to its success.

The project coordinator is appointed by the CEO or executive team. In some organizations, a director of diversity is appointed initially to fill this role. In other organizations, the facilitator gets the initiative off the ground, ensures that key people are involved, and coordinates the communications strategy. Most typically, the project coordinator is either a member of the executive team (giving tremendous organizational weight and power to the position), a human resources professional (giving greater access and knowledge as to how personnel data have been gathered and tracked in the past), or the task force leader (ensuring a strong link between the task force and the major players of the organization).

The ideal candidate must have strong interpersonal skills, a collaborative work style, strong written and verbal communications skills, the confidence of the leader and the trust of others with whom he or she must interact, and a solid understanding of the business imperative and the dynamics of working with diversity issues (e.g., how to work through resistance and gather support for the effort). Further, the individual must realize the full business impact of effectively working with diversity; understand the big picture; be able to identify resisters and supportors who might not be clearly visible; be interpersonally effective; and have relationships with diverse members of the organization.

The project coordinator:

- Manages all aspects of the initiative on a day-to-day basis
- Understands and articulates the vision for this diversity initiative and the business rationale for undertaking it
- Is the communications link with the CEO, the executive team, the task force, and the external consultant if there is one
- Manages necessary administrative tasks (letters, memos, invitations to focus groups, etc.)

- Coordinates and directs all activities (e.g., the scheduling of focus groups and executive interviews)
- Communicates fully and effectively with the task force members
- Manages the resources allocated to the task force
- Leads and possibly facilitates task force meetings
- Receives data from focus groups and interviews

Human Resources

The human resources department provides support to the diversity initiative in the following ways:

- Gathers relevant employment data
- Identifies areas in human resources where ongoing diversity initiatives have already begun (for example, diversity retention and community outreach) and provides feedback in these areas
- Offers support to the data collection phase

Employees

Employees provide the information on which the organizational assessment is based. They can be invited to participate in several ways, such as by:

- Answering the questionnaire
- Participating in focus/listening groups
- Hearing the findings and recommendations in feedback sessions
- Volunteering to serve in the implementation phase of the diversity initiative

External Consultants

Many times in large organizations, there are teams of internal consultants in the human resources, organization development, and training departments. The diversity task force is likely to work with these internal consultants in some way. In those organizations that do not have a consulting team or similar resources in-house, the diversity task force may decide that the use of external resources would be helpful.

Consultants (external and internal) are particularly helpful for tasks such as:

- Strategizing the overall approach to the diversity initiative
- Presenting information on the business imperative and fostering commitment by educating and building awareness
- Assisting with the design of the written survey for employees (use consultants with skills in statistical analysis)
- Conducting the focus groups (use consultants with facilitation experience)
- Assisting with summarizing and analyzing the information from employees and synthesizing the recommendations from the findings
- Designing a prototype feedback session based on the draft final report
- Assisting with conducting some of the feedback sessions
- Delivering some of the services identified in the implementation plan, such as designing and conducting training programs, establishing an alternative work schedule program, and setting up a day care facility

Developing a Communications Strategy

A communications strategy is a multifaceted plan to keep members of the organization informed throughout the organizational assessment. The objectives of the communications strategy are to: broadcast the business rationale for working with diversity, build and maintain support, involve the whole system, and provide continuous feedback and ongoing communication about what is happening and why to members of the organization.

In thinking through a strategy, consider organizational politics. Ask questions such as:

- What are we trying to achieve at this point?
- Who do we need to involve?
- Who needs to know and when?
- Who are the gatekeepers who could block or support the assessment?
- How will a particular person or group be able to really "hear" what is being said?
- How can we communicate the leadership's commitment to the diversity initiative?

The first step in any communications strategy is to outline the business rationale and the benefits to the organization for moving in this direction. The challenge is to communicate frequently at the beginning of the initiative to assure people of leadership's commitment. This can be done through newsletters, regular meetings, at management retreats and at staff and town meetings. These communications initiatives set the tone so people will understand the overall effort and the rationale behind it. As a result, when people are asked to participate (e.g., through task force involvement, listening/focus groups, surveys, and interviews), they will understand how important their involvement is and how it will be linked to the overall effort.

Clear commitment creates a safe space for people to speak about their perceptions and experiences. Without this commitment, valuable information about the current state of the organization may be missed. In turn, employees may express cynicism or skepticism about meaningful organizational change.

Listed below are six key points to remember in thinking through a communications strategy.

1. Ask and listen.
2. Keep the channels of communication open throughout the diversity initiative.
3. Spread good news.
4. Be creative when addressing resistance.

5. Provide a realistic time frame for change to occur.
6. Be flexible.

Each point is discussed below.

Asking and Listening

It is important to tell people that they will be invited to participate through focus groups, surveys, and/or interviews. This prepares people and helps them to know what to expect. Ask and listen throughout the organizational assessment. The success of the assessment depends on how willing people are to share their stories. Meaningful change can begin to occur when people talk openly about their experience and are heard.

Keeping the Channels of Communication Open

During each phase of the organizational assessment, people desire information about what is happening and why. Continual updates can be provided in staff meetings and newsletters and during other organizational functions. Other forms of communication include making resources available to employees, such as relevant articles, videos, and publications. These can be distributed to individuals or to central offices or made available in the corporate library.

Communication not only helps establish an accurate picture of organizational progress, it also can correct misconceptions when they occur. In one large federal agency, the office grapevine was hard at work attributing to the diversity task force all kinds of power it did not have or want. It was rumored that this task force was changing an agency policy that would negatively affect some employees in regard to having the opportunity to work at home. As the rumor spread, more and more people began to suspect the task force of misusing its power. This misconception was countered with a memo to all employees reiterating the task force mission and the parameters of its responsibilities. Task force members also diffused the problem by talking with people throughout the organization to correct their perceptions of what activities the task force was actually working on at the time.

People must understand what is going on and why and how their involvement will be linked to the overall effort. A sound communications strategy combined with task force involvement from the beginning of a diversity initiative helps create a safe place for the organization's "story" to be told.

People who are involved in the planning and strategy development often become important champions of the effort who can help move the initiative forward. They become the bearers of good news—the "town criers" who go from group to group communicating positive stories, reconfirming tales of commitment and sponsorship from the leaders.

For example, Terry, a high-powered woman in a large organization, attended most upper-level management meetings and retreats in her division. She used these experiences to relate positive accomplishments of the task force and tied the examples to a proactive benefit for the division. Her strategy was to always relate the initiative to the organizational goals, framing the effort as having significant payoffs to the organization rather than being an end in itself. She found opportunities for people to participate in the diversity initiative by suggesting specific things they could do in their own departments or teams. She believed in people being proactive, asking themselves and others around them what they could begin doing right away to get the group moving in the right direction. She was a true advocate of this diversity initiative by tying it to the organization's larger mission and sparking action in her colleagues.

Spreading Good News

As the communications strategy is put into place and people hear the message that organizational change—even transformation—may be at hand, champions come forward in support of the effort and are willing to help move it forward. Recognizing support and celebrating successes are essential to moving the diversity initiative along expediently. For example, one company set aside funds for their scholarship program due to the diversity initiative and then announced this good news in their company newsletter.

Support is present when you hear phases such as:

- "It's about time!"
- "This organization has to begin to work on the barriers preventing minorities from moving into management jobs."
- "We must diversify at all levels."
- "Where are the upward mobility programs?"
- "This effort is a wonderful idea. I hope some racial bitterness will be dissolved."
- "Everyone must work united, not divided, for this organization to get the job done."
- "This questionnaire is a good step in the right direction."

Capitalizing and building on that support is crucial. Sometimes support comes from sources you may not have anticipated. Often it comes from people who can bring a solid commitment or some special awareness to the effort.

For example, Alan, an African American from the warehouse section in his company, was invited to participate on the diversity task force. At a meeting when concern was expressed that few employees would take the time to fill out the diversity questionnaire, Alan volunteered to take the questionnaires to his group at the warehouse. He distributed them and then returned two days later to collect them. He was aware of feelings of isolation on the part of the warehouse staff and felt this strategy would encourage employees to respond by directly communicating that their input was valuable. Alan believed this would increase the response rate, and he was correct. The return rate for the completed questionnaire was much higher than in previous efforts to gain employee participation. Contributions such as Alan's deserve to be acknowledged and highlighted by the organization.

Being Creative When Addressing Resistance

Resistance to anything often means that the individual or group is not being heard or considered. When the organization takes the time to listen and actually work through the resistance, the long-term payoff is a much richer, more deeply rooted set of core values that reflect an inclusive environment and profitable organization.

Resistance that prevents people from making a commitment to working with diversity is present when you hear:

"This is a waste of time and money."
- "You won't change anybody's attitudes with official, boring programs."
- "This must mean quotas are on the way."
- "This country is a melting pot. This focus on diversity is divisive."
- "If you are in America, you should be American, not African, Japanese, Italian, etc."
- "You are creating a problem that doesn't exist by asking these questions."
- "Any time a subculture refuses to integrate itself into the greater culture, there is revolution."
- "What is wrong with the way we do things now?"
- "Who are you, the P.C. [politically correct] Police?"
- "We are a merit system and the only thing that should be considered is performance."

Some individuals who have been resistant will become involved and supportive as soon as they are asked to participate. A core principle of social scientist Kurt Lewin's theory[1] for organizational change is that people are more likely to modify their own behavior when they are involved in identifying problems and finding solutions. In fact, employee involvement promotes more workable solutions and has the additional benefit of reducing resistance to change.

Some resisters will never get behind the effort. But remember, the organization does not need the buy-in of every single person in order to make significant progress. Once the initiative develops enough momentum, it will move forward under its own steam. We have seen the person at the head of the organization jump in front of the parade, once he or she realized it was moving without him or her.

Try to unearth the reasons for the resistance. Many women and minorities have worked hard their whole lives to fit in and be perceived as successful. Some do not want to risk their own standing by championing a cause that looks unrelated to business goals. Many potential champions choose to bide their time even though their own past experiences in the organization underscore the need to work more effectively with diversity.

For example, Denise, an African-American woman who has risen up through the ranks of a major U.S. corporation, is keenly aware of the need to raise the corporate consciousness about the issues of diversity. She knows the internal and external impact of not addressing these issues. However, she has decided not to take a stand in support of a long-term diversity effort because she believes her career will be at risk. Until the organization's leadership strongly and openly supports working with diversity, this potential champion is unwilling to become an outspoken advocate for organizational change. Denise may look for allies who can provide a safety net or who will join forces to strengthen her message. When trust and confidence are built, then it is likely that people like Denise will actively assist in raising the consciousness about diversity issues.

In some organizations, white men feel resistant because they feel excluded from the diversity effort. If white men become the "excluded" ones as the result of diversity work in organizations, then we will have learned nothing for all the time, energy, and effort spent over the last fifty years. Remember, the goal of working with diversity is to create an inclusive community. Fully considering the feelings, thoughts, and perceptions of white men will reduce the likelihood of backlash and make it easier to facilitate discussions around backlash if it occurs.

Many organizations have begun to directly address potential backlash by white men by developing training workshops to address their issues or concerns. AT&T has a course entitled "White Males: The Label, the Dilemma" in which members of all groups have the opportunity to share their values and reactions to how white men feel about what is happening in the workplace. This seminar reminds people that the diversity initiative includes everyone, not only members of diverse groups.

In another large corporation, white men formed a group called Hear Us Too because they felt excluded and left out of the diversity effort. Initially, they expressed their feelings of exclusion, anger, and frustration as participants in a multicultural effort that focused primarily on women, people of color, and people with disabilities. As they continued to meet, they realized that many of the younger men in the organization, who were part of dual-career couples, were experiencing a great deal of frustration in regard to responsibilities of parenthood. These younger men were concerned about flextime and paternity leave, desired better work/family balance, and were worried that taking paternity leave would create the impression that they were not dedicated to their careers. The group recognized that these were similar issues to those expressed by women during the organizational assessment. When the men realized this, they communicated their findings and realizations to the organization through an employee bulletin to voice their support for the diversity initiative.

Sometimes resistance occurs as a result of the frustration and anger of the members of one group in relation to another group. In one organization, a focus group provided the first formal opportunity for a group of African-American women from varying levels in the organization to surface their frustration about the diversity effort. They stated that only one group had unequivocally benefited from the diversity initiative: white women. The African-American women perceived that although some minorities and people with disabilities had made minor strides as a result of the diversity effort, white women had received the significant payoffs. The African Americans perceived white women as being the ones to advance in greater numbers, be repeatedly promoted over their African-American counterparts, and gain greater access in large numbers at higher levels in traditionally white-male jobs.

The frustration felt by the African-American women was summarized by one woman who said that white women were best able to be tolerated by white men because of their common race. The African-American women expressed bitterness about still being on the bottom of the organizational hierarchy after so much effort and money had been spent to work with diversity. The results of the initiative had added pain to years of frustration of trying to be included in a closed system. The information from this focus group was filtered back through the organization so the leaders could see that the organization was still not addressing one of the deeper issues at the heart of diversity—the issue of race.

Providing a Realistic Time Frame

Remind people that things will not change overnight and that the organization is committed to a long-term effort. It can lead to frustration when people have unrealistic expectations about the speed with which positive change can occur. One way to counter these expectations is to acknowledge small steps and celebrate successes as they happen. For example, it is a success when the organization's leader publicly acknowledges for the first time the commitment to work with diversity.

Based on recommendations from an organizational assessment, one government agency announced that a plan was being established to enable employees to participate in the creation of their own career development plans. The organization's challenge was to train managers who would guide this new plan and to set up clear procedures to make sure it was implemented. To avoid frustration on the part of employees who wanted to begin this career development plan immediately, the agency established and publicized realistic target dates for the plan's implementation. The agency chose one office in which to pilot a trial career development plan, which was implemented within the first six months after the organizational assessment.

Being Flexible

Working with diversity is a fluid process that unfolds in often unpredictable and surprising ways. For example, in a large manufacturing company, the need to consider flextime emerged from focus groups and an organizationwide survey. To the surprise of employees, management gave them the option of flextime in response to this expressed need. Employees had thought such a policy change would never be allowed. The fact that management was willing to change this policy gave employees hope that other important issues would be addressed by the organization. People began to link their participation and involvement in the organizational assessment with the possibility of long-awaited, desired action. This one policy change had a positive and powerful impact on the entire diversity initiative.

It is common to discover in the midst of an organizational assessment that previously unidentified groups of people will come forth to request a focus group. Subgroups of an organization are often unwilling to identify themselves or claim membership until they perceive that the diversity effort is sincere, safe, and effective. For example, there were few African-American employees in a research division of a major telecommunications organization. During an assessment, an open invitation to meet with them to hear their views on the division went unanswered. However, once the assessment was into its final stages and was receiving "good press" from other employees, the African-American group came forth with a direct request to be heard.

It is appropriate to expect and welcome the participation of groups who come late to the diversity initiative. Be prepared to respond to unpredicted events and accommodate the emerging needs of the organization. Be more committed to the overall mission of your diversity initiative to create an inclusive community than to the specific details of your plan to achieve it.

Conclusion

As you move through the diversity initiative, remember that communication is the central theme that must be present. A solid base of support and commitment from leadership and effective communications mechanisms enable the organization to successfully manage the critical tasks described in the next two chapters: gathering and analyzing perceptual data from employees and managers.

Note

1. Kurt Lewin, *Field Theory in Social Science: Selected Theoretical Papers*, D. Cartwright, ed. (New York: Harper & Row, 1951).

7

Involvement:
How Do We Get People
Involved and Collect Data?

When planning has been completed and organizationwide communication has begun, it is time to invite the rest of the organization into the conversation. The involvement phase is where the real story of the organization begins to unfold.

People at the head of organizations—those who set the formal and informal policies—often believe employees are satisfied because they continue to show up for work. Typically, they are unaware of how employees feel and the degree to which they produce in spite of specific obstacles and barriers. Further, many executives have not experienced significant barriers to their own success (such as being a single parent, participating in a car pool, having to hold down two jobs, or having elderly parents living with them).

Many people in minority groups long ago lost their faith and trust that the organization would be open to their concerns. The data collection point in the diversity initiative is the time to involve as many people as possible. The request to come forward and speak will challenge those who have gone underground to avoid retaliation or exclusion from a culture that they perceive to be limiting in its model of success.

This phase invites employees to discuss freely how they feel about working in the organization and to identify any barriers they have encountered. As a result of hearing and assimilating others' experiences, managers and employees can begin to create a more inclusive environment. Senior managers gain insights and deeper understandings from the data and can see what changes are necessary in the organization. Employees benefit from seeing ways in which the experience of others has been similar to or different from their own. Employees also benefit by being able to work more closely and successfully with one another on teams. The ongoing benefit to the entire organization will be actual changes in the work environment on a daily basis that ensure inclusion.

Further, through their willingness to hear this information, managers and executives are also better able to maintain a strong position in recruiting employees. Upper management is better prepared for the competitive global environment when it knows how strong or weak its internal system is. If the system is divisive or people are demoralized, the organization will not have the impetus to survive. This phase keeps the organization's leaders informed of potentially troublesome issues that might occur if this information was not gathered and considered.

What This Chapter Does

The purpose of this phase is threefold: (1) to involve as many people as possible in the conversations around diversity, (2) to gather information directly from managers and employees about diversity issues, and (3) to broaden the horizons of policy makers in the organization by making them aware of employees' perceptions.

As a result of the steps described in this chapter, employees will be able to communicate the extent to which they feel they are valued, appreciated, included, and able to contribute fully. Through these discussions, the organization will identify the specific organizational barriers that prohibit people from full inclusion, participation, and contribution. The result is that organizations can create a more inclusive environment, where inclusion and participation drive management decisions.

Sample letters to employees and their supervisors are provided, as well as sample questions from the focus group guide, interview guide, and survey.

Many organizations find it advantageous to bring in external consultants to handle all or part of the data collection. First, because data collection is time-consuming, the organization may not be able to afford to release people from their jobs to perform this task. Second, people within the organization may not have the experience necessary to conduct interviews and focus groups or to customize a survey to access the information desired. Third, and most important, it is sometimes difficult for people within the organization to maintain objectivity during the data collection phase and create trust among the people from whom they are collecting data.

This chapter provides the guidance and specific techniques to address problems that can arise during this phase of the organizational assessment. It is written both for organizations that will collect the data themselves as well as those that choose to partner with an outside consultant. Careful planning, adequate preparation, and ongoing guidance to the people responsible for data collection enable this component of the organizational assessment to be conducted successfully.

This chapter covers the five primary ways information is gathered:

1. Walk-throughs
2. Focus groups
3. Interviews
4. The survey
5. Employment data

Walk-Throughs

In walk-throughs, also called site visits, the project coordinator, diversity task force members, and external consultants (if they are included) observe the organization's culture and climate. Walk-throughs are helpful if the people conducting the organizational assessment are unfamiliar with certain departments or divisions. They are allowed to get a sense of what it is like to live in this organization by spending time in this environment.

Walk-throughs are not critical if the project coordinator and diversity task force members have a solid and up-to-date understanding of the functions and organizational culture and climate. However, it is advantageous if changes have occurred that could affect the climate (e.g., changes in management or in the physical environment).

For example, on a walk-through in a finance and accounting department, the people conducting the organizational assessment noticed a marked change in the environment since a new department director had been appointed. Employees seemed friendlier and more open than before. When questioned, the employees said that lately customers were feeling more comfortable about stopping in to ask questions. When the observers asked the director what was different, he commented that he had recently taken down a door that used to block the hallway where most of the employees sat. This change in the physical environment had produced a significant change in the climate of the department.

If the project coordinator and task force members decide to conduct walk-throughs, they can begin by identifying which parts of the organization to walk through and then contacting the head of each department/division to arrange a brief meeting and site visit. Employees can be notified through E-mail, staff notes, a staff meeting, or a notice on the bulletin board. Formal notification of each individual is not necessary because this will be an informal tour of the site.

On the day of the walk-through, task force representatives can spend about half an hour with the senior person to understand the purpose of the department and the types of jobs employed by the department. As representatives walk through the site, they can direct their attention to aspects of the environment, such as:

- *The physical environment.* Is it nourishing? Depressing? Are there plants, pictures of family members, personal mementos? What is the proximity of offices/work spaces to one another? Are offices open, or can they be closed off? Do offices/work spaces have windows and natural light? Is there visible debris? Is the environment safe and clean? Are there any visible inappropriate pictures or posters, suggesting any type of harassment?

- *The diversity of the culture.* What is the visual image? Heterogeneous? Homogeneous? Who sits near whom?

- *Camaraderie.* Is this a place where people interact openly? Are people isolated? Are office doors kept closed? Are there central spots for employees to meet socially? Who is in conversation with one another?

Figure 7-1. Sample focus group questions regarding role of assignments and barriers to advancement/inclusion.

Role of Assignments

A. Are you aware of a job posting or vacancy notice system in this organization? If yes, is it readily accessible to you?

B. Are there certain assignments that are crucial to success? If yes, what are they?

C. How are assignments made? (How do you receive assignments?) Objectively, based on a set of known critria? Subjectively?

D. How often do you think you or others have received a particular assignment for reasons other than your qualifications or experience (e.g., gender, ethnic/racial background, physical capability, or age)? Please explain.

E. How often do you think you or others have been passed over for a particular assignment at least in part because of your/their gender, ethnic/racial background, physical capability, or age?

Barriers to Advancement/Inclusion

A. Do you perceive any barriers to inclusion/advancement for women in this organization? If so, what are they?

B. Do you perceive any barriers to inclusion/advancement for racial/ethnic minorities in this organization?

C. Do you perceive any barriers to inclusion/advancement for people with disabilities in this organization?

D. Do you perceive any barriers to inclusion/advancement because of age in this organization?

E. Do you perceive any barriers to inclusion/advancement for people of different sexual orientation in this organization?

Focus Groups

A focus group is a guided discussion that spotlights a given topic and gathers information relevant to that topic. In studies of this nature, focus groups are used to gather employees' thoughts, opinions, and perceptions about the organizational culture and how it affects job satisfaction. This is the opportunity to help the organization come alive in the conversation. A selected sample of questions typically asked in a focus group is provided in Figure 7-1. The full focus group guide is provided in Chapter 13.

Catherine, the diversity manager for a large federal agency, has utilized the term "listening groups" very successfully. She found that within her organization, the term "focus groups" evoked a negative response. People had concluded that in focus groups you were asked to express opinions, yet no one really listened because nothing ever resulted from the effort. In contrast, the listening groups were facilitated in such a way that people contributed more freely because they felt they were being heard. Further, Catherine was careful to communicate to participants the changes that were taking place within the organization as a result of the employees' comments and suggestions.

For purposes of this book, we use the terms "focus groups" and "focus/listening groups" interchangeably. Organizations can select the term that is accepted and understood by their workforce.

Focus groups typically include eight to ten people and can be as small as three or four people. They are often homogeneous in nature, i.e., involving people with the same gender and racial/ethnic makeup. They are facilitated, if possible, by a person of the same gender and race.

Benefits of Focus Groups

Focus groups are the most powerful component of the entire organizational assessment. They provide a rich source of information and are a place to capture the story of a group. In almost every case, they have a positive impact on the initiative. Positive reactions include the following:

- Getting people involved in a direct and meaningful way
- Triggering people's curiosity as to how other groups responded to the questions
- Generating momentum in the diversity conversation
- Highlighting issues that might originally have been missed in developing the questions for the focus groups, interviews, and survey
- Bringing enthusiasm from the group back to the work environment, thereby encouraging others to participate in the organizational assessment

The focus group represents an invitation to speak. For some, this is the first time a conversation such as this has been legitimized. People often feel encouraged by being asked to participate in focus groups. They feel the organization desires information from them. In one organization, an employee, Bob, commented that this was the first time in seventeen years that someone had asked him about his experience of having a disability and working in his organization.

When focus groups are conducted in a sensitive, caring manner, where individual anonymity is ensured, people feel they can honestly share their experiences in a formal setting as they might in an informal setting. For example, in one client setting, a group of African-American women were initially hesitant to speak, although many said they would share their real feelings with a friend. However, as the focus group continued, there was a tremendous outpouring of frustration because of feelings of disconnection and isolation from the management of the organization. At the end of the focus group, many commented that the formal sanctioning of the focus group (being able to participate on company time) gave a level of support not previously experienced.

In organizations where these discussions do not occur informally (e.g., highly technical environments where people are sometimes isolated from one another due to the nature of their work), people feel they are given a vehicle for starting these conversations. Often, managers in high-tech companies and research environments comment that "our people are too introverted; they won't talk." The opposite is true. These people are almost always eager to talk about their issues, even though they might be uncomfortable initially.

The focus group provides a safe, loosely structured, open environment where employees feel legitimate permission to share what is on their minds. As a result, focus group participants often communicate well past the time allotted for the meeting.

People begin to feel more comfortable speaking truths about their feelings and their perspectives when they have a facilitator to guide the discussion and a safe environment for the conversation. During the focus groups and more typically during the feedback sessions, having loosely structured conversations about difficult topics helps people see the commonalities across gender and race. They learn new information about one another and begin to have these important discussions informally.

Negative reactions can occur after focus groups if the organization takes no initiative to acknowledge and respond to employees' input, or when focus group members communicate a misinterpretation of the group discussion or betray confidentiality.

Conducting Focus Groups

To conduct focus groups, task force representatives and the project coordinator can begin by determining the total number of focus groups and selecting people to participate. The employment data can be used to determine the composition of the focus groups. The primary selection criterion is diversity of all types (gender, race, level, function, physical capability, and sexual orientation, if gay/lesbian task forces exist in the organization). Ideally, focus groups will represent the full spectrum of the workforce, except the senior executives who will be interviewed.

Keep in mind that the intention is to create a "big" conversation. The focus groups give depth and momentum to the initiative. It enhances the overall effort to include as many people as can reasonably participate in focus groups.

Typically, approximately 10 to 20 percent of the entire workforce participates in focus groups. It is appropriate to overrepresent employees from the minority cultures relative to their proportion of the workforce. For example, suppose you have an organization of 300 people, with 240 men and 60 women (an 80:20 ratio). The organization wants to select 30 people to participate. To get good representation of gender issues, the organization might request 15 women and 15 men (a 50:50 ratio).

Overall, the focus groups will represent the diversity in the organization. However, within each focus group, it is effective to encourage as much homogeneity as possible. For example:

- Group people together by gender, race/ethnicity, etc. (e.g., conduct separate focus groups for African-American women, African-American men, white women, white men, Latinas, Latinos, people with disabilities, etc.).
- Conduct separate focus groups for management and support staff.

- Make sure that people in direct reporting relationships are not invited to the same group.
- Emphasize repeatedly that confidentiality will be maintained.

Homogeneity and confidentiality are important because these factors create as nonthreatening an atmosphere as possible, and they minimize the potential (and perceived) risks as employees express their feelings. Further, when people have the opportunity to express their views in a homogeneous group, the data are cleaner and more accurate.

In some organizations, it is appropriate to hold a mixed minority group discussion (e.g., of African-American, Asian-American, Latino/Latina, and Native American employees) after the homogeneous ones to discuss shared perceptions, compare experiences across groups, and build commitment to the initiative. This is particularly helpful in organizations where the percentage of minority employees is small, since this can help to ensure anonymity when the information is presented to the entire organization.

Be aware, however, that a mixed minority group may blur the perceptions from individual groups and diminish the facilitators' ability to collect accurate data. In one focus group of Asian women that initially appeared to be homogeneous, the group members discovered that there was a combination of people born in the United States and those born in other countries. The participants' responses differed significantly and were related to this distinction.

If an organization has only a few representatives of a group, conduct one-on-one interviews with these individuals. To increase the trust level in an interview setting, stress that anonymity will be preserved. The interviewer must then review the interview data and combine it with the focus group data from all employees to find general themes.

To ensure the necessary gender/racial distribution from the majority and minority cultures, task force members set parameters for the focus group participation (e.g., the percentage of men and women). Then the organization can use a random selection within each group to identify specific individuals. It may also be appropriate to select participants "randomly" after controlling for specific parameters. For example, first determine the gender mix desired (e.g., 50:50), then randomly select individuals within each gender group. In addition to gender and ethnic group, grade and job function are frequently used as parameters to first define the group before using random selection.

In addition to employees selected, others may volunteer to participate in focus groups. Voluntary participation is accepted in the spirit of inclusion.

Inviting Participants

Once employees have been selected, the next step is to design the letter inviting them to participate. Employees should receive a formal letter from the task force inviting them to participate (a sample letter is shown in Figure 7-2). When employees are invited, emphasize the confidentiality issue. Explain that their "story" will be told in a composite.

Encourage supervisors/managers to support employee participation in the focus groups. Provide a way for people to bill their time, if necessary. Particularly in a manufacturing environment, it is important to have the full and active support of supervisors and line managers to account for the possible loss in productivity. The benefits of including employees in the dialogue far outweigh the one or two hours off line.

Supervisors/managers should be sent a memo from the head of the organization asking them to encourage their employees to participate and giving them instructions about how employees can bill this time. A sample letter is provided in Figure 7-3. Individual supervisors should be given names of the employees who report to them who have been invited to participate in focus groups.

Selecting Facilitators

The next step is to select focus group facilitators. A number of factors should be considered in choosing people to serve as facilitators.

- Select people who have a high level of credibility and trust in the organization. Employees must have confi-

Figure 7-2. Sample focus group invitation to employees.

Date:

To:

From: Diversity Task Force

Subject: Workforce Diversity Focus Groups

You are invited to participate in a focus group to look at issues relevant to workforce diversity in our organization. Our
organization is conducting an assessment of diversity issues,
as described in the Employee Bulletin dated _____.
    With the increasing mix of cultures and backgrounds in
our workforce, we believe it is important to understand how
well our current management practices and culture are working with diversity. We will identify possible areas for improvement that will enhance workplace diversity for the future.
    A "focus/listening group" is a guided discussion that spot-
lights a given topic and gathers information relevant to that
topic. In this case, you can share the thoughts, opinions, and
perceptions you have relative to our culture and how it affects your level of job satisfaction.
    You will be meeting with a facilitator who will guide the
discussion. We believe it is important that the information
shared in these groups be held in the strictest confidence.
Therefore, the consultants will not ask your names, and your
responses will be considered as a group, not individually.
    Your participation is important to this effort. This meet-
ing is scheduled for _____. Please confirm your participation
by calling _____ no later than _____. If you choose to participate, please charge the time to charge number _____.

dence in the facilitators to freely share critical information.
For example, consider union representatives and employee
leaders of women's groups and minority groups.

   • Choose people with skills and experience in facilitation. (Guidelines and skill development can be provided, if
appropriate.) For example, people in employee assistance
program (EAP) offices often have these skills.

   • In many instances, it is advantageous to match the
facilitator to the group in terms of gender and race (i.e.,

Figure 7-3. Sample focus group letter to supervisors.

Date:

To:

From: Head of the Organization

Subject: Workforce Diversity Focus Groups

To assess the openness and effectiveness of our current culture as it relates to our increasingly diverse workforce, we have assigned facilitators to conduct a number of focus groups. This group input is critical to our ability to adapt our management practices and culture to attract and retain a high-quality workforce now and in the future.

These groups will be composed of employees selected randomly based upon gender, racial/ethnic background, job level, etc. If any of your employees are invited to participate in one of these focus groups, please encourage their participation (their input will be anonymous). If necessary, have them charge the one and one-half hours of participant time to the charge number provided in their letter of invitation.

I will advise you of the employees from your department who are asked to participate. A report on the outcome of this assessment will be made available to you and all employees.

Thank you for your cooperation.

an African-American male facilitator could lead all focus groups for African-American men). This can create a deeper access to the information and possibly a more thorough understanding of the issues presented. If the facilitator is not of the same gender, race, etc., it is particularly important that she/he be a skilled facilitator who is aware of interpreting the information through her/his own cultural lens and be willing to continue the dialogue until the group members feel understood.

• Avoid assigning people who could create role confusion or conflict if they served as facilitators. For example, avoid choosing people in the human resources department or EEO offices since their official roles might make them appear threatening to focus group participants.

• If the organization decides it is appropriate to use an outside facilitator or consultant to conduct focus groups, select someone who has experience in the area of diversity and facilitation and in conducting focus groups.

If the facilitators are new, it may be appropriate to have two facilitators conduct the focus groups, one to facilitate and one to record.

Scheduling Focus Groups

The next step is to schedule focus groups. Scheduling is typically done by a support person in the office of the project coordinator.

Allow two hours of time for each focus group in case they run longer than the scheduled one and one-half hours. One hour of time is allotted between focus groups, for the facilitators to finish writing and organizing their notes.

The Role of the Facilitator

Explain the roles and responsibilities to the focus group facilitators. They are responsible for welcoming participants at the start of the meeting and giving a statement regarding the mission of the organization and the purpose of conducting the project. They explain the purpose of the focus group: to hear everyone's viewpoint and to create an atmosphere where hearing one another's perspective has the possibility of enriching everyone present. The facilitators emphasize confidentiality. They explain that they will be taking notes as people talk and that employees can request that the notes be edited, if there is something they would like excluded from the formal record.

Facilitators explain and enforce the ground rules, such as: Each person will have the opportunity to complete his or her thoughts; destructive or judgmental comments are not allowed; employees cannot use the information discussed in a negative way; and no one has to defend what he or she says.

Facilitators create an atmosphere conducive to honest and open employee communication. This includes the room setting (e.g., a circular table is much more conducive to a conversation than classroom style seating) and the tone set when starting and guiding the group. It also includes avoiding things that make people uncomfortable, such as tape recorders and video-taping.

The facilitators follow the focus group guide (provided in Chapter 13) to collect the necessary information. They ask questions to clarify a person's response, when appropriate. They record the information presented without interpretation (e.g., they write down the anecdotes verbatim). It is important that facilitators avoid any negative reactions (verbal or nonverbal) to what is being said. They report in a neutral way the statements and behavior. The facilitators themselves become the invitation to everyone to speak. The quality of the facilitators' listening in a curious, nonjudgmental way will be felt in the entire room.

The facilitators are not aiming for consensus from focus group members. For example, in focus groups in one agency, employees described how people got assignments. There were three or four differing perceptions of how assignments were made, all from people in the same office. Focus groups are an opportunity to hear differences in people's perceptions of the same issues.

Facilitators encourage participation, particularly among employees who may be less vocal. They mention that employees are not obligated to participate and share with the group. Facilitators are aware that there is sometimes resistance in focus groups, and they are trained to handle the resistance effectively.

After the focus groups have been conducted, each facilitator prepares a summary of the data collected. The summaries capture the essence of the discussion, relevant anecdotes, and any observations by the facilitator. It is vital to maintain a distinction between data from employees and comments/observations from the facilitator to keep the data clean.

It is most useful when the facilitators summarize the data by subject area (e.g., keeping comments related to feedback and communication separate from those related to work environment). Further, by organizing the data by subject area, inconsistencies can more readily be identified.

Focus group guides and summaries are submitted to the project coordinator.

Interviews

Interviews are conducted with executives to gather their perceptions regarding the diversity issue. Meetings can be structured as one-on-one interviews or small-group interviews.

During the interviews, executives are asked to define "success" in the organization and to describe the characteristics of a typical employee who will "make it" in the organization. They are asked to describe many aspects of their own career. Through interviews, the organization can find out whether executives think there are any organizational barriers to people's advancement and if the organization structure itself is easier for some people to navigate more effectively than others. Executives may also discuss what actions to take to expand the ways in which people in the organization can succeed.

Sample interview questions for senior managers are shown in Figure 7-4. The full interview guide is provided in Chapter 14.

Because the people at the top in hierarchical structures are the authors of the culture, they often reflect the cultural roots of the organization. They can contribute rich information about the cultural perceptions of the system. Often, the conversations with these people point out dilemmas and inconsistencies in the system.

For example, in an interview with John, a senior official in a large government agency, he described moving from one powerful mentor to another over the course of his career. The image emerged of this man swinging to the top of the organizational structure with the helping hands of many strong, powerful people. John readily admitted that he would never have been exposed to the opportunities and inside information had it not been for these people. When asked if he thought mentoring was important for people of the minority culture, he said, "Of course." However, John felt it was hard to create a successful mentoring program because so much depends on chemistry. Through this interview he identified a dilemma: Mentoring is vital to success in his organization, yet he does not believe that the organization can create a formal mentoring program that would be equally available and effective for all people.

Figure 7-4. Sample interview questions for senior managers.

When you think about your career as a manager, certain events or episodes probably stand out in your mind, things that shaped your career as a professional. We want to discuss these items with you. Our purpose is to understand the profile of success within this organization, based on people's individual careers.

Please review these questions in preparation for our interview with you:

1. What are the qualities, skills, strengths, and characteristics critical for your success? Is knowledge of official guidelines for promotion, assignment, and training processes important? Did you have that knowledge?
2. What was your first managerial job? What did you learn from it?
3. Please describe the person who taught you the most during your career. What did that person do that made him/her so special? How did this relationship start? Do you consider this person a mentor/coach? If not, have you ever had a mentor/coach?
4. Have you ever been a mentor/coach to anyone? If so, to whom (race, gender, job function, grade level, age)?
5. What was your first important assignment? How was it obtained? What were subsequent important assignments? How were they obtained?
6. What training courses did you take? Were they important? Why?
7. How did you first become visible to people at higher levels in the organization? How did you benefit from this visibility?
8. What barriers did you face in your career path? How did you overcome them?

Selecting Interviewees and Interviewers

If interviews will be conducted, task force representatives and the project coordinator can begin by selecting people to be interviewed. Typically, interviews are held with the "top slice" of the organization, the people who set the formal policies and informal tone of the organization.

Interviews can also be conducted with:

- The sole woman or minority employee who has broken through to a level of the organization where the majority of incumbents are white men

- Leaders of parts of the organization where things are working particularly well or poorly
- Key players in the organization who can provide valuable feedback and/or who could be major resisters if excluded

After identifying who will be interviewed, the next step is to select people to conduct the interviews. Interviews are conducted typically by the same people who facilitate the focus groups. Given the sensitive nature of the information collected, it is preferable to have an external consultant gather the data, although this is not imperative. It is critical that the person/people conducting the interviews be given strong sponsorship from the organization's leaders. Further, when selecting interviewers, ensure that they are skilled in asking clarifying questions and gathering data of a sensitive nature.

Inviting Interviewees

Invitations to people to be interviewed can be made at a special meeting related to the diversity initiative or at a regularly scheduled executive staff meeting. In the meeting, the head of the organization indicates his/her support for the effort, explains that interviews will be taking place, and asks for full cooperation. The leader can then send a formal letter to each interviewee to explain who will conduct the interviews and encourage their full cooperation and participation. A sample letter is provided in Figure 7-5.

Interviews are typically scheduled by a support person in the office of the project coordinator. Allow between one and one and one-half hours for each interview, and allow thirty minutes between interviews.

Conducting the Interviews

During each interview, the facilitator follows the interview guide (provided in Chapter 14) to collect the necessary information. As with the focus groups, the facilitator concentrates on recording, not interpreting, the information provided.

At the beginning of the interview, the facilitator explains

Figure 7-5. Sample interview invitation.

Date:

To:

From: Head of the Organization

Subject: Workforce Diversity Interviews

I invite you to participate in a confidential interview to discuss
issues relevant to workforce diversity in our organization.
With the increasing mix of cultures and backgrounds in our
workforce, we believe it is important to understand how our
current management practices and culture are working with
diversity. We also plan to identify possible areas for improvement that will enhance workplace diversity for the future.
     Your participation is important to this effort. This meet-
ing is scheduled for _____ with _____. Please confirm your
participation by calling _____ no later than _____.

---

the purpose of the interview and the general agenda for the
session. The facilitator sets an appropriate tone so that the person feels comfortable and secure in speaking honestly about
his/her perceptions.

Summarizing the Interviews

After all the interviews have been conducted, each facilitator prepares a summary of the data collected. The summaries
capture the essence of the discussion, relevant anecdotes, and
any observations by the facilitator. It is important to maintain a
distinction between data from employees and comments/ob-
servations from the facilitator. Further, distinguish between fac-
tual information (e.g., the history of someone's career, the
assignments held, the number of people supervised) and perceptions (e.g., the interviewees' perceptions of what it takes to
get promoted).

Facilitators then summarize the data by subject area and
submit their interview guides and summaries to the project
coordinator.

The Survey

The purpose of the survey is to gather many perceptions from employees in an accurate, complete, and expedient way. The data demonstrate the numbers of employees who perceive similar patterns about the workforce and reflect the degree to which these perceptions differ from group to group. The survey is structured to ensure anonymity.

Designing the Survey

The first step in using a survey is to select an existing survey that can be modified to reflect your specific organization, or to design a new one. A sample of a typical employee survey is shown in Figure 7-6. A full survey is provided in Chapter 15. The survey is designed to measure the effects of various differences, such as gender, race, ethnicity, disability, age, sexual preference, job level, and job function.

As you modify or create a survey, consider the following guidelines. Be sure to encourage employees to provide demographic data. At a minimum, this includes gender, race, ethnic background, disability, age, and education. Grade or level is also important, although employees may be uncomfortable providing it because of concerns about confidentiality. By collecting this information, the organization can "cut" the data using demographic variables (gender, race, grade, etc.). Without these responses, the organization loses rich information. For example, in response to the question "Is this workplace accessible?" it is important to know who is speaking. Is it a person with a disability, for example? By stressing the confidentiality of the responses, you can encourage employees to provide their demographic data.

Use a survey that has primarily closed-ended questions (e.g., multiple choice) that can be tabulated. These can be supplemented by open-ended questions that give employees an opportunity to provide their own responses.

Consult with someone (e.g., a statistical analyst or social scientist) who has knowledge of surveys and survey analysis. Discuss the purpose of the survey and the questions you intend to answer with this information; then determine whether the survey as currently designed will meet those objectives. Also

Figure 7-6. Sample of survey section related to career advancement.

This section of the questionnaire is designed to obtain information and opinions regarding your advancement in this organization.

Please rate how satisfied you are with each aspect of working in this organization that appears below in items 1 through 25, using the following scale:

(A) Very satisfied
(B) Somewhat satisfied
(C) Neither satisfied nor dissatisfied
(D) Somewhat dissatisfied
(E) Very dissatisfied
(F) Not applicable or don't know

How satisfied are you with:

1. Your organization as a place for someone of your gender to work?
2. Your organization as a place for someone of your race/ethnic background to work?
3. Your organization as a place for someone of your physical capability to work?
4. Your organization as a place for someone of your age to work?
5. Your organization as a place for someone of your sexual orientation to work?
6. Your organization as a place for someone of your gender to develop a career?
7. Your organization as a place for someone of your race/ethnic background to develop a career?
8. Your organization as a place for someone of your physical capability to develop a career?
9. Your organization as a place for someone of your age to develop a career?
10. Your organization as a place for someone of your sexual orientation to develop a career?
11. Your ability to discuss work-related matters with your current supervisor?
12. Your freedom to voice concerns/ideas to your current supervisor?
13. Your freedom to voice concerns/ideas to management above your current supervisor?
14. The appreciation you receive from your current supervisor for your contributions?
15. Organizational policies regarding care for dependents (e.g., staying home with a sick child or taking time off to help an elderly parent)?

Figure 7-6. *(Continued).*

---

16. Your promotion rate throughout your career?
17. The amount of control you have over your career?
18. The way you have been treated throughout your career because of your gender?
19. The way you have been treated throughout your career because of your race/ethnic backbround?
20. The way you have been treated throughout your career because of your physical capability?
21. The way you have been treated throughout your career because of your age?
22. The way you have been treated throughout your career because of your sexual orientation?
23. The classroom training you have received?
24. Opportunities throughout your career for developmental assignments?
25. The cultural diversity of your immediate work environment, e.g., the mix of people from different racial and ethnic groups?

---

check whether the wording of the questions and their response choices will allow a clear and unambiguous analysis.

Administering the Survey

After you have selected a survey, determine the mechanism to administer it. Surveys can be administered by mail or in person. If the organization expects resistance from employees who are completing the survey, invite employees to a one-hour session during which the survey is administered on-site. This sends the message that the survey has received a high level of sanctioning from the executives.

If the survey will be mailed or handed out for employees to complete at their convenience, allow only a brief turnaround time (e.g., three days) so that the survey is treated as a priority. It is helpful to have a representative or informal leader of a group hand out the surveys to people in their area/group. These small groups can also check on people's progress and encourage participation. Be sure to have a mechanism for employees to anonymously submit their completed surveys (e.g., an internal mailbox).

Selecting Recipients

Selecting who will receive the survey is the next step. Small organizations can administer the survey to all employees. Large organizations may survey 15 to 25 percent of their workforce. When selecting a sample, use a demographic cut first (e.g., identify that you want 50 percent men and 50 percent women), and then use a random selection process within that to identify specific individuals to participate.

To design the sample, first decide on the percentage of the entire workforce you want to cover. Select a percentage, e.g., 20 percent, that will give you a reasonable sample size in terms of effort and cost. Then determine whether that overall percentage will provide enough people within the demographic and/or organizational groupings you want to analyze.

It is desirable to survey a minimum of roughly twenty employees of a particular gender and ethnic group within a particular department or grade level. If fewer than twenty employees in a particular group are surveyed, the survey responses may not be representative of the whole grouping and may instead reflect individuals' perceptions. If there are fewer than twenty employees in a particular grouping (e.g., American Indian employees), invite all employees in that grouping to complete the survey.

Organizations must "oversample" employees to get the desired response rates. All targeted sample sizes must be increased by a factor of 1.5 to 2 to account for the expected rate of nonresponse. Typically, only 50 to 60 percent of the people who receive the survey actually complete and return it. This means that if you want twenty completed surveys by people of a particular ethnic group, you must sample and send the survey to about thirty-five people of that group.

To supplement the sample, the organization may also encourage voluntary participation. This reinforces the commitment to be inclusive. It is critical not to purposely exclude any employees from completing a survey.

Inviting People to Complete the Survey

After all of these preliminary decisions are made, invite people to complete the survey. The communications strategy is

Figure 7-7. Sample survey invitation to employees.

Date:

To:

From: Head of the Organization

Subject: Workforce Diversity Survey

    You are invited to complete the attached survey as part of our Workforce Diversity Initiative. This is your opportunity to give us in writing your perceptions of how this organization is addressing and valuing diversity. We want to know your thoughts, opinions, and perceptions about our culture and how it affects your level of job satisfaction.
    The survey is anonymous. You can give your name if you choose. Please include demographic data as requested, so that we may tabulate your responses as a group.
    The survey takes approximately forty-five minutes to complete. You are permitted to complete the survey on work time.
    Your participation is important to this effort. Please submit your completed survey to Mail Box _____ by _____. If you have any questions about the survey, please contact _____.

vital in making this effort successful. Employees will be more likely to participate if they understand the purpose of the diversity initiative, what has transpired to date, what they are being asked to do, and that confidentiality is ensured. To increase the likelihood of employees responding to the survey, it is important to authorize work time in which employees can complete the survey and to communicate support from management. The sample letter provided in Figure 7-7 can be used to invite employees to participate.

If the questionnaire is administered in groups, the primary role of the facilitator is to create an atmosphere of quiet, with time for employees to reflect and think about the questions. Typically, it takes forty-five minutes to one hour to complete the survey provided in Chapter 15.

After the surveys are completed, they can be submitted for

data entry. The data will then be analyzed and interpreted by the individual(s) responsible for the statistical analysis.

Employment Data

Employment data are simply the quantitative information about the organization. They allow the organization to look at itself as a community and answer two questions: "Who lives in this community?" and "Who occupies certain levels in the organization, certain functions, line and staff?"

Employment data include information such as demographic data (total number of employees and number of employees distributed by gender, race, disability, grade, level, etc.) and attrition data (number of employees leaving, noting any patterns by gender, race, grade, function, department, job title, etc.).

The employment data are used to:

- Select people to interview and to invite to focus groups.

- Assess glass ceiling issues (this analysis is described in more detail in Chapter 8).

- Identify any areas of the organization where support for diversity is demonstrated or is lacking (i.e., departments where white women, minorities, and people with disabilities actively elect to work and tend to stay for significant periods of time, or departments people avoid because of perceived harassment or discriminatory behavior).

- Identify functional areas that are inhabited by one group or another (for example, in many organizations, support staff positions are held by women, and security forces are composed primarily of men and women from racial/ethnic groups, such as African Americans).

Collecting Employment Data

To collect employment data, task force representatives and/or the project coordinator can talk with the appropriate department (e.g., human resources and EEO) about the types of employment data available in hard copy or on computer. Then they can make an initial request for data including:

- *Workforce composition.* Collect information on the total number of employees and number of employees distributed by gender, race, disability, age, grade, function, department, and job title. These variables are referred to below as "standard information." Observe clusters or pockets in which people of a particular gender or race predominate.
- *Attrition data.* Collect standard information on employees who have left the organization.
- *Promotion data.* Collect the standard information described above for employees who have been promoted. Calculate the length of time between promotions; determine the old and new grade levels.
- *Hiring data.* Collect the standard information for all employees, as well as the grade level at which the incumbent was hired.
- *Complaints of sexual and racial harassment.* Collect the standard information for employees who have filed informal or formal harassment claims.
- *Salary data.* Review the placement of employees by salary. Note any patterns by gender or race. Are women clustered in lower grades? Are minority employees clustered at the lower end of the salary ranges?

Analyzing the Data

After the data are collected, analyze to determine patterns, for example, across gender, race, ethnicity, and age. Look for any areas of the organization that appear to be experiencing a higher percentage of problems (higher attrition rates, a greater number of harassment complaints, etc.).

During the project, make additional requests if supplementary information is required. Keep notes regarding data that would be helpful to review and is unavailable at present. Later in the project, this list can be used to develop recommendations about the types of data that would be useful to collect and track in the future.

Conclusion

After finishing the work described in this chapter, the organization will have the data necessary to answer questions such as: Is this an inclusive organization? Is there a glass ceiling? Are there specific barriers to advancement for various groups? The next chapter provides instructions on how to analyze the employment data and data from the survey, focus groups, and interviews to answer these questions and many others.

8

Data Analysis:
What Does It All Mean?

This chapter takes the reader through a step-by-step process to synthesize raw data collected from employees, analyze it, and then produce findings and recommendations. The chapter provides a nuts-and-bolts approach to a task that is often time- and labor-intensive and considered overwhelming.

The analysis described in this chapter enables the organization to answer the following questions:

- Is this a good place for people of diverse groups to work?
- Is this an inclusive organization?
- What are the supports and barriers in this organization in relation to working with diversity?
- What does it take to be successful?
- Who is advancing in the organization? Who is not?

The analysis enables the organization to look at itself through the eyes of its own employees and determine what in the organizational structure/process contributes to employees' perceptions.

The analysis of the raw data is typically conducted by the task force (or selected members), the project coordinator, and a statistician or statistical analyst. An external consultant may be helpful in completing this task by giving an outside perspective and looking at the data with an objective eye.

The statistical analyst conducts the first level of analysis of the employment data and survey data. This person's role is to analyze both the employment data and the survey data using various demographic variables (i.e., looking for trends relating to gender or race), and then analyze how the trends observed in the employment data and survey data relate. The statistical analyst also is instrumental in looking at the relationships between findings from the focus groups and interviews, as compared to the employment and survey data.

What This Chapter Does

The purpose of this phase is to look for relationships between themes and the functions of the organization (e.g., the data from employees as it relates to performance review, promotions, assignments, and treatment. As a result of this phase, the organization will have an understanding of what the data mean, whether barriers seem to exist, and which organizational issues need to be addressed.

During this time, the picture of the organization looks bleak to many people. This is particularly true when employees have responded openly and honestly to questions about problems and barriers in the organization. This is an opportunity to manage the feelings of hopelessness, anxiety, and disappointment and to handle the actual information that has been brought forward.

Being overwhelmed is a typical reaction during the analysis phase. People may be overwhelmed by the sheer volume of data, the sensitivity of the information (which can make employees and the organization as a whole feel vulnerable), and bringing out into the open information that has been discussed previously only in private, homogeneous groups. These feelings can be handled most effectively by sorting through the data in a sequential, organized fashion and taking the time to go through each step.

This chapter describes the steps an organization takes to analyze data. The chapter covers six essential steps:

1. Summarizing data separately for the four types of information (focus groups, interviews, the survey, and employment data)
2. Comparing trends across the data collection methods (e.g., comparing trends in the survey data to trends in the focus group data)

3. Determining categories and themes
4. Developing findings
5. Developing recommendations
6. Writing the final report

The analysis is based on information from four sources: focus groups, interviews, the survey, and employment data. Each data collection method has its own purpose and strengths. For example, strengths of the survey are that the sample typically is much larger than the focus group sample and that the survey is completely anonymous. The survey tells the extent to which experiences and perceptions are common across different groups and the proportions of people who experience a given situation or hold a particular perception.

In contrast, the focus groups are an opportunity for people to express themselves without the constraints of survey response choices, describe their own experiences, and respond to one another. The strengths of the focus groups are that they are an invitation to speak in a legitimate way about topics that may have been previously taboo.

The combination of the survey and focus groups is much more powerful than either one of them alone in painting an accurate picture of the perceptions of the workforce.

Summarizing Data

In most projects, the analysis begins by assembling the data collected and the focus group and interview summaries (as described in Chapter 7). Have the statistical analyst tabulate numerical data from the survey and the employment data.

Summarize findings from each data collection method used. This will allow you to work with smaller, more manageable pieces of information. These summaries are used for three purposes: (1) Some will be included in the final report as appendices, (2) some will be woven into the body of the report, and (3) all will be used for further analysis. Descriptions and samples of the summaries are provided in this chapter for the four data collection methods: focus groups, interviews, the survey, and employment data.

Focus Groups

The focus group data are the heart of the initiative, as described in Chapter 7. In every diversity initiative, there are common categories that are addressed in the focus groups, interviews, and survey, including what it takes to be successful, recruitment, advancement, assignments, feedback and communication, career development, stereotyping, harassment, and work/family issues. The write-up for focus groups consists of approximately one page (sometimes two or three) per category. A sample is provided in Figure 8-1.

Within each category, write several paragraphs that capture the essence of the response from African-American men, African-American women, Asian-American men, Asian-American women, white men, white women, people with disabilities, etc. These provide a picture of what each group thinks and feels about the issue.

As you can see from the responses summarized in Figure 8-1, feedback and communication is an issue for all groups in the organization (although it manifests itself slightly differently for each group). An organizationwide initiative to improve feedback and communication would be warranted based on this type of employee response.

Interviews

There are three steps to analyze the data from interviews. First, thoroughly read all data collected in the interviews. Second, analyze the content and look for common themes. The purpose of the analysis is to note comments that are repeated frequently across interviews, as well as comments that are noted by all interviewees of a particular subgroup. For example, in one organization all women interviewees noted that actively networking was vital to success in the organization, whereas male interviewees did not mention this factor. After reviewing this finding, the organization's leaders realized the organizational climate allowed men many opportunities to network informally, whereas women had to actively find ways to network. Therefore, women saw networking as a separate and vital component of their jobs, while for men networking was

Figure 8-1. Sample focus group summary on feedback and communication.

Employees believe that feedback and communication from one's supervisor are critical to advancement.

African-American Women

The majority of African-American women responded that they do not receive useful feedback. For most employees, feedback is verbal and primarily negative. Many have encountered silence, reluctance, or cursory comments such as "things are fine" when requesting feedback. Most feel that African Americans and other minority groups are evaluated unfairly and with less enthusiasm than whites.

African-American Men

Most describe feedback and communication as nonexistent. The only formal feedback mechanism is the annual performance review, which most described as ineffective. Many participants noted that supervisors do not know how to communicate with African-American employees. The general feeling is that white men are rated more favorably than women and African Americans.

Employees with Disabilities

Some employees talked about the responsibility to constantly educate others, including supervisors, about how to communicate with and work effectively with them. Some mentioned that they do not get feedback, even when they request it.

White Women

Almost unanimously, white women feel that they do not get useful feedback from their supervisors. Feedback is generally verbal, with the exception of the written performance review. A few participants stated that their supervisors' feedback improved dramatically after upward appraisals were implemented. The majority said they were not aware of any differences in the ways women and men were evaluated. Many had a feeling that they were evaluated differently, although it was hard to prove.

White Men

Many participants perceive a lack of feedback and communication. With some exceptions, individuals receive little individual, constructive feedback unless it is solicited. A sentiment expressed by some participants was "never a thank-you, always a spanking." Some employees noted that there have been recent efforts to increase communication between employees and supervisors.

Figure 8-2. Sample interview write-up.

> Interviews were conducted with twelve senior managers. When asked to describe the keys to success, senior managers said they believe that natural leaders will rise to the top through their own performance, instinct, intuition, and savvy. They believe that people advance by taking risks, avoiding specialization, being mobile, doing an outstanding job, and establishing themselves in line positions.
>
> Senior managers stressed the importance of skills that were concretely job-oriented, such as technical and interpersonal skills and speaking and writing ability. Both minority and women managers mentioned networking. Women managers also felt that working long hours and getting support from their managers were very important. Minorities also emphasized team building and knowing "the system."

an integral part of their culture. The third step of the analysis is to summarize the findings on paper.

The interview write-up consists of between one and three pages summarizing the executives' perceptions of the keys to success. An example is shown in Figure 8-2.

The write-up also includes a paragraph or two detailing senior managers' perceptions of each category (advancement, assignments, etc.). The information collected in interviews can be kept together as a single document or inserted throughout the report in the discussion of each category.

The Survey

There are six steps to analyze the survey.

1. Clean the data by checking the percentage of missing responses for each survey item. For items with a high missing percentage, obtain the survey identification numbers of the surveys with the missing responses. Then review the actual survey forms to determine whether the person left the answer blank or whether it is a data entry error that can be corrected. If the latter, make the correction to the data file.

2. Compute cross-tabulation tables for each survey item, including the percentages for each response choice

Table 8-1. Sample cross-tabulation table.
Survey Item 3: How satisfied are you with your career advancement in the organization?

Item 3 Response Choices	African Americans		
	Men	Women	Total
Very satisfied	0	0	0
Somewhat satisfied	10 20%	0	10 10%
Neither satisfied nor dissatisfied	20 40%	20 40%	40 40%
Somewhat dissatisfied	20 40%	10 20%	30 30%
Very dissatisfied	0	20 40%	20 20%

Item 3 Response Choices	Whites		
	Men	Women	Total
Very satisfied	10 20%	0	10 10%
Somewhat satisfied	10 20%	10 20%	20 20%
Neither satisfied nor dissatisfied	20 40%	20 40%	40 40%
Somewhat dissatisfied	10 20%	10 20%	20 20%
Very dissatisfied	0	10 20%	10 10%

across the entire organization and by the demographic groups of interest.

For example, the results of a survey given to one hundred African Americans (fifty men and fifty women) and one hundred whites (fifty men and fifty women) are shown in Table 8-1. The plain number in each box is the number of people who responded with the particular answer

Table 8-2. Sample cross-tabulation table showing summarized survey responses.

Survey Item	African-American Men	African-American Women	White Men	White Women	All African Americans	All Whites	All Women	All Men
3. Percentage dissatisfied with career advancement	40	60	20	40	50	30	50	30

choice, e.g., ten African-American men responded "somewhat satisfied." The percentage under each number is the percent out of the total number of people in that demographic group, e.g., the ten African-American men answering "somewhat satisfied" are 20 percent of the entire group of fifty African-American men surveyed. These percentages can be compared across demographic groups to examine whether, for example, the percentage of African-American women responding "somewhat satisfied" is different from the percentage of African-American men or the percentage of white women responding "somewhat satisfied."

3. Summarize the numbers from these cross-tabulation tables in a table containing a single line for each item on the survey. An example is shown in Table 8-2.

4. Compute cross-tabulation tables for each survey item, including the percentages for each response choice within organizational groupings, such as departments and grade levels, by the demographic groups that are pertinent within each grouping. For example, within the organizational grouping of clerical employees, examining responses only by race (because clerical employees are primarily women) would be appropriate. These cross-tabulation tables can also be summarized by tables, with one such table for each organizational grouping.

5. If necessary, weight the percentages in the cross-tabulation tables to account for different groups being sampled at different rates and for different response rates. For example, in a diversity assessment in a federal agency,

African Americans were oversampled, i.e., a larger proportion of all the African-American employees and managers were chosen for the survey sample than the proportion of all whites. To make the percentage of African Americans responding a particular way to a survey item comparable to the percentage of whites responding the same way, the percentages were adjusted by their respective sampling rates because an African American in the sample represented fewer other African Americans in the population than a white in the sample.

6. Prepare a write-up to summarize the survey results. The summary tables, such as Tables 8-1 and 8-2, are the basis for the write-up. The summary statements come from examining each summary table within itself, as well as from comparing different summary tables (e.g., summary tables of different organizational groupings).

Survey Response Rates

A high response rate (e.g., over 50 percent) is a good sign that the organization is ready to have this conversation and give input. A well-developed, visible communications strategy can often be the key to a high response rate. The response rate is typically high when employees understand that management is committed to taking some action based on the data, anonymity is ensured, and there is support for the survey effort itself. In these cases, there is usually an overwhelming amount of information from employees on the open-ended portions of the questionnaire. Many employees see open-ended questions as an opportunity to share their experiences and stories firsthand.

A low survey response rate can suggest that something is wrong in the organization. It could be that the organization is saturated by questionnaires or by work pressures that make it difficult for employees to find time to complete the survey. It may suggest concern about lack of anonymity or indicate that employees think these issues are unimportant. It could be a symbol of people's hopelessness, cynicism, or resistance to the issue. It could also indicate the lack of commitment or support by the organization for the survey effort.

When the response rate is significantly lower for one group as compared to all others, it usually suggests that the group members feel hopeless and frustrated and do not believe the situation will improve or feel that the topic is not worthy of their attention. Response bias would arise if those who responded were different (e.g., more satisfied) than those who did not. It is important to note in the write-up if the response rate is very low (i.e., less than 50 percent), since this could result in response bias.

Using the Survey Results

The write-up of the most significant survey results can be condensed to a few pages. It includes information about the number of people surveyed, as well as the percentage response rates by gender, race, etc. The write-up also captures the major findings of the initiative, describing results that are interpreted as surprises, inconsistencies, or particularly significant. The write-up is supplemented by tables presenting the percentages that support the data mentioned. Figure 8-3 is a sample survey write-up. One supplementary table is shown in Table 8-3.

Survey results are also used to support or question the findings from focus groups. For example, in one organization, few employees talked in the focus groups about their own experiences with sexual harassment or said they knew someone who had been harassed. However, on the survey over 50 percent indicated they had been harassed sometime in their career. The anonymity of the survey allowed employees to share information that would not have come out in the focus groups alone.

In focus groups in another organization, African-American employees reported that the work environment was sometimes difficult to work in or hostile. The survey reinforced this, because in response to a question about racial harassment, over 60 percent of African Americans indicated they had experienced harassment. In this case, the survey and focus group data reinforced one another, with the survey shedding light on the depth of the problem.

Employment Data

The employment data serve two primary purposes. First, the data provide an objective measure of whether there is a

Figure 8-3. Sample survey write-up.

A total of 128 employees completed the survey: 70 women and 51 men. Seven surveys were excluded from the analysis because gender data were missing. Racial/ethnic representation was provided from employees who are African American, Asian American, Latino/Latina, Native American, and white. Nine employees with disabilities also participated in the survey. The grade range for employees who completed the survey ranged from grade four to grade thirteen.

Most employees are basically satisfied with working in the organization, although more women than men felt their gender was a hindrance or barrier to promotion (45 percent versus 26 percent). More women than men felt their level of assertiveness was a hindrance or barrier to promotion (73 percent versus 48 percent).

Assignments

Employees feel that they have relatively little control over receiving assignments. Between a third and a half of all survey respondents felt that they had little or no control, and 89 percent of Native Americans felt this way.

Stereotyping

One piece of survey data that supports stereotyping is the extremely high percentage of Latinos/Latinas and foreign-born Asian-Pacific Americans who report using foreign language skills on the job (64 percent and 51 percent, as compared with 30 percent or fewer of the other groups). These data support the stereotype that some Latinos/Latinas and Asian-Pacific Americans may be perceived as being capable only of doing jobs using their language skills. Table 8-3 shows an example of a table that would support this write-up.

Harassment

The survey data concerning harassment revealed that between one-third and one-half of the women in every racial group reported having experienced some sexual harassment. Racial harassment was also felt to be prevalent, particularly by African Americans.

glass ceiling. To calculate whether there is a glass ceiling and where it is, ask questions such as:

- How many women are at each level (pay grade) of the organization? How many people from each minority group are at each level of the organization?

Table 8-3. Sample supplementary cross-tabulation table showing survey response.

	Whites	African Americans	Latinos/ Latinas	U.S.- Born Asians	Foreign- Born Asians	Native Americans
Percentage Who Use Foreign Language Skills on the Job	30	26	64	28	51	24

Figure 8-4. Write-up of the sample glass ceiling.

The employment data show that glass ceilings exist for minorities and women. For example, although women constitute nearly 50 percent of the professional workforce, they hold only 20 percent of the senior management positions. Similarly, minorities constitute about 15 percent of the professional workforce and only 4 percent of the senior management positions.

Other data also suggest that glass ceilings exist. Women are concentrated in lower grades or levels than men. The distribution of women peaks at grade nine and then drops. As a point of comparison, men peak at grade ten and remain fairly constant through grade twelve before dropping off at grade thirteen. Minorities are concentrated in lower grade levels than whites. Whites (men and women) peak at grade ten; other racial/ethnic groups peak at grade nine.

Data show that for new hires with a bachelor's degree, men and women of age 21 or 22 start at the same grade. However, as they get older, newly hired men start at higher grades than women with comparable experience. The difference widens as the age of the new employee increases.

- What is the ratio of men to women, whites to minorities, etc., at each level?
- Are minorities, women, people with disabilities, and people from other diverse groups in positions where they will likely be promoted into positions above the glass ceiling over time?

In terms of writing up the employment data, the information related to the glass ceiling is usually summarized in one or two pages and included in the final report. An example is provided in Figure 8-4.

The second purpose of the employment data is that the data can be contrasted and compared to the qualitative data collected from employees. For example, the organization can compare actual complaints of sexual or racial harassment to the perception of the degree to which people report it. When these are different (and they often are), it is appropriate to ask: "What does this mean?" In some organizations, the low rate of formal harassment complaints indicates a fear of reprisal.

The most helpful ways to use employment data are to answer questions such as:

- Are actual rates of promotion for various groups similar to or different from people's perceptions of who is advancing?
- Are actual rates of hiring for various groups similar to or different from people's perceptions of who is being hired?
- Are the number/percent of reported cases of harassment smaller or larger than the frequency with which harassment is perceived as an issue in the focus group discussions or on the survey?
- Are career development opportunities (such as training and mentoring programs) provided to certain types of employees more than others? What are the perceptions about the accessibility of these career development opportunities?
- Are attrition rates different for different groups? What are the perceptions regarding attrition in the organization?

Drawing Conclusions from Employment Data

It is easy to draw misleading conclusions from numerical data. By drawing upon the talents of an experienced statistical analyst and asking members of the task force to review preliminary conclusions, the facilitators will reduce the likelihood of error.

Do not place too much emphasis on comparisons of percentages of small numbers of respondents. This can happen easily when the data are cut too finely (e.g., by racial/ethnic and gender groups within two grade-level groupings within a department, such as when comparing African-American women clerical employees to white women clerical employees within a particular department). Once you fall below twenty people (e.g., fewer than twenty African-American women clerical employees in a particular department), the percentages may reflect the perceptions of individuals rather than represent all African-American women clerical employees in the organization.

Remember that survey responses are perceptions of the people who completed the survey. Use language in the write-ups to reflect this.

Consult with a statistical analyst about the specific cross-tabulations desired. This is important since each organization is different and each initiative is different, with its own peculiarities (e.g., problems with the numbers of different demographic groups, sampling issues, problems with the makeup of different organizational groupings).

In addition, more sophisticated statistical analyses are possible that would relate respondents' perceptions about different issues. Whether or not these additional analyses are conducted depends on time, money, the requirements of the initiative, the number of completed surveys to work with, and the level of sophistication of the audience for the initiative results.

Criteria to Use When Preparing Summaries

The write-up is an opportunity to condense and synthesize a great deal of data. As you prepare the write-ups:

- Focus on issues of most concern to employees.
- Capture the emotional intensity.
- Document supporting data.
- Notice inconsistencies that arise.

In the write-ups, begin with issues about which there was a lot of energy and discussion. Drop those categories around which there was very little discussion or interest. However, provide a summary of any categories in which some employee groups responded strongly yet in very different ways. For example, the downsizing issue is often of concern to white men, who see it as a threat to advancement. In contrast, white women may be more concerned about downsizing because of the potential loss of recent gains, like flexible hours and work/family policies. The concern is that these policies will be viewed as expendable when the organization is trimming its budget. People from racial/ethnic minority groups are concerned that they will be let go first and in larger numbers than are whites.

Capture the emotional intensity, to the extent possible. This can be achieved by using selected quotes and anecdotes that represent the essence of a group. To maintain confidentiality, make sure that any anecdotes are edited so as not to identify the speaker.

Document supporting data so that it is possible to track down the source document for any quote, percentage, or number. This is a quality control measure, enabling the writers to identify the source for every specific statement that ultimately is included in the final report.

As you summarize, notice any inconsistencies or questions that arise. Often the data from one method appear to contradict information from another. Make notes of these so they can be explored further in the next step.

An analysis of Asian-American employees on one survey indicated that they were satisfied with management and the organization as a whole. However, in focus groups with an Asian-American facilitator, much greater dissatisfaction surfaced. Also, it was observed that turnover was higher than average for Asian-American employees than for other groups. Upon further analysis, it appeared that many Asian-American employees were hesitant to criticize management and the organizational structure on their own, when completing the survey, but not in the group. One employee noted that rather than criticize or confront the authority in the system, it was easier to leave the organization and go elsewhere.

In this organization, the true level of dissatisfaction emerged only when a safe atmosphere was created where people could honestly express themselves—a focus group with an Asian-American facilitator. This benefited the employees by providing them with a level of support beyond what they had experienced in the past. It benefited management by providing insights into what was actually causing turnover among members of this racial/ethnic group and giving management the opportunity to take steps to address concerns of the Asian-American employees.

Comparing Trends

After summarizing the data from each source (focus groups, interviews, etc.), compare the data across sources to get a fuller picture of what is happening inside the organization. The focus group data tell orally what is going on in the organization. The survey tells the extent to which it is occurring. Both types of information are extremely valuable, as they give a point of comparison. Anecdotes in the focus groups and interviews and open-ended questions on the survey also add richness to the quantitative data.

There are four basic ways to make comparisons. Each is listed below with an example.

1. *Compare information between focus groups to see how different groups perceive the same issues.* This approach highlights issues in which people have different perceptions and experiences. This step often yields some surprises. There may be content areas that are viewed very differently by different groups. For example, in the area of advancement, which asks employees to describe who advances in the organization, there is often a range of responses. Ethnic minority employees often think white men and women advance most quickly, while white men often perceive that minorities and women advance more quickly. Each group perceives another to be more advantaged at this time.

When asked about getting adequate feedback and communication from their supervisors, minorities and women often perceive that they do not get feedback and that white men do. However, at the same time, white men perceive that they do not get feedback. Analyzing the information gives the organization an opportunity to look at truths. The organization can begin to acknowledge that both perceptions may be right and can use this information as an indication to look further. With this feedback issue, for instance, minorities and women often miss the subtle cultural cues of the white male culture that are valuable feedback. Most white men perceive these cues on a subliminal level by virtue of being a member of that cultural group. So, minorities and women are right that they are not "getting something that white men are." In addition, white men are right that they are not getting explicit verbal feedback.

2. *Compare focus group information to interview data to contrast how employees and executives view the same issues.* Comparisons between focus groups and interviews can be enlightening since they highlight the differences between employees' and managers' perceptions. Subjectivity, for example, often makes employees feel that assignments, promotions, and training opportunities are mysterious processes; many employees feel disadvantaged by the perceived lack of fairness in the processes. On the other hand, upper management often focuses on the benefits of subjectivity: It allows flexibility and avoids the feelings of having one's hands tied by bureaucratic policies.

3. *Compare qualitative data (focus groups and interviews) to survey data to determine how many people experienced the things mentioned in focus groups and interviews.* The survey offers a concrete point of comparison. It gives a baseline that the organization can use in the future to monitor its progress. Use the survey data to corroborate or question the focus group data.

4. *Compare all data collected from employees (through focus groups, interviews, and the survey) to the employment data tracked by the organization.* This provides a reading into employees' perspectives versus the organizational record. For example, in reviewing the data about the assignment process, you would look at the following information:

- *Comments in focus groups.* "Assignments are critical to anyone's success," "If you don't have the right assignments, you aren't visible," "Visibility is a key issue."
- *Comments in interviews.* "I succeeded because I got critical assignments. I don't know how I got them. One thing led to another."
- *Statistics from the survey.* How many people believed they got the assignments they did because of gender? Because of race?
- *Employment data.* Where are women, men, whites, racial/ethnic minorities, and people with disabilities

employed in the organizational hierarchy? Which types of people hold line positions? Staff positions? Which are in the high-visibility and critical assignments? What jobs are stepping-stones to advancement? Which types of employees are in those slots?

Determining Categories and Themes

After completing the steps described above, synthesize the data into themes. The themes give a manageable way to understand the data and feed it back to the organization.

A theme is any comment or perception that is expressed repeatedly. For each category, there are often numerous themes. In the assignment category, there might be themes such as: There are many perceptions of how the assignment process works; certain assignments are crucial to success; women and minorities are not getting the assignments white men are; difficult, visible assignments go to white men; and there is risk aversion on the part of managers to giving difficult assignments to people with disabilities, minorities, or women. From the themes, organizations can take a leap to the finding.

Developing Findings

A finding is a bottom-line statement, a root cause, and a basic operating principle. For every category (recruitment, assignments, etc.), there are usually one or two findings. Findings are unique to each organization. To continue the example from above about the assignment process, the finding might be that the process is mysterious (people do not understand how it works) and is not equitable (it treats people differently based on gender and ethnicity).

Findings are simply synthesized themes and serve to enable the organization to more comprehensively understand what the data uncovered. The findings point out the parts of the organizational structure to be eliminated or changed in order for the organization to work effectively for all members. Although findings are unique to each organization, there are certain findings that typically occur.

Given the sheer volume of data collected, it helps to put findings through a "filter" to determine their importance. One recommended approach is to ask:

- *What did we find out that the organization needs to know and needs to handle right now?* These may indicate places where the organization is vulnerable. Be sure to report these critical findings orally and in the final report.
- *What did we find out that the organization would like to know about because it is important?* Addressing these will help create an environment that genuinely supports working with diversity.
- *What did we find out that is simply nice to know and has no significant cost if we do not address it?* Exclude these from the written report, for the sake of brevity.

One of the more subtle findings is stereotypical thinking. Because of its subtlety, it may be difficult to identify directly and may be embedded in the answers to other questions. For example, when focus group participants are asked to describe barriers to advancement that women could confront, some might say "work/family responsibilities" and indicate that "women are not as dedicated to the job as men because of their families." This would be considered stereotypical since it is a generalization to assume that all women have family responsibilities and that these responsibilities would interfere with work.

Another example is the stereotype that graduates from African-American colleges are not well educated or prepared, because the participants do not consider historically African-American colleges equivalent to "white colleges." This could affect many aspects of the organization (where recruiting efforts are made, who gets challenging assignments, etc.).

To identify findings and uncover the meaning(s) in the data, ask the question: "So what?" The answers provide insight into the barriers to be confronted in the organization. These could be policies and procedures to be modified or new programs to be explored. The data also reflect the supports in the organization—the people, programs, and policies that support the initiative to work with diversity.

Figure 8-5. Sample recommendations for the final report.

Recommendation: Examine the career assignment process. Create a system that ensures fair representation of people from diverse groups at all organizational levels. More specifically:

- Develop a procedure to ensure that minorities, women, and people with disabilities are systematically considered for key assignments, particularly in line positions, early in their careers. Create a tracking system to monitor results.
- Ensure that there are clear, consistent, and objective criteria for promotions and assignments. Communicate criteria to all employees.
- Develop a training and development program to enhance the advancement potential of minorities, women, and people with disabilities.
- Use the annual review as an opportunity to ask employees about their interest in management positions.
- Encourage interested employees to pursue management/leadership training.

Recommendation: Explore more-effective feedback and communication policies and practices.

- Design a performance feedback mechanism.
- Hold supervisors accountable for regular communication and feedback to employees.
- Clarify for employees what criteria they will be evaluated on.
- Provide supervisors with training on giving feedback (both positive and negative).
- Provide training for supervisors on coaching a culturally diverse workforce.
- Consider ways to improve and expand existing reward systems, including rewards for effective teamwork.

Developing Recommendations

Recommendations are constructive actions that can be taken to further strengthen the organization. They include steps to eliminate or reduce the barriers.

Sample recommendations are provided in Figure 8-5. Each recommendation includes a general statement committing the organization to address a finding and then describes specific ways to approach the issue.

Writing the Final Report

Preparing the draft report is the next task. The draft—and final—report consists of the following sections:

1. *Executive Summary.* The Executive Summary is a one- or two-page summary of the entire report. Typically, it includes one paragraph summarizing each major section of the report (the introduction, background, findings, and recommendations).
2. *Introduction.* The Introduction puts the initiative in context and explains why the organizational assessment was undertaken.
3. *Background/Methodology.* This explains how the initiative was conducted. It describes the organizational commitment, establishment of the task force, the dates/time frame when the initiative began, and the methods used to collect information from employees.
4. *Findings.* Findings are synthesized themes that emerged from the data. They may be broken up into general findings that apply to all employees and specific findings (e.g., those that pose particular barriers to certain groups).
5. *Recommendations.* Recommendations are provided in response to each finding. These recommendations become the basis of the implementation plan.
6. *Appendices.* Appendices typically include the data collection instruments (the focus group guide, interview guide, and survey) and relevant reference information, such as articles or a recommended reading list.

After the report is drafted, select readers to provide comments and feedback. Readers are typically the task force members, executives, and people in the organization who can serve as representatives of each diverse group. Readers should be given approximately five days to read and respond to the draft report.

Readers can submit written comments individually to the lead writer(s) of the report. If comments and suggestions conflict with one another, it may be appropriate to have a meeting with the selected readers to come to a consensus on revisions to the report.

As a final step in this phase, prepare the final report. The final report can be reviewed and approved by two or three selected readers before it is distributed. Options for distribution are described in Chapter 9.

Conclusion

As you go through the steps in this chapter, be aware that people often experience shock, are overwhelmed, and may feel defensive when reviewing the findings. In addition, if the people who are analyzing the data lose perspective on the data or feel that the situation is unsolvable, it is helpful to bring in outside assistance.

9

Feedback:
How Do We Talk about This Information?

Organizational change takes place in many ways and often begins with language and the way we talk about things. Our language changes as we begin to move toward new ways of thinking and acting. Encouraging conversations about ways to create full inclusion of all employees powerfully promotes new attitudes and behaviors in the everyday work life of employees. Those conversations begin with the feedback to the organization about the data collected from focus groups, interviews, and the survey.

The purpose of giving feedback is to present important organizational information to the people who provided that information in a way that they will hear it, think about it, begin to understand its implications, and do something about it.

Feedback enhances the diversity initiative in a number of ways. First, it allows the diversity conversation (initiated by the focus groups, interviews, and survey) to continue in an organized, structured, safe way. The feedback of organizational data collected during the organizational assessment gives a mechanism for formal and informal communication to take place throughout the system. This supports the continuation and growth of the diversity initiative and enables people to become increasingly more comfortable talking about sensitive issues. Second, feedback sessions provide an excellent forum to gather suggestions and recommendations from employees in regard to what goals they would like to achieve for themselves and the organization through the diversity initiative.

What This Chapter Does

The goals of this chapter are to explain how an organization can continue the dialogue with people about the meaning of the data collected in the organizational assessment; describe the possible ways feedback can occur (through written materials, such as a report, newsletter, or project update, and through oral communication, such as feedback sessions and oral presentations); identify benefits of having feedback sessions in which the diversity conversation can develop; and identify ways to gather suggestions and recommendations during the feedback sessions to address the diversity issues surfaced.

As a result of conducting feedback sessions, organizations will give back synthesized information about people's perceptions collected during the organizational assessment, continue the diversity conversation supporting organizational change; bring crucial issues and concerns into the open where they can be worked and dealt with; explore and discuss the findings of the initiative in greater depth in order to understand their meaning and the implications to the organization; relate the findings to one's department, work group, team, or self; and generate solutions and identify goals for the diversity initiative.

In giving the feedback from the organizational assessment, the organization has the perfect opportunity to communicate the inclusiveness that is the heart of the diversity work. By reporting and honoring the concerns and feelings of all employees, the organization effectively facilitates the organizational conversation.

This chapter addresses three guidelines:

1. Understanding that people respond to feedback in many ways.
2. Communicating feedback to senior management first.
3. Giving feedback as soon as possible.

Each is described below, as well as methods of giving feedback.

Understanding People's Responses

Many people are likely to be validated by the feedback, while others may find the information unsettling. The relationship with the organizational leadership that has been built in the early phases of the diversity initiative governs how fully the organization will communicate the feedback to the members of the organization. The organizational assessment sometimes reveals perceptions that are different than expected. Organizations may think they are doing a better job than their membership perceives.

For example, the human resources (HR) department for a high-tech corporation had addressed the issue of recruiting women and minorities over a period of some years. From the perspective of the HR staff members, a significant effort had been made to make managers aware of the desirability of broadening the pool of potential employees to include more people from diverse groups. In addition, the HR staff had identified candidates with the requisite educational background and experience whom they believed were overlooked by those managers doing the actual hiring.

Despite their efforts, this hardworking human resources staff was alarmed to hear that many senior managers perceived them as not doing an adequate job. When the HR staff members became defensive, the diversity task force became concerned. The members were concerned that an adversarial relationship between management and HR would undermine the possibility of diversity initiatives getting started. The task force set up a meeting and invited HR and several senior managers. In this meeting the HR staff was recognized for its recruiting efforts and, together with senior management, new recruitment strategies were developed.

Watching for Backlash

Be prepared for potential backlash from white men during the feedback phase. White men may be frustrated, angry, and resentful about the focus on diversity issues. A climate of backlash in the organization can subtly sabotage this phase unless it is acknowledged and addressed. When concerns are expressed up front, there is less likelihood that backlash will occur. People conducting the feedback sessions can take steps to ensure that white men are heard, their contributions are recog-

nized, and the barriers they face in the organization are acknowledged. The organization can communicate that the point
of the diversity initiative is to be inclusive of everyone, not to
change or disregard white men.

One organization effectively explained the range of reactions of white men by placing them on a continuum. At one
end of the continuum was the belief some white men expressed
that the diversity effort would increase awareness and bring
issues out into the open. These men acknowledged that the actions taken to address common concerns of "diverse groups"
often directly benefited white men (e.g., through better training, mentoring, coaching, career development). Therefore, their
perception and experience with diversity issues was positive
and personally beneficial.

At the other end of the continuum was the perception of
other white men that the effort would create further separation
between people and might adversely affect morale and produc-
tion. The greatest concern typically expressed was that preferential treatment would be given to people who might not have
earned it and that competent employees would suffer. Ironi-
cally, this is a similar concern of people from diverse groups.
They do not want to be "given" anything because they are
women or minorities; instead, they want to be offered assignments and promotions because they have earned them. By
using a continuum, many of the reactions, feelings, and experiences of the white men in the organization were captured.

Until recently, white men were discussed as if they were of
one mind with one personality, a stereotype that fueled many
people's biases. White men are no more the same than individuals in any other racial/ethnic group. Treating any group as
such may call forth defensiveness and backlash.

Promoting Understanding

Understand that certain issues can be the distinct experience of one group and be absent or misunderstood by other
groups. The feedback sessions can open the door to greater understanding by representing the concerns of each group in a
rational and sensitive manner. This enables the participants in
the feedback session to discuss what to do with the information
in a way that will increase understanding, inclusion, cohesive-

ness, and productivity for the organization and its members. It also creates a situation where no single individual has to be the champion for an issue or have the issue perceived as his or her concern alone.

In a high-tech lab, several women approached the director and described their concerns about women gaining access to working on "hot" projects. In the past, there was little understanding of these concerns, and management seemed reluctant to look at women's issues too closely. There was concern that a close review would create a backlash from white men in the organization. After much discussion, the director decided to use a broader approach and look at a variety of quality of work life issues.

A survey was sent to employees. Some of the most powerful information that came out of it involved sexual harassment. There seemed to be little understanding on the part of the men in the organization as to the behaviors that were offensive to women and, in some instances, to other men. The leadership realized that sexual harassment was a critical issue and was made aware of the organization's vulnerability because of people's lack of understanding and sensitivity to it. For this reason, the organization decided to conduct sexual harassment prevention training as the first step in the implementation phase. The sexual harassment problem was addressed constructively, in a way that improved overall communication between men and women. This provided the groundwork for addressing other challenging issues related to women in the high-tech lab environment while continuing to work with issues that were more generic to all—issues such as career development, creating a more collaborative work environment, alternative work schedules, and part-time employment.

Communicating Feedback to Senior Management

Executives should receive the feedback before anyone else in the organization in order to have time to digest the information and absorb its meaning in a constructive way. Be sure to give them the good news first to help them put the other information into context. Use the feedback sessions at the executive level to strengthen commitment. With clear and visible continued commitment from the leadership, the rest of the organization will be better able to receive the information.

Depending upon the nature of the feedback, be sensitive to and be prepared for varying responses from leadership and management. Leaders who believe they have worked diligently to manage the organization affirmatively and with sensitivity to diversity may experience disappointment if they hear feedback to the contrary. Management may be surprised or even hurt by the perceptions of the people in the organization, especially when managers believe they have tried to create an environment that is fair and works for everyone. Differences in perception occur for numerous reasons. Executives may have not communicated their own concerns about these issues. They may have tried to "fix" things without involving the people affected. Although some progress might have been made, the executives may have missed those things that would have had the greatest impact on employees.

One chief executive who had worked very hard to make the performance evaluation process fair and constructive was devastated when he heard that many people in his organization perceived that the appraisal process was biased. This well-intentioned leader struggled to understand the bias around race and gender that prevented certain people from moving up the career ladder. Through a closer look at the evaluation process, he was able to see some of the reasons it could be perceived as unfair.

Giving Feedback as Soon as Possible

When feedback is given as quickly as possible upon completion of the organizational assessment and final report, it satisfies people's curiosity about what was learned. If there are delays, people have a tendency to make assumptions about the cause—thinking, for example, that management is stalling. Delays may have disruptive effects on the successful movement of the diversity initiative. You may hear comments such as, "I knew nothing would come of this study. Things don't change around here," and "What are they trying to hide?" Giving feedback promptly ensures people that something is being done with the information. It also maintains momentum, keeps the flow of communication open, satisfies people's curiosity, and makes use of data that is valid and reflective of the current issues that are most significant to the organization and its employees.

Feedback Mechanisms

Feedback can occur in two ways: (1) a written report and (2) oral presentations. People take in data in different ways. Providing feedback in both a written and oral format is most effective since some individuals are more receptive to data that is spoken, while others absorb information more readily when it is in written form. Suggested approaches are provided below.

Written Feedback

Once the final report has been written (as described in Chapter 8), it can be disseminated in several ways:

1. Everyone can receive a copy of the full report.
2. One copy can be made available in the central office.
3. One copy can be available for each department.
4. A summary can be distributed to employees.
5. A summary can be included in the newsletter or in the electronic mail system.

Some organizations demonstrate the importance of the initiative by distributing copies of the full report to every individual. Other organizations disseminate one copy to each department and ask the department heads and supervisors to make sure the information is shared with all employees. At a minimum, distribute a summary of the findings to all employees. This can be done by directly mailing a short report or by including a summary in an employee newsletter or bulletin to each employee. Be sure to identify where employees can review a full copy of the report if they are interested.

The value of giving employees an opportunity to review the written materials prior to attending an oral feedback session is that it gives people time to reflect upon and integrate information. They come to the oral feedback sessions better prepared to discuss issues and share recommendations for improvement.

Oral Feedback

The primary reason for conducting oral feedback sessions is to create a conversation based on employees' perceptions as collected in the organizational assessment. Feedback sessions provide an opportunity for employees to share feelings about the results of the organizational assessment with one another and begin to identify how they can take action. As a general rule, people have never had this type of conversation before except in homogeneous groups. Oral feedback sessions provide the opportunity for these conversations to occur in diverse groups.

The oral feedback session is one of the most powerful moments in the change initiative. When people hear the data together, at the same time, it gives the data validity. People have a feeling of safety knowing they will not have to personally author any statement or disclose any experience. The disclosure has already occurred; now the information speaks for itself. People have the opportunity to be in the presence of rich information and to have potentially deep discussions about it, without having to personally defend their perceptions and convince people that their own perceptions exist on a wider basis. Moreover, when a group of people receive feedback about themselves, they begin to take ownership of the aspects that are relevant to them.

In one organization, a feedback session conducted for a department of approximately sixty people resulted in tremendous learning for all participants. Upon hearing the feedback that African-American women throughout the organization were feeling frustrated and isolated in regard to getting feedback from their managers, Dave, one of the managers, asked if African-American women in the department agreed with the data. Two of the African-American women in the group openly expressed their agreement and shared their perceptions and feelings about feedback and communication with management. This was new information for managers in the room and opened an ongoing dialogue in the department. In this department there was enough of a basis for communication that the managers of the group members were able to take the feedback, apply the parts of it that were relevant to themselves, and use the information in a constructive manner.

In some departments where people might not feel as comfortable working with the information immediately, the feedback session can serve as a basis for discussions that people might have with one or two other people. In the situation in which African-American women felt frustrated and isolated in regard to getting feedback from management, the data could be a useful point of discussion in a meeting between one of the women and her supervisor. In addition, the African-American women's feelings could be discussed with people who supervise and manage African-American women to determine how they perceive the feedback issue. These kinds of discussions can lead to better understanding of a difficult issue.

By modeling openness and honesty, the presenters in feedback sessions foster an attitude of receptivity to the information and honor differences in perception. Some people will be uncomfortable hearing the information, even if it clearly and objectively represents people's experience. The presenter can encourage dialogue, letting people know that this discomfort is a normal response to hearing the feedback the first time, and provide a safe space in which to express differences of opinion and resistance to accepting the information.

After the feedback is delivered, facilitators can use Outcome Facilitation® to focus employees and managers on their desired outcomes, generate possibilities regarding having an improved workplace, and create additional momentum among employees for moving forward to their desired state. During this part of the discussion, the facilitators emphasize the importance of having clearly defined, vivid, personal outcomes.

Content of Formal Feedback Sessions

Formal feedback sessions include a presentation summarizing the organizational assessment, followed by a question and answer session and time to brainstorm and discuss possible solutions. The sessions range in length from forty-five minutes for a presentation to a small group to ninety minutes to two hours for a comprehensive presentation to larger groups. These can be set up as special sessions or conducted as part of regularly scheduled staff meetings.

The summary includes the impetus for the diversity initiative, background and methodology, findings, recommendations, and overview of the implementation strategy, with discussion, questions, and answers throughout. This format can be used in the small or large group setting. If your goal is to inform everyone of the findings at once, a large group presentation is an effective approach. However, because of the emphasis on presenting information, there is no time for in-depth dialogue. The presenter uses relevant anecdotes and examples so the flavor and feeling of the feedback is communicated effectively.

A team presenting the data to a large group in one company prepared twenty transparencies, wallcharts, and graphs about employment data, promotion rates, attrition rates, etc. Although this information was important, the employees commented at the end of the session that the charts and graphs could have been handed out for people to review on their own. The employees observed that it was the qualitative findings, issues, concerns, and discussion among participants in the session that really communicated and integrated the organization's story.

When facilitators tell the story in an objective yet comprehensive manner, people have a chance to hear the experiences of others in the organization. This has the potential to foster feelings of compassion and understanding for others' experiences, rather than trigger defensiveness and guilt. Use the quantitative and qualitative data in a balanced way to provide meaning and direction to the overall effort.

Feedback sessions are particularly powerful when they take place in an intact work group. Use the small-group format to conduct informal presentations for work groups, teams, and departments, followed by a period of time for extensive discussion. Because people in intact work groups work with one another on a daily basis, this is where some of the most significant issues of exclusion and inclusion take place and where some of the deepest problems occur. If a work group can hear the information together, then there is an opportunity for people to get a sense of how the findings relate to their group. This is also an opportunity for people to share honestly their own experiences if they choose.

Often, in smaller groups, the presenters/facilitators can ask questions, guide an in-depth discussion of the findings, and help the group discuss their goals for dealing with the findings in their own creative way. Typical questions might be:

- Has this been your experience?
- How has your experience been similar to or different from this finding?
- What can you do as an individual and group to create a more ideal state?

The major benefits of this format are that constructive dialogue can occur and that people are more likely to be open to the feedback and integrate the information. On the other hand, it may take weeks or months to inform all members of the organization when feedback is presented in smaller groups. Making the written report available will compensate for the length of time it takes by allowing people to read the report while waiting to participate in a small-group feedback session.

The feedback sessions can be an appropriate time to ask people to focus on the future and for people to describe what the organization is like in the outcome, coming from the perspective that the organization has already healed and achieved success with regard to diversity. Possible questions include: If you assume success with regard to the diversity initiative, what do you have? What is different about the organization that you now experience? How are you different?

Now stay in your outcome and remember back. How did the organization do it? What specifically did the company do? What was your role? What did you do?

Outcome Facilitation® enables the organization to have a clear and collective understanding and agreements about where it is heading. Outcome Facilitation® requires that individuals take personal responsibility for contributing to the success of the initiative. The exercise is most effective when it occurs at a time when the organization is celebrating its successes ("Look how far we've come") and planning the next round of initiatives ("Now where do we go?").

If the feedback session includes extensive discussion, an

additional session could be scheduled to focus on future outcomes. The diversity initiative benefits in three ways from having employees generate outcomes through the Outcome Facilitation® exercise.

1. By involving all employees in designing the outcome, each person recognizes his or her own level of ability and responsibility to make this outcome come true. The best place to capture these personal revelations after the initial sessions is to have some ongoing opportunity at staff meetings for people to share results and keep their enthusiasm and commitment alive. People realize that the work they do in terms of examining their own beliefs and attitudes, adopting empowering beliefs, and taking action on their commitments contributes to making the desired outcome a reality.

2. By assuming that success is achieved and asking people to step into their desired feelings and ideal reality, the organization demonstrates that success is both possible and probable. The experience of success generates excitement, particularly among those who have doubted that the organization is truly committed to the initiative or that change will ever occur. Excitement increases people's commitment to the initiative.

3. Coming from outcome saves time, energy, and resources. When people are in the mind-set of a problem ("This is the way it is," "This is reality"), it is a struggle to solve it. By shifting perspective and stepping into solution, people generate solutions more quickly, easily, and creatively.

Who Receives Feedback and How

Feedback is given to everyone in the organization: the executives, task force, managers, supervisors, and all employees.

One approach is to have members of the same racial, cultural, and ethnic groups hear the feedback together. Some groups are more comfortable hearing the information this way, which may allow for a more spontaneous conversation. If your organization chooses this approach, then it is advisable that individuals also participate in mixed feedback sessions with members of their teams or work groups. As previously described, the mixed sessions organized by work group serve a different purpose. They help to ensure that members of the same work team have an opportunity to discuss these sensitive issues in a structured forum.

If there is some very difficult and sensitive feedback to be discussed, it might be wise to feed the information back through homogeneous groups. The facilitators might determine it is best to have each group hear the information separately, react to it, and then come together to hear and work with feedback in a mixed group.

After analyzing the data, one small company that was having some problems between their men and women sales agents found it useful to have separate sessions of men and women to hear the feedback. The company also scheduled a session the following day where the two groups could get together to discuss the information. The opportunity to hear the information in homogeneous groups gave the men and women time to discuss some of the frustration they had been experiencing with one another and to strategize some ways to move the discussion in the mixed groups in a more positive direction. One important thing this mixed group did in the feedback session was determine they needed a half-day session devoted solely to improving communication between men and women on the same work teams. They planned a half-day workshop on gender communication.

The decision to give feedback to a homogeneous group can be something as simple and straightforward as the following. The Latino/Latina group in one organization was having its annual conference. The decision was made to offer a feedback session on the results of a diversity initiative the organization had recently completed. The leaders in the organization felt it was a perfect opportunity to reinforce the commitment to the diversity initiative by communicating the results of the initiative to this group in this setting. The leaders also believed that the reactions of this group would provide valuable information that could be incorporated into future sessions for other groups. As a result, the Latino/Latina group members felt included in the ongoing initiative to work with diversity and knew they were valued as important contributors to the continuing organizational conversation.

Whether the feedback sessions are in small or large groups or are given to homogeneous or mixed groups, some people feel hope for the first time in these feedback sessions that their organization is creating structures, programs, and policies that are inclusive of all individuals. These dialogues leave people with a better understanding of each other and a sense of direction for the organization.

Who Delivers the Feedback

The sensitivity, integrity, organizational understanding, and continuity of the feedback delivery team affects the success of this phase. Those delivering the feedback should be able to present data clearly and concisely, facilitate and encourage in-depth discussion, and recognize and help participants work through potential problems caused by discomfort or resistance to the data. Ideally, the feedback team models a healthy and honest way of interacting and encourages individuals to openly share their feelings and perceptions. Facilitators who have an understanding of organizational dynamics will recognize many of the potential issues that arise in a typical feedback session as healthy for the organization and employees to express.

Feedback can be delivered by individuals selected by the organization's leadership or the task force, or it can be delivered by members of the task force itself. External consultants, if they have been previously involved, can also help deliver feedback sessions. It is helpful to use two-person teams that are diverse in race, gender, ethnicity, position, rank, etc. These teams become models of the diversity that is being fostered. Task force members tend to make effective feedback presenters/facilitators because they have been selected on the basis of their diversity, are intimately involved with the diversity initiative from the beginning, are experienced with working with diversity issues among themselves as they have interacted, and are experienced from guiding a diversity initiative full of unknowns and fraught with challenges. By the time the organizational assessment has been completed and the report written, these individuals are well qualified to manage this critical phase of delivering the feedback.

A diversity task force in one organization decided to deliver the feedback. They established diverse pairs (e.g., a Latin woman and a white man). The feedback sessions were particularly powerful because the presenters had been involved in the initiative since its inception. They had designed the survey themselves and had analyzed the data thoroughly with the help of consultants. Further, as the task force continued to meet, the members discussed employees' varying reactions to the feedback with one another. These employees' perceptions were then integrated into subsequent feedback sessions. The cross-pollination of ideas strengthened the impact of the feedback effort and deepened the ongoing organization conversation.

Thorough preparation by the presenters increases the likelihood that the information will be presented in a clear, comprehensive manner. Even with thorough preparation, presenters may meet challenges and resistance from the participants. Suggested approaches for handling the most common issues that arise in feedback sessions are presented in Figure 9-1.

What Follows the Feedback

Once the feedback for the entire organization has been communicated to the managers and employees, people will begin to find solutions and become motivated to take action. In fact, it is a sign of health for the individual department or group to respond to the data immediately, rather than wait for someone from above to direct them. Of course, this will work better if some of the issues directly relate to a specific department, rather than affect many in the organization. If the issues cross many departments or the entire organization, it makes sense that the parties work together to coordinate an organizationwide effort to resolve the issues. The following is an example where one department responded quickly and effectively to feedback from the employees.

A small research and development company conducted an organizational assessment to identify ways that it could serve its customers better as the company diversified its products and services. Upon completion of the organizational assessment, the computer center received feedback about its lack of responsiveness to internal customers. It appeared that there was a lack of cooperation among employees in the computer

Figure 9-1. Recommendations for handling issues during feedback sessions.

Issue:	Some people will question the validity of the data.
Response:	Make sure facilitators are familiar with the data and the analysis so they can answer challenging questions.
Issue:	Some people will question the methodology and analysis.
Response:	If a survey was conducted, the responses can be written so any statistics can be understood easily. If any complex analysis was done, the statistical analyst can participate in presenting feedback or be available to answer questions.
Issue:	Some people will deny the data.
Response:	Facilitators can respond by restating the data. They can explain that although the data might not be true for every member of the group, the data are true for the majority of the members of that group and are important to recognize as such. Facilitators may ask people who deny the data to share their own perceptions so a discussion can occur.
Issue:	Some people will think the analysis has diffused the issues or reduced the intensity of the data.
Response:	Facilitators can give relevant anecdotes in order to have the feelings and intensity of the data come alive.
Issue:	If the data are reflective of many problems, some people will feel overwhelmed by the job ahead.
Response:	Facilitators can reassure people that it is useful to get clear on the current state of reality, so people in the organization can create and move toward their ideal state in a measurable way. In addition, it is more powerful having things in the open, even when the information is uncomfortable or painful, rather than having issues remain undefined. Issues that are suppressed can affect the organization in an ongoing, insidious manner.
Issue:	People will be interested in knowing the dates when these changes will be addressed.
Response:	Facilitators can present the implementation strategy and share the proposed timeline of when the recommendations will be finalized. This is a good time to remind people that the initiative is a long-term process and to reassert the commitment to action.

department itself and that their conflicts were being felt by the rest of the organization. It surfaced that the hardware and software professional services staff had little appreciation for the support staff function. The support staff felt that they were treated as second-class citizens.

During a focus group discussion, the support staff mentioned that one of the Ph.D.s from professional services had publicly yelled at them for having made a mistake on one of the computer systems. They noted that this type of treatment was not unusual. This treatment angered members of the support staff, yet they felt they had little recourse because of their role in the department. In addition, they felt that their ongoing concerns in regard to career development issues and career laddering were easy to ignore because of their lack of importance in the organization.

Before the assessment, Vernon, the director of the organization, had sensed that there were problems. After receiving the specific feedback from the assessment, he realized that things required immediate attention. Vernon decided to have a team building training session for the employees in the computer center, so they could address their specific problems. He believed the team building would enable the computer center employees to better appreciate all job levels and functions and work more effectively together. Then the employees could discuss how their department could better serve the organization's goals and product development. In addition, Vernon assembled a mini-task force, consisting of managers and support staff, to work on the issues of job descriptions and career laddering for the support staff. These efforts elevated the role of the support staff in the department.

Efforts such as those initiated by Vernon help to create a forum for discussing the sensitive issues that are often present when there are class distinctions preventing members of the same department from working effectively together.

Conclusion

Feedback holds a mirror up to the organization. The feedback allows the organizational story to be told openly, honestly, and publicly. People begin to say, "This is who we are. This is our story." These discussions often lead to empowerment and appropriate action ("If it's our story, then we can do something about it"). Organizational change begins in a major way when the system believes its own feedback. Some people will believe the feedback immediately. Others may require some time, and some may never believe it. But for many, feedback sessions are magical because positive change begins immediately, simply because these conversations are taking place.

If desired, people in the organization can act upon suggestions made by employees in the feedback sessions without waiting for a formal implementation plan to be developed. Employee suggestions can also be communicated back to the project coordinator or task force leader, so they can be addressed formally in the implementation plan. Instructions for preparing a comprehensive implementation plan are provided in the next chapter.

10

Experimentation and Implementation:
How Do We Move into Action?

Many of us are accustomed to the traditional steps in conducting a diversity initiative: gathering data, analyzing the information, developing recommendations, and then delegating the implementation of these recommendations to the appropriate parties. But to address diversity issues, we must actively experiment with new policies, procedures, and initiatives that achieve the desired results of inclusion, collaboration, and full participation.

An attitude of experimentation enables organizations to approach implementation in a more fluid manner. It is important to test the assumptions underlying the plan and look at the results with an intent to assess what is working. This is not the time to settle on a single diversity plan. Rather, this is a time to approach the recommendations with the philosophy of "let's experiment, be open to the possibilities, and be willing to make some mistakes," and most important, "let's collaborate with one another in learning how to work with diversity."

When reviewing the approaches and implementation initiatives described in this chapter, remember that they may take place over several years. This perspective enables you to stay focused on moving forward one step at a time.

The diversity plan builds upon the strengths of the organization's culture and takes into account the particular challenges or problem areas identified in the organizational assessment. It requires careful consideration of resources by finding ways to utilize existing systems and practices whenever possible, rather than inventing new and different ones that could add costs or create unnecessary resistance. In addition, the plan is flexible and evolves and changes as new information becomes available. Most important, the plan is developed with input from everyone in the organization.

What This Chapter Does

The purpose of this chapter is to provide guidance and structure as you develop strategies to implement diversity initiatives. Specifically, the chapter describes how to move from recommendations into implementation. As a result of completing the steps in this chapter, you will have a comprehensive diversity plan, with action steps, assignments, and timelines. Further, your organization will actively experiment with solutions to address diversity issues.

This chapter covers the information needed to develop a diversity plan. It includes:

- Guidelines to successful implementation of the diversity plan
- Developing the diversity plan
- The four components of the plan:
    1. A vision statement with organizational goals and objectives
    2. Roles and responsibilities
    3. Implementation initiatives
    4. Accountability statement

A sample diversity plan is also presented.

Guidelines to Successful Implementation

Follow these five guidelines to ensure successful implementation of your diversity plan:

1. Understand who you are as an organization, and build on your strengths.

2. Incorporate diversity goals into the business plan.
3. Link working with diversity to other corporate initiatives.
4. View working with diversity as a long-term initiative.
5. Focus on desired outcomes and results.

Understanding Who You Are

The diversity plan takes into consideration what is known about the organizational culture, especially in terms of where supports and resisters to working with diversity might exist. The plan is built upon the findings and recommendations of the organizational assessment. Frequently, the assessment identifies champions of the effort within the organization who can become advocates, advisers, and participants in the actual development of the diversity plan itself. In many cases, departments are identified where successful practices are being used to work effectively with diversity. These practices can be applied across the organization.

For example, in a company with offices in sixteen locations around the country, the human resources department learned that one of the satellite offices was successfully attracting recent graduates with degrees in engineering and computer science who came from diverse cultural and racial backgrounds. The HR department called upon the manager of this office to provide guidance to managers in other locations. In addition to developing a successful recruiting and hiring strategy, this manager vocally championed the benefits of a more diverse organization.

Sometimes, the diversity implementation team must set priorities based upon what has been learned about specific barriers. For instance, issues relating to work/family concerns might have a longer cycle and require further in-depth investigation. Problems that surface in the area of sexual or racial harassment would require immediate attention.

A federal agency learned of widespread sexual harassment when it conducted an organizational assessment. As a result, management decided that the first component of the diversity plan would be to remedy the situation immediately. The highest level of management issued a strong policy statement and mandated that training be given to all managers and employees. While this training was being delivered throughout the organization, the diversity implementation task force continued to move forward on other initiatives.

Incorporating Diversity Goals into the Business Plan

The organization that understands that diversity issues are business issues establishes diversity as a corporate objective by including it in the organization's business/strategic plan. All systems, from individual development plans to performance appraisal systems and salary review systems, can then be reviewed to ensure consistency with the commitment to diversity.

In a large technical services company, interviews of corporate executives revealed a strong resistance to anything resembling quotas. The CEO recognized the advantage to be gained if the composition of the company's workforce more accurately reflected the customer base. The CEO and director of diversity developed a strategy whereby each division designed its own plan for becoming more diverse. Each division's plan was based on its employment data, its customers, and the community in which it was located, and each plan had to reflect the overall corporate objectives established for the organization. The key element was that the division leaders were empowered to take responsibility for making needed changes to achieve the corporate objectives. Inclusion of key players and placing responsibility at the local level increased the likelihood that they would become fully participative of the overall diversity initiative.

Linking Diversity to Other Corporate Initiatives

A realistic diversity plan utilizes organizational systems that are already in place. Eventually, the concept of working with diversity becomes integrated into the strategic thinking of all aspects of the business. Rather than adding another costly plan to the corporate agenda, the plan to work with diversity takes advantage of existing programs such as total quality initiatives, management training programs, and employee networking groups. The concept becomes interwoven in the fabric of the organizational structure and philosophically permeates all training programs.

Strategic thinking in all areas of the business will create

the necessary links to fully integrate diversity. A natural place for diversity work to be done is to connect it to the total quality initiatives already under way in so many organizations. Quality management, a systematic approach to maximizing customer satisfaction by optimization of the thinking and acting of all players, is clearly linked to working with diversity.

Viewing Working with Diversity as a Long-Term Initiative

"This is the way we will be doing business from now on" is the message that employees, managers, customers, and the community need to hear from the organization's leadership. To be most effective, the message must be supported by the core values upon which the business is built.

The organization may meet with resistance from some employees who are skeptical about the organization keeping its promises to improve the quality of work life and create more equitable environments. Skepticism can be overcome by continual reinforcement of the strong commitment of organizational leaders to work effectively with diversity and by broadcasting and celebrating successes, small and large.

This is an appropriate time to write an article for the company newsletter highlighting how people might be feeling and that being discouraged at the beginning of the implementation phase is normal. The article can focus on the need to recommit to the long-term goals and identify all of the steps being taken that are keeping the diversity initiative alive (task force work, any specific successes, etc.). As people are kept informed via the overall communications strategy, some of the cynicism begins to fade.

Focusing on Desired Outcomes and Results

As you develop specific strategies to address diversity issues, stay focused on desired outcomes and results that are presented in the final recommendations from the diversity task force. The diversity implementation team can use outcome thinking just as it was used by employees in the feedback sessions.

For example, with regard to recommended meetings between employees and supervisors on career development, the diversity implementation team can ask the question: "How did we do it?" They may conclude that the approach was phased in over time. In the first year, all supervisors received a refresher training course on providing career development, and one-half of the employees had a career development meeting with their supervisor. In the second and third year, every employee had a one-hour career development meeting with his or her supervisor. By the fourth year, the full outcome had been achieved: Each employee had a one-hour meeting with his or her supervisor every six months. They would then write these steps in the appropriate sections of the implementation plan under the "career development" heading. At a later point, each department will develop more specific, detailed steps to accomplish the career development goals.

Developing the Diversity Plan

The diversity implementation plan is developed using multiple sources: results from focus groups, interviews, and the survey; employment data; the analysis and recommendations provided by the diversity implementation task force; the desired outcomes described in the feedback sessions; and strategies used successfully by other companies.

Typically, the diversity implementation plan identifies immediate action steps, as well as tasks to be completed over a one-to-three-year period. The steps to follow in developing a diversity plan are outlined below.

1. Designate and officially appoint a person—the director of diversity—to facilitate implementation. This individual has direct access to the leadership of the organization. This person is different from the project coordinator who guided many aspects of the organizational assessment. (The director of diversity's duties are described in more detail later in this chapter.)

2. The director of diversity, with approval from the leadership, creates a diversity implementation team. The team may include members from the original task force to

provide continuity. The primary role of the new team is to prepare suggested implementation strategies. This group is composed of a diagonal slice of the organization and has a diverse membership in terms of job function, grade level, gender, race, physical ability, sexual orientation, cultural background, etc.

3. Invite employees to participate in the diversity implementation team. Give employees the names and telephone numbers of the people to contact if they are interested in participating. Employees may be given the option of submitting their recommendations for action steps in writing to these individuals and/or being physically present during the development of the implementation strategies. This involvement enriches the plan by including creative ideas from the full workforce.

4. The diversity implementation team members separate into small groups of two or three. Assignments may be made by the director of diversity, or individuals may volunteer for assignments. Each group includes people with particular expertise in the subject matter and those who have particular jurisdiction over allocating resources to a given area. Groups may also include employees who have volunteered to participate.

5. Each small group is assigned (or volunteers) to research a recommendation or set of recommendations. For each recommendation, the group researches possible implementation strategies and develops a written proposal for the most effective way(s) to address the issues. The group identifies action steps that need to be taken and who is responsible for each step. The group also provides input on prioritizing the steps, noting which action steps may be completed simultaneously. To prepare this information, the group draws upon its knowledge of the organization, the data collected from employees, additional suggestions provided by employees in feedback sessions, and information about how other similar organizations have addressed these issues. The sample diversity plan provided in this chapter can serve as a resource as the groups prepare their proposals.

6. Each group submits its proposals to the director

of diversity, who then meets with the entire diversity implementation team to review the information. Based on these proposals, the team develops a draft diversity plan, with a detailed timeline, assigned roles and responsibilities, and an estimate of resources required. This chapter includes guidelines about assigning roles strategically and provides a sample diversity plan to use as a prototype.

7. The draft diversity plan is shared with the organization's leadership for input and review, and a suggested timeline is submitted for approval.

8. After approval, the draft plan is shared with the executive team, senior management, and management to solicit their ideas and support.

9. The final plan is developed by incorporating appropriate changes and feedback.

10. The plan is disseminated to all people who are directly involved in the initiative.

11. Highlights of the plan, including the organization's priorities and the timeline for addressing various issues, are communicated to all employees.

12. The director of diversity guides and shapes the implementation of the diversity plan and evaluation of the success of these efforts.

Be sure that the leadership allocates sufficient time, money, and empowerment to enable people to develop the diversity plan. The development of the plan can be lengthy and require that people be pulled away from their jobs for meetings. The task is less intrusive when the work is spread out among many people, each having a piece of the development plan.

Assign Roles and Responsibilities Strategically

Send a strong, clear message about the importance of the diversity initiative by selecting a highly visible person from the leadership to serve as the director of diversity. Appoint someone outside of the human resources department, who is not connected with EEO, affirmative action, or training. In the early critical stages of implementation, the sponsorship and attention should be held at the corporate (rather than departmental) level, where the individual is seen as a successful business-person concerned about the bottom line.

To illustrate the significance of strategically assigning roles, consider these two scenarios. Joan is the diversity coordinator for a large public sector organization. She is also the assistant to the director of the Management Institute, the training arm of the organization. Prior to this assignment, Joan had chaired the diversity task force, which had conducted an organizational assessment and produced a report on diversity issues in the organization. Joan, an African-American woman, appeared to be the perfect choice for the role of diversity coordinator, at least from the perspective of the organization's leadership. Joan will tell you otherwise. She struggles to keep the diversity issues alive and on the table, and she meets often with resistance from senior management and line managers.

Without sufficient sponsorship, resources, or commitment from the leadership, Joan is not able to implement the comprehensive recommendations of the diversity implementation team. Although the organization issued a strong diversity policy statement in support of building a fully inclusive organization, it had not changed any internal systems that were identified as barriers to women and people of color. Joan feels there is lip service to diversity but that she has been given no real access to the white power structure in her organization. Joan is typical of many people selected to manage diversity efforts in large organizations. She is talented and keenly aware of the issues that must be dealt with but is often powerless to influence decision making because she has no connection to the inner circle of senior executives who run the organization.

Joan is now spending her time developing connections and building relationships with key people in the organization. She sees her job as having to communicate and repeatedly sell the concept and benefits of diversity to these people. She cannot move to implement initiatives because the sponsorship and support are not yet in place.

Tim, on the other hand, has had a very different experience. He has been with his telecommunications company for seventeen years. An electrical engineer, Tim developed the business acumen to bring millions of dollars in contracts to his company over the years. A corporate vice president by the time he was forty, he was viewed as one of the company's success stories. When Tim lost two talented women from his staff who felt they had hit the glass ceiling, he became an early advocate of removing barriers to women's career advancement in the company. His frustration led him to discuss glass ceiling issues with other women and later with people of color on his staff. Tim worked to create a diversity task force that became the coordinating group for an organizationwide assessment.

When the results of the assessment indicated the presence of significant barriers to advancement and career development for women and people from other minority groups, the CEO was moved to take action. He appointed Tim as corporate vice president for diversity management. Tim's first task was to develop a strategic plan to address diversity issues and incorporate them into the overall business strategy for the company. Tim was given the authority and the resources to move forward. A clear message was sent by this appointment that the company took the results of the assessment seriously and that it was going to make some dramatic changes in the way things were being done.

The director of diversity needs to be an official appointment by the leader in the organization. This sends a strong message to the entire workforce that this initiative warrants a full-time, corporatewide position. There are instances where people have attempted to keep a diversity initiative alive by structuring their time to be the unofficial director of diversity. Over time, these individuals have burned out and the initiative has lost momentum because of the person having so many demands placed on his or her time. Also, if the management above this person is not a strong advocate of diversity, the decision to do the diversity work can reflect negatively on the individual and may be seen as a misuse or waste of time.

The assignment of a director of diversity as a corporatewide position indicates to the organization that diversity is seen as a key business factor and will therefore get the recognition and positioning required to root it firmly in the organizational structure. Clear linkages and collaborative relationships are then created among the individuals and departments that have been key players in the diversity initiatives. Linkages are created among four key areas:

1. The organizational leadership that sponsored the initiative
2. The diversity implementation team that has given momentum and guidance to the initiative
3. The human resources and EEO departments that have addressed these issues for years
4. The director of diversity

With this support structure in place, the diversity effort is positioned to have a great impact and to result in widespread organizational change.

The Four Components of the Plan

When creating a diversity plan, you focus on four components: (1) a vision statement with goals and objectives, (2) roles and responsibilities, (3) implementation initiatives, and (4) an accountability statement. These four components are included in the sample diversity plan that appears in this chapter.

Vision Statement with Goals and Objectives

The vision statement includes goals and objectives that are established by the management with input from the diversity implementation team. Goals are based on information gathered in the organizational assessment. In this way, everyone is involved in setting the goals and objectives. A vision statement from the leader at the outset demonstrates strong commitment to the diversity plan. Continued communication of the commitment to the established goals and objectives reinforces the message, encourages participation in the initiative, and increases the likelihood that the diversity initiative will take hold and the diversity plan will accomplish the desired goals.

Roles and Responsibilities

To ensure that the diversity initiative will take hold, there must be clear role definition, delineation of responsibilities, and accountability for all members of the organization. Senior managers, working with the CEO or executive director, can review and provide input about roles and responsibilities. In this component, suggested roles and responsibilities for members of the organization are described.

Implementation Initiatives

Initiatives address action steps to be taken for the organization to work effectively with diversity in areas such as education and training, recruitment and hiring, retention, career development, mentoring, and community outreach.

Accountability Statement

As with any organizational change effort, there must be ways to track and measure success. The organization must show commitment to personal accountability for attaining organizational goals and objectives. Here are examples of ways to hold people accountable:

- Identify goals and objectives for diversity in the annual business plan, and then measure them on an annual basis. Were the goals and objectives achieved? If so, how? If not, why not?
- Managers can identify measurable ways that they will facilitate valuing diversity in their own departments and teams. They can review these results with their managers (both above and below them) on a quarterly basis.
- Each time the leadership states goals and objectives and gives a time frame, an opportunity is created for tracking and measuring the results. To the degree possible, these results should be publicized to the organization to reinforce momentum.

Specific ways to maintain accountability can be discussed and determined by each organization.

We strongly recommend that the business plan contain specific reference to the diversity goals as determined by the CEO and senior managers, such as those provided in the sample diversity plan. Other important considerations include allocation of resources and a projected time frame for accomplishing goals and objectives.

Sample Diversity Plan

The sample plan presented here includes a composite from different companies about ways to address a variety of diversity issues, including training, recruitment and hiring, etc. The sample plan is a big picture perspective of many possible ways of putting a diversity initiative into place.

We recommend that you use the sample plan to trigger ideas for your own diversity plan, determine which initiatives to address first, and assess which tasks have already been accomplished. The plan you develop will be more customized to your specific needs, based on your goals and the feedback received from employees.

For some organizations, the diversity plan will be much longer and more detailed than the sample plan (for example, under training, you could list specifically how many people will attend training, how often, and in what subject areas). For other organizations, the diversity plan will be much shorter than the sample plan and will focus on the one or two areas the organization determines are most critical to address during the coming year.

The significance of the diversity plan is the strong message it sends to the organization's members about the commitment and willingness to take action. Whether the diversity plan comprehensively covers every area of the organization or focuses more specifically on a few key priorities, the commitment to take action is a powerful and positive sign.

Sample Vision Statements

_____(Name of organization)_____ envisions creating a work environment in which all individuals are valued, feel their ideas have merit, and feel their talents are fully utilized to benefit customers, the organization, and themselves.

_____(Name of organization)_____ is dedicated to eliminating barriers based on race, gender, ethnicity, religion, age, disability, and sexual orientation and to create a work environment in which every employee is able to achieve his/her full potential in support of organizational goals.

Sample Statements of Goals and Objectives

- Attract, retain, and develop a diverse workforce to meet the needs of a changing work environment and marketplace.
- Redesign reward and recognition systems to reflect valuing diversity.
- Help all employees to fully develop in their careers to meet individual and organizational goals.
- Develop an assignment process that ensures fairness and objectivity and provides the best match of employees' skills, strengths, development needs, and job requirements.
- Become the employer of choice of all groups, including women, minorities, and people with disabilities, by attracting the finest talent available to our workforce and retaining employees by providing opportunities for career development and advancement.
- Create a work environment free from harassment of any kind and based upon mutual respect. This includes taking steps to define and promulgate organizational policy prohibiting harassment and establish and publicize procedures for handling harassment concerns, internally and externally.

Roles and Responsibilities

The CEO establishes goals, provides leadership, and creates the vision and rationale for working with diversity. Senior managers develop the plan, managers execute the plan, and employees participate in the plan. Representatives from human resources facilitate and support the overall effort, particularly with regard to implementation. The diversity implementation team guides the implementation of the plan and develops and manages the communications strategy.

Detailed descriptions of roles and responsibilities are provided for the:

- CEO/Executive Director
- Director of diversity
- Senior management
- Management
- Human resources department
- Employees
- Diversity implementation team

The board of directors also participates in the initiative by lending overall support to the effort and reaffirming the business imperative. The board can do this by ensuring that at least one board member is a stakeholder in efforts to promote workforce diversity. The stakeholder can be a member of the EEO or human resources staff. Alternatively, the board can commit that an established percentage of its membership be from diverse groups.

CEO/Executive Director

Ongoing Responsibilities

- Create the vision of Workforce Diversity = Profitability for All.
- Advocate, encourage, and provide incentives to management to support the diversity initiative.
- Set the policy and corporate goals for effectively working with diversity.
- Build commitment to diversity issues through ongoing communication.
- Continue to work with the diversity implementation team.

Immediate Responsibilities

- Appoint a director of diversity.
- Approve the diversity implementation team.
- Communicate the business imperative for working with diversity in the organization.

- Communicate a vision for working with diversity in the organization.
- Communicate a working definition of diversity for the organization.
- Discuss the diversity initiative and present the draft diversity plan at senior staff meetings and at regularly scheduled meetings throughout the year.
- Publish a memorandum to the entire organization in regard to the diversity initiative.

Responsibilities during First Calendar Year

- Identify quantitative items for the business plan goals for diversity.
- Guide senior managers in developing diversity goals for their departments.
- Hold senior managers accountable for implementation of diversity plans.
- Codevelop a diversity education plan, and monitor its progress.

Responsibilities during Next Calendar Year

- Expand the role of human resources to monitor and support workforce diversity issues.
- Hold quarterly meetings between senior management and various network groups of minorities, women, people with disabilities, and white men. Forum may vary.
- Extend the commitment to valuing diversity to the community at large. This could take the form of becoming an advocate for diversity in the community (e.g., ensuring that country clubs encourage a diverse membership).
- Encourage employees to be involved in community programs.
- Demonstrate commitment to diversity by evaluating managers on human resources management skills and behaviors that are now considered as important as other factors.

Director of Diversity

The director of diversity should be an individual who is close to the head of the organization so that the effort is seen as a corporate organizationwide initiative.

Ongoing Responsibilities

- Serve as a liaison among organizational leadership, diversity implementation team, management, employees, and diversity efforts in other areas in the organization, if applicable.
- Guide the development of the diversity plan, based on recommendations from the organizational assessment.
- Be a point of contact for all diversity initiatives that are under way in the organization.
- Coordinate communications strategy with the diversity implementation team.
- Talk with or informally interview members of the organization regarding how they are responding to the effort.

Responsibilities during First Calendar Year

- Function as the project manager for diversity in the organization.
- Coordinate actions throughout the organization to implement the plan.
- Communicate successes in one area of the organization to other areas in order to share successful models, etc.
- Monitor the evaluation process to ensure quality and timely implementation.

Senior Management

Ongoing Responsibilities

- Ensure that the organization provides all employees with an atmosphere that values continuous learning, diversity, empowerment, and creativity.
- Actively support recruitment and retention of women, minorities, and people with disabilities.

- Communicate with and listen to concerns of white men who may be feeling disenfranchised and left out.
- Communicate commitment to and progress on workforce diversity at town hall meetings and staff meetings.
- Establish an environment that fosters open communications flow among employees, managers, and customers.

Responsibilities during First Calendar Year

- Provide input and develop strategies to move the leadership's vision into the comprehensive business plan for the company and respective organizations.
- Establish accountability by establishing each manager's diversity plans and targets based on his or her own demographics, geographical area, and customers.
- Build commitment in support of the diversity plan.
- Execute the diversity plan.
- Work in partnership with human resources to ensure that policies and procedures are in place to support the new vision and direction.
- Develop understanding of the business imperative for working effectively with diversity.
- Gain/broaden understanding about issues and concerns related to working with the full range of diversity issues at the organizational level.
- Establish point of contact to work with human resources in regard to diversity issues.
- Strengthen commitment to placing qualified minority and women student interns in the organization.

Responsibilities during Next Calendar Year

- Demonstrate commitment to diversity by evaluating managers on human resources management skills and behaviors that are now considered as important as other factors.
- Reward managers who effectively serve as role models and translate the organization's value of diversity into action.
- Report to the organization's leadership semiannually on managers' progress with implementation of the diversity plan.

- Define and include effective diversity management as part of the evaluation of line managers.
- Sponsor coaching/mentoring programs, and recognize mentoring in performance evaluations.

Management

Responsibilities during First Calendar Year

- Continue to recruit, retain, and encourage people from all diverse groups and white men to use their unique skills to excel in the organization work environment.
- Continue to create an environment that is sensitive to all aspects of diversity.
- Establish an environment that fosters open communications flow among employees, managers, and customers.
- Regularly coach individuals on strengths and weaknesses.
- Act as coaches, mentors, and resources to employees of all groups.
- Take a proactive approach to encouraging and—where appropriate—placing women, minorities, and people with disabilities in positions that will break stereotypical molds.
- Strengthen commitment to placing qualified minority and women student interns in the organization.

Responsibilities during Next Calendar Year

- Assist employees in career development.
- Recommend training for high-potential employees of all groups.
- Support training programs designed to increase awareness of multicultural, gender, and diversity issues.
- Be willing to develop coaching/mentoring relationships.
- Consider evaluating benefits of "shadowing," that is, assigning someone to follow around another employee in order to discuss issues the employee is working on, attend meetings with the employee, etc. Mid-level managers often shadow those at higher levels, for varying lengths of time.

- Offer employees the opportunity to formally evaluate management in regard to diversity issues, such as through the use of a 360-degree evaluation process (see Chapter 11) or through upward feedback.

Human Resources Department

Ongoing Responsibilities

- Partner with the director of diversity and diversity implementation team to ensure the feasibility of all new policies and procedures and to see that they are implemented in a timely and accurate manner.
- Support the leadership's reviews on the progress made by the senior managers on implementing the diversity plan.
- Enforce a recruitment policy that will ensure the attraction of women, minorities, and people with disabilities.
- Promote hiring practices based on job criteria and skill of applicant versus experience and credentials.

Responsibilities during First Calendar Year

- Include the plan for working with diversity in the strategic human resources plan, and link it directly to the organization's business plan.
- Periodically issue information about the job vacancy, EEO, and grievance processes.
- Conduct an internal assessment based on exit interviews or follow-up data to determine why employees who leave to go to another employer selected that organization.
- Continue to encourage managerial responsibility to ensure that the policies and procedures regarding a harassment-free environment are clearly understood and implemented.
- Develop training curriculum to support awareness and skill development in workforce diversity issues for managers and all employees.
- Ensure integration of diversity principles into all training.

Responsibilities during Next Calendar Year

- Examine reward systems to make sure they benefit all employees equally. Specifically, track promotions, merit increase percentages, and cash awards by group (gender, racial/ethnic, people with disabilities, etc.) to make sure they are given equitably across groups. Report findings to the organization.
- Set up benefit options that address the varying needs of the organization.
- Provide training that reflects the goals and values of the organization in regard to diversity.
- After initial organizational assessment on workforce diversity, expand employee opinion survey to include diversity issues and conduct every two years.
- Ensure that both managers and employees make greater use of network groups in bridging racial, ethnic, and gender differences, as well as differences based on physical and mental ability and sexual orientation.
- Periodically publicize the importance, purpose, and value of mentoring experiences.
- Review training and development sessions, programs, and materials for adherence to current working with diversity vision and philosophy.
- Create an organizationwide AIDS policy.

Employees

Ongoing Responsibilities

- Participate in networking events.
- Appreciate and value the breadth and depth of diversity and the variety of skills people bring to the workplace.
- Fully participate in diversity training.
- Seek coaching/mentoring relationships with people who can provide perspective on and guidance to your career.
- Be open and honest in providing feedback on how well management is working with diversity.

Diversity Implementation Team

This group may also be referred to as the diversity council or the diversity advisory board. The group may include the project coordinator who was involved in the original task force. The project coordinator often serves as the day-to-day liaison between the director of diversity and the diversity implementation team.

Responsibilities during First Calendar Year

- Support the positive momentum of the diversity initiatives by communicating and celebrating successes.
- Actively promote and support the diversity initiatives outlined in the diversity implementation plan.
- Help direct the assessment of the current state of the organization's workforce.
- Work with human resources to define training needs and strategies.
- Assess organizational barriers and supports that affect recruiting, retention, inclusion, and promotion.
- Help implement the communications strategy described below.

Objectives of the Communications Strategy

- Keep channels of communication open.
- Communicate the leadership's commitment to the diversity initiative by outlining the business rationale and benefits to the organization.
- Communicate the draft plan to all levels of the organization.
- Celebrate and acknowledge the importance of the contribution of all employees, so that they understand that the diversity effort is critical to the overall success of the organization and that future success will derive from the full utilization of the creativity and skills of all employees.

Actions Regarding the Communications Strategy during First Calendar Year

- Update all employees with current and correct information about the initiative and the diversity plan.
- Provide a realistic timetable for change to occur.
- Use mechanisms of communication (including electronic mail, videoconferences, town meetings, staff meetings, newsletters, and management forums) that are already in place to inform the organization of the vision, goals, objectives, and actions.

Implementation Initiatives

The following list summarizes the initial steps for implementing the plan to work with diversity:

- Establish goals for working with diversity, and identify measures of accountability. Determine additional methods to measure the effectiveness of this plan.
- Communicate strong commitment to this initiative from the organization's leaders.
- Have senior managers review the draft plan and give input.
- Use education to develop awareness and skills. Educate to increase awareness of the business imperative and to build commitment to the initiative on the part of senior management.

Specific initiatives with recommended actions have been provided for the following areas:

- Recruitment and hiring
- Retention
- Training and development
- Career development
- Mentoring
- Community outreach
- Work/family issues
- Harassment-free environment

Organizations can calculate cost and time estimates for each initiative based on the available resources (training departments, human resources staff, EEO department, etc.) and other organizational initiatives that are well developed and link to the diversity effort (e.g., quality initiatives, self-managing teams, high-performance work teams, and reengineering designs).

Recruitment and Hiring

Recommended Actions

- Emphasize minorities, women, and people with disabilities in college recruiting efforts.
- Emphasize competence-based credentials rather than past experience.
- Meet with professors from minority schools. These meetings allow professors to assess the organization's culture and later to recommend the organization to their students. Professors will also be able to recommend students who are best suited for the type of work and the culture.
- Encourage the placement of interns and co-op students who are members of diverse groups.
- Recommend policies for providing selection feedback to applicants.
- Encourage senior minorities, women, and people with disabilities in the organization to assist in providing names of possible recruits.
- Hire people from all groups to ensure solid representation at all levels of the organization.
- Assess the internal organization to see if minorities, women, and people with disabilities are available as candidates for upper-level jobs.
- Meet with local professional organizations for minorities and women to ask their input as to what the organization can do to attract more people from diverse groups and to discuss potentially tapping their databases.

- Meet regularly with advisory groups of women, minorities, and people with disabilities. Encourage these groups to reach out to their own networks for recruitment purposes.
- Extensively advertise the organization as a leader in diversity.
- If it accurately represents the organization, include minorities, women, and people with disabilities in addition to white men in corporate publications such as annual reports, recruiting brochures, and advertisements.
- Create a progressive image in the media.
- Advertise in magazines and literature that cater to women and minority groups.
- Publish articles on the efforts the organization is making in the area of diversity. (One company published an article announcing the opening of an on-site day care facility and flextime for employees.)
- Distribute press releases focusing on diversity work that the organization is currently doing.
- Continue to create internships with minority colleges that encourage minorities to work at the organization for a period of time while earning college credit.

Retention

Recommended Actions

- Encourage participation in mentoring activities (cross-cultural, cross-gender, etc.).
- Encourage participation in network groups that represent the full diversity of the organization.
- Design and conduct exit interviews with women, minorities, and people with disabilities to assess reasons for leaving and to gain insight into perceptions of invisible organizational barriers and strengths.
- Conduct an assessment based on exit interviews or follow-up data to determine why employees who leave to go to another employer selected that organization.
- Develop a user-friendly job posting system to alert

employees to job openings throughout the organization.

Training and Development

Recommended Actions

- Provide educational programs on diversity to increase awareness and self-assessment by participants.
- Ideally, develop and conduct skill building programs to teach people how to more effectively work with diversity.
- Provide training to enhance interpersonal effectiveness and teamwork while dealing effectively with all differences: racial/ethnic, gender, physical capability, sexual orientation, personality style, age, etc.
- Ensure that supervisors are effectively trained to provide both positive and constructive feedback, coaching and counseling to a diverse workforce.
- Provide training for those people who manage and are involved with individuals with disabilities so the managers and coworkers can help enhance their working effectiveness.
- Supplement ongoing training programs with modules on career development and mentoring.
- Train managers to handle workforce issues that if not handled properly could have a negative impact on working with diversity at the organization. For example, teach managers to handle harassment complaints effectively by dealing with them first at the local level and/ or by referring them on to the formal complaint process in the organization.
- Train employees to handle harassment issues assertively and confidently, whether at the local level within the chain of command or through EEO and the formal complaint process.
- Provide team building sessions that focus on capitalizing on the diversity of members.

Outlines for the following skill building training workshops are provided in Chapter 16 under five categories:

I. Foundation Courses
- Facilitating Organizational Change
- Building a Diverse Workforce
- Prejudice and Conflict: Distant Cousins or Close Relatives?
- Valuing Diversity
- People with Disabilities: Our Untapped Resource
- Eliminating Sexual Harassment in the Workplace

II. Management and Supervisory Development
- Developing Your People
- Supervising in a Diverse Workplace
- Managing Men and Women
- Advanced Interview Techniques
- Job Descriptions: The Key to Legal Management of Employees
- Introduction to Task Force Management

III. Professional and Career Development
- Career Development
- Mentoring in a Diverse Workplace
- Strategies for Breaking the Glass Ceiling
- Image and Personal Power
- Personal/Professional Balance

IV. Professional Development for Women
- Women in the 1990s: Competition, Leadership, and Integrity
- Career Strategies for Women
  - Module I: Generation and Transitions—A Historical Perspective
  - Module II: Stages of Feminine Identity
  - Module III: Understanding and Appreciating Gender Differences
  - Module IV: Women as Leaders:
  - Module V: Challenges to Women as Team Members
  - Module VI: Negotiating Differences
  - Module VII: The Internal and External Barriers to Women's Career Success

- Module VIII: Political Awareness within Organizations
- Module IX: Working with Integrity
- Module X: Mentors—Finding One, Being One
- Module XI: Networking
- Module XII: Building Support Systems/Personal Nourishment

V. Interpersonal Effectiveness
  - Building Intercultural Skills
  - Building Cross-Gender Communication
  - Conflict at a Crossroads: Resolving Conflict in a Diverse Environment

Career Development

Recommended Actions

- Establish the criteria for managing people in support of a diverse workforce.
- Evaluate current position descriptions for mid- and senior-level managers to see if the descriptions reflect what is needed to effectively manage people and support a diverse workforce.
- Take a more proactive approach to placing women, minorities, and people with disabilities in positions that will break stereotypical molds.
- Encourage and reward those who take rotational/exchange assignments.
- Train managers and supervisors in how to coach employees to support career development.
- Consider and evaluate benefits of shadowing assignments for women, minorities, and people with disabilities.
- Encourage senior women, minorities, and people with disabilities in the organization to assist in providing names of interested minorities, women, and people with disabilities to designated points of contact for assignment purposes.

- Determine and publicize the number and percentage of women and minority candidates considered and chosen for senior-level vacancies and first-line managerial positions on a yearly basis.
- Develop an organizationwide assessment procedure to identify the career potential early in their careers of all employees, including minorities, women, and people with disabilities.
- Reward or give special recognition to employees whose actions or recommendations are instrumental in removing or reducing career development barriers for people with disabilities.

Mentoring

Mentoring provides the opportunity for continued employee growth and development that builds competence and commitment. A mentor is usually a more experienced, tenured, or senior-level person in the organization who serves as a coach, teacher, exemplar, counselor, and provider of moral support. Mentoring programs can enable people to contribute more fully and perform more effectively over the course of their careers. Mentoring relationships can be fostered informally and formally and can be planned or spontaneous.

Recommended Actions

- Periodically publicize the importance, purpose and value of mentoring experiences (specifically include cross-cultural and cross-gender).
- Include mentoring and acting as a resource for new and current employees as part of management's responsibilities.
- Value and reward mentoring in performance evaluations.
- Have divisions sponsor mentoring programs and education about the mentoring process.
- Include a module on mentoring in an ongoing management program that creates awareness of the benefits and helps develop mentoring skills.

Community Outreach

The organization is part of the community in which we live. Sharing resources through community outreach can enrich the lives of both the community and the organization.

Recommended Actions

- Partner with community and educational institutions.
- Invest time and money in local career days at high schools and colleges, offer work/study programs for high school and college students, and/or create a stay-in-school program that encourages young people to get an education while working part-time.
- Donate old computer equipment, calculators, furniture, and other useful business items to a local school or minority association.
- Work with local chapters of associations (minority associations, Girl Scouts, Boy Scouts, etc.) to develop programs that help youth develop the skills needed to become employed at the organization.
- Meet with diverse professionals in the business community to elicit ideas for outreach opportunities.
- Participate in Adopt-a-School programs.
- Provide cross-cultural tutoring to community members.
- Make opportunities available for in-school volunteers.

Work/Family Issues

Recommended Actions

- Establish a work/family policy reflective and supportive of a diverse workforce.
- Communicate the work/family policy to the entire organization.
- Ensure uniform implementation of policies on work/family issues, such as treatment of part-time employees and use of leave (annual leave, sick leave, or leave without pay) following childbirth.
- Have upper management send a powerful message to the rest of the organization by supporting flexible work schedules and work/family policies.

- Develop flexible work schedules and communicate them to supervisors and employees.
- Make an employee assistance program (EAP) available to all employees.
- Develop a mandatory training segment in management courses on work/family issues.
- Implement education awareness training about the hidden bias against people with mental and emotional disabilities.
- Provide education on AIDS.
- Provide job-sharing opportunities for women and men.
- Offer day care for children on-site.
- Offer care for aging parents.

Harassment-Free Environment

Recommended Actions

- Publicize an organizational policy statement on how to create a harassment-free environment.
- Clearly determine and communicate appropriate behavior to comply with a harassment-free environment.
- Provide training for managers on handling many types of workplace harassment, both informally at the local level and through the formal complaint process.
- Address issues regarding fear of reprisal in regard to filing harassment complaints with EEO.
- Create a corporate ombudsman to handle harassment issues of all kinds.

Accountability

Building accountability into the diversity initiative is critical to its long-term success. Suggested approaches to establish accountability are listed below:

- Create an environment where the organization can quantify the diversity initiative.
- Establish individual diversity plans and targets based on demographics, geographic area, and customer base.
- Evaluate managers on human resources management

skills and behaviors that are now considered as important as other business factors. Take appropriate developmental and corrective action.

- Use annual employee feedback to assess progress with diversity initiatives.
- Hold senior managers accountable to diversity goals by means of the business plan.
- Report on the number and percent of women and minority candidates considered and chosen for senior-level vacancies and first-line managerial positions on a yearly basis.
- Establish a procedure to ensure that women, minorities, and people with disabilities are systematically considered for line assignments early in their careers. Establish a tracking system to monitor the results of this.

Conclusion

An organization can successfully create and put into effect its diversity implementation plan by following the prototype outlined in this chapter. The next chapter describes various evaluation methodologies to track the organization's progress in meeting the established goals and objectives.

11

Evaluation:
How Do We Know We Have Succeeded?

The purpose of the evaluation phase is to hold the organization accountable to make the changes recommended and described in the diversity implementation plan. The final phase in the diversity model, evaluation provides an opportunity to assess the effectiveness of the strategies, policies, and practices that the organization has implemented. In this phase, the organization compares its progress to the desired outcomes and goals. If it has established critical success factors in the diversity implementation plan, these can be used as specific evaluation criteria.

There are numerous ways to track and evaluate progress. To gather valuable perceptual data, the organization can ask its employees, managers, and customers about their perceptions of how the organization has changed in response to the diversity initiative and what, if any, changes are still desired. The organization can also revise the performance evaluation standards to reflect valuing diversity. The organization may choose to implement a 360-degree evaluation tool, described later in the chapter. These approaches can be supplemented by quantitative evaluation methods, such as tracking employment data.

This phase requires recommitment to the diversity initiative from the leaders of the organization, the director of diversity, the diversity implementation team, and all other critical players. Once the findings have been fed back and the plan established, the hands-on work of implementation begins. Integrating new policies and procedures and behaving in more inclusive ways present challenges on a daily basis. Recommitment is critical; it allows the dialogue to remain open, allows momentum to be maintained, and enables the organization to push through the inertia that sometimes develops. Continuing the diversity initiative requires staying committed for the long haul, continuing to view the initiative from a long-term perspective, and using evaluation approaches to assess progress and maintain accountability.

Because the organizational initiative takes time, we suggest that the organization monitor its progress informally on a quarterly basis by assessing how managers' diversity plans are doing in their respective departments. Reports on the status of these managers' plans would go directly and solely to the head of the organization. A more formal progress report might occur every two years.

What This Chapter Does

The purpose of this chapter is to demonstrate methodologies of evaluating the organization's progress with respect to the diversity initiative. Evaluations allow the organization to assess its progress to date, acknowledge those areas where there have been successful outcomes, and identify areas that still require attention and correction. Because evaluation is nearly as important as the initiative itself, it requires the necessary attention and allocation of resources to adequately track the results. The use of periodic evaluations increases the likelihood that the diversity initiative will remain on course and maintain momentum over time.

The chapter covers guidelines for approaching the evaluation phase, methods of evaluation, recommended timing for evaluation approaches, and suggestions for maintaining the momentum of the diversity initiative.

Guidelines for Approaching the Evaluation Phase

There are three guidelines during the evaluation phase: (1) publicize accomplishments, (2) recognize that whatever has not been addressed will be revealed, and (3) remind people that the diversity initiative is ongoing.

Publicizing Accomplishments

An important aspect of the evaluation phase is to identify those things that have been achieved based on the goals identified throughout the entire diversity initiative. It is empowering for people to know that their suggestions and issues are being actively addressed and may result in changes in the organization. By linking actions to the diversity initiative and publicizing them on an ongoing basis, the organization generates additional enthusiasm, communicates solutions that are working in one department or work team to the rest of the organization, and gives people tangible validation that their contribution to actively work with diversity is having positive results for the organization and its members.

Identifying Overlooked Issues

In the evaluation phase, critical issues and current problems are identified that may have been overlooked during earlier phases of the initiative. The evaluation phase may reveal pockets of resistance to implementing diversity initiatives and to support the objectives outlined in the diversity implementation plan.

Individuals or groups may come forward with specific issues that have not yet been addressed directly. The evaluation process is similar to peeling away layers of an onion. Once the top layer of an issue has been pulled away, new layers are revealed. These deeper layers of problems are often felt intensely by individuals in the organization.

For example, in a large government agency, the evaluation process revealed that the organization had taken significant strides to address sexual harassment issues but had overlooked racial harassment as a barrier. A group of African-American employees at the midmanagement level formally requested that racial harassment be addressed. The organization is currently conducting prejudice reduction training for all employees to correct this oversight and address what has been clearly identified as a very real problem.

The evaluation phase will likely reveal areas where more data need to be collected, where other policies must be revised to be more inclusive, and where additional resources must be allocated. For example, employees in one midsize organization were dissatisfied with the existing work/family policy. Some people noted that although a local day care facility was provided, people were on waiting lists for years before being able to place their children there. This was a source of frustration to many employees. Upon further study, the organization learned that people would prefer vouchers that could be used at day care facilities near their homes. This workable solution enabled the organization to provide day care to employees who desired it for their families.

Reminding People the Initiative Is Ongoing

Although evaluation is the last phase of the diversity model, it is also part of an ongoing cycle. The evaluation process may reveal that some employees are still dissatisfied with the slow progress being made to resolve diversity issues. When this happens, better communication to the organization's members is usually needed from the leadership, director of diversity, and diversity implementation team, explaining to employees what has been accomplished, how accomplishments relate to the initiative, and what is planned for the future. It may be appropriate to underscore that changes take time and the implementation initiative will move along more rapidly when individuals are in full support and take an active role. The organization can also design ways for employees who would like to be involved in implementation and/or evaluation. For instance, employees can join the implementation task force or a subcommittee of the task force, become involved in advocacy groups, or participate in community outreach programs. Evaluation will continue on a regular basis, as will the implementation initiatives and formal and informal communications strategies.

Methods of Evaluation

Evaluations take a number of forms. Eight suggested methods are described below:

1. Compare progress to the diversity implementation plan and the desired results.
2. Reassess employees' perceptions through focus groups and surveys.
3. Conduct management assessment.
4. Use customer feedback.
5. Modify performance evaluation factors.
6. Use a 360-degree evaluation tool.
7. Track employment data.
8. Communicate with networking groups and special interest groups.

Comparing Progress to the Diversity Plan and Desired Results

Using this approach, the organization holds itself accountable to achieving the desired outcomes identified during the feedback sessions and described in the recommendations in the diversity implementation plan. The organization can evaluate its progress by using the critical success factors established during the feedback sessions and finely crafted by the diversity implementation team as its members developed the diversity implementation plan.

Reassessing Employees' Perceptions through Focus Groups and Surveys

In this approach, the organization uses both focus groups and written surveys to gather data from employees to determine their perceptions two to five years after the original assessment. You can use a subset of the original questions that were used in the organizational assessment and incorporate additional questions, such as those in Figure 11-1. Collect data in particular about how employees are feeling, as well as their beliefs, attitudes, and perceptions about the progress of the diversity initiative. The data collected give the organization a basis for comparison from the point at which it began the initial effort. The survey can be a stand-alone initiative or it can be woven into an employee opinion survey, if one is used by the organization.

Figure 11-1. Recommended evaluation questions for all employees and managers.

The following questions can be used as a starting point for conversations with employees to evaluate the effectiveness of the diversity initiative. The questions are designed for discussion in focus groups and interviews or can be tailored to fit a questionnaire.

- Has management articulated its philosophy and set of principles for managing the organization in regard to diversity? Do these include valuing diversity and respecting differences?
- Is the organization addressing all types of diversity, not solely gender and race?
- Is valuing diversity part of the strategic business plan?
- Does management understand that diversity is a competitive advantage (in terms of competing for employees, customers, innovation, and creativity and of reducing costly turnover)?
- Does management provide a positive example of respecting and valuing diversity? Are actions congruent with the messages to employees?
- Does the organization reward managers who value differences and work well with diverse teams of people?
- Are all segments of the workforce population represented at each level of the hierarchy?
- Is this organization considered family-friendly? Minority-friendly? Friendly to people with disabilities? Friendly to women? Friendly to men? Friendly to older, more tenured employees? Friendly to younger employees?
- What has happened formally to address diversity? How are things taking root informally?
- Is this a workplace where all employees have an equal advantage?
- Are there any patterns in promotion that are a concern? Patterns within certain groups?
- Are there any patterns in turnover that are a concern? Patterns within certain groups? Patterns with particular pockets in the organization?
- Are people hearing each other? Are diverse people working better together?
- Are employees more willing to engage in honest discussions about diversity issues?
- Do collegial relationships exist between people of diverse backgrounds?
- Has cultural harmony increased in the workplace? How do you know?
- Have staff members been trained to recognize and understand all types of cultural differences?

Figure 11-1. *(Continued.)*

- Are intercultural conflicts handled effectively?
- Has the organization established and enforced a policy prohibiting harassment (sexual, racial, etc.)?
- Has the organization made it explicitly clear that inappropriate jokes about any person/group are unacceptable?
- Is there a clearly publicized and safe complaint procedure for dealing with harassment issues?
- Has the organization as a whole bought into the initiative? Are there any pockets of resistance? What strategy is in place to work with the resistance?
- Are celebrations of the organization's diverse cultures a regular occurrence?

Conducting Management Assessment

We recommend management assessment and evaluation on a yearly basis. All levels of management can develop goals and objectives that tie the business unit, division, department, or team objectives to having and fully utilizing a more diverse workforce. In order to track their diversity goals and objectives, managers can be asked such questions as:

- Are you achieving goals set forth in your annual business plan and individual management development plan?
- Are you supporting goals set forth in the diversity implementation plan? If yes, in what specific ways?
- Are there effective and profitable results of diversity in your business unit, division, department, or team?
- How would your business unit, division, department, or team be improved if you worked more effectively with diversity?
- Are there diversity issues causing you concern in your business unit, division, department, or team? Whom in the organization could you contact to help you?

Managers may also be evaluated by higher management or through the use of a 360-degree feedback tool (discussed below) to determine those who excel in human resources management skills, particularly with respect to diversity issues.

If the organization takes the diversity initiative seriously, then within two to five years it will be starting to dismantle some of the system's institutional barriers. Within this time frame, the organization might implement succession planning programs for women and minorities; employ more minorities, women, and people with disabilities at all levels of the organizational hierarchy; expand the performance review process to include measuring teamwork; and reward people for better capitalizing on diversity.

Using Customer Feedback

To optimally meet customers' requirements and expectations, the organization must have an effective way to collect feedback from its client base. With respect to diversity, the feedback can include asking customers questions about whether their needs are being met by the products, services, and employees. The organization can ask customers if there are any steps it could take to make its products, services, and employees more accessible and desirable. Questions about the future are also appropriate. These could include questions such as:

- If we were meeting all of your needs, what would be different? What additional services would be provided for you?
- How would you be treated over the telephone?
- How would you feel about doing business with this company?
- What languages would you prefer to communicate in?

Modifying Performance Evaluation Factors

Performance evaluation factors reflect the core values of each organization. One of the most powerful ways to integrate and effectively promote working with diversity is to link it to the performance evaluation system. It is through the performance evaluation process that individuals are held accountable to demonstrate the values that the organization espouses.

After conducting an organizational assessment, one organization determined that the factors on its performance evaluation procedures did not reflect the diversity issue in a tangible way. To remedy this, they added a factor called Valuing and Managing Diversity. It was defined as "the degree to which a manager views differences as assets and utilizes these differences to accomplish organizational goals by identifying the balance between developing shared organizational values and valuing diversity, and challenging assumptions that limit opportunities." Although this factor could be more behavior-specific to help directly shape managers' behavior, this organization has begun to hold its managers directly accountable through its performance appraisal process.

Using a 360-Degree Evaluation Tool

Many companies are using a 360-degree evaluation tool to conduct management and employee assessments. Although the 360 feedback tool has been around for several years, it is now being used in many more organizations as a measurement tool for diversity work.

In the 360 feedback process, feedback is collected via questionnaires from "all around" an employee—his/her supervisors, subordinates, peers, and customers. The feedback is then compared to the participant's own perceptions of his/her skills, abilities, or styles. Organizations use these assessments in a variety of ways: in training programs, for individual development, in team building, for succession planning, in needs analysis, as a form of upward feedback to management, and as a part of total quality management initiatives. The most prevalent and meaningful way the tools are used is to develop, rather than evaluate, individuals.

A 360 feedback tool is a strong mechanism to integrate into valuing and working effectively with diversity because it can be customized to fit the needs of the organization. Specific behavioral items that address diversity, teamwork, empowerment, and interpersonal effectiveness across differences can be included. Ideally, the feedback is behavior-specific and provides managers with feedback that is specific enough to improve skill deficiency. For example, "Does not allow others to finish what they have to say" is more specific than "Should improve communications skills." The more specific and descriptive the feedback is, the greater the likelihood for continued positive behavior and for skill improvement.

The 360-degree evaluation process can also serve as a centerpiece for a dialogue between members in a work group and on a team. Its ability to enhance communication between employees can be dramatic. Members can come together in small or large groups, discuss the feedback they received, and identify what they would prefer take place. People who have avoided issues of differences over time can now have a structured discussion that can guide them through what could formerly have been a difficult feedback session. People can then develop ways to hold one another accountable for the behavior changes that are requested.

When implementing a 360 feedback tool, make sure that training is provided to all participants about ways to give feedback in empowering ways. Further, training may be necessary to create a climate where employees feel safe and confident about providing feedback to their supervisors and peers.

Tracking Employment Data

Review employment data to determine where improvements have been made (e.g., in terms of the glass ceiling, turnover rates, and hiring/promotion rates). For example, review the numbers of people from diverse groups at all levels of the organization, especially as they are represented in high-level ranks.

In an effort to conduct a thorough evaluation of diversity, one organization created a database with the current demographics of its employees. The database was very comprehensive and included data on the performance evaluation for each individual; the position the person now holds; the number of years in the same grade or level; the person's education, including all degrees and certificate programs from recognized training programs; whether the individual had supervisory or management experience; and the types of critical assignments the individual had held. Being able to compare individuals across demographic groups allows the organization to isolate variables and measure statistically what is happening with its people. For instance, the organization is able to compare the length of time African-American men are employed at a certain grade level, as compared to white women, with all other variables being equal.

The organization intends to review this data comprehensively every two years. It will also distribute an opinion survey to employees at two-year intervals. This approach enables the organization to compare the subjective perceptual data from the survey with the objective employment data.

Communicating with Networking and Special Interest Groups

Many organizations have informal networking/support groups before a diversity initiative begins. Often, more groups are formed as the organization begins to fully embrace and support a diversity initiative. Groups can develop around all kinds of special interests. Typically, these groups have a clear, formal, and vocal way of coming forward and sharing their experiences. Because of these characteristics, the groups are an excellent resource for the evaluation process. Specifically, they can communicate regularly with the director of diversity and the diversity implementation team. They can also be asked to complete a survey or participate in a focus group on an annual or biannual basis.

Recommended Timing for Evaluations

We recommend that evaluations of the organization as a whole in relation to the implementation plan should occur at intervals of two and five years. A two-year evaluation will unearth information about the short-term effects of a diversity initiative, whereas a five-year evaluation can provide more depth about how the changes in attitudes have permeated the organizational culture and the way people interact on a day-to-day basis.

The results of these types of evaluations should definitely be distributed to the entire organization in a formal report.

Some of the recommendations, such as the implementation of new policies or training programs, may be accomplished over a relatively short period. Others that require more in-depth work, such as revision of the career advancement process, may require several years before progress is recognizable.

After two years, there should be work in progress (or completed) on most of the recommendations.

Maintaining Momentum

The most powerful and effective strategy for maintaining momentum is for the director of diversity to play the leading role in carrying out the diversity implementation plan and the evaluation of the organization's results. The director coordinates all aspects of the plan and knows how the effort is progressing throughout the organization. This individual helps drive action by working with the diversity implementation team, going back to each department and asking people how they are progressing, tracking the diversity implementation plan, and gathering pertinent information and reporting quarterly to the leadership.

The director of diversity tracks the initiatives that are under way, setting timelines, documenting when they began, where they are now, and where they are going. It is important that people be reminded regularly of the business imperative throughout the implementation strategy, the benefits of specific initiatives, and how activities in which they are engaged are part of the overall organizational plan. This clear communication maintains momentum and helps prevent people from feeling overwhelmed or isolated with their own piece of the work.

The director is the clearinghouse for information who links people and resources to one another. This includes helping people maintain the vision of the bigger picture of diversity and coordinating meetings for people working on different issues to come together and share information. The director also tracks accountability to the particular initiatives assigned, which includes reviewing goals, keeping people focused, and checking to make sure deadlines are met. The diversity implementation team and upper management also play an important role in maintaining the momentum and sharing in some of these responsibilities. The director of diversity has ongoing meetings to report on progress to the executives and management team.

The director of diversity can further increase momentum with publicity about the organization's successes internally to employees and management and externally to field offices and those overseas. The director can then link these successes to the diversity implementation initiatives. An effective communications strategy will allow employees, as well as management, to see the link between the actions taken (new types of training, new policies and programs, etc.) and the diversity implementation plan.

Conclusion

As you review your progress during the evaluation phase, you will recognize that what was initially your desired outcome has now been achieved. To be most effective, the people who are guiding the diversity initiative will look ahead and define new desired outcomes at established intervals. These conversations can occur annually or at any point at which the organization has a significant amount of data about its progress.

The director of diversity and the diversity implementation team have a responsibility to include others in these conversations. The communications strategy and evaluation approaches offer an opportunity to be inclusive.

The organization can also create a formal mechanism for employees, supervisors, and managers at all levels to come together annually to discuss, share, and create a collective vision for the organization's future. In these meetings, participants can receive updates on the progress made during the previous year. They can develop specific goals for the next year, discussing their responses to questions such as: "If you could assume even more success in the area of diversity, what would you have? How would you feel?"

In closing, the evaluation phase is part of the ongoing cycle of the diversity initiative. Evaluation marks the end and the beginning of the cycle. Successes in the first cycle become the new baseline for the current reality as the organization enters the next cycle.

Evaluation brings the organization to a place where it can see its successes and then create a re-vision for the future, with new goals and implementation initiatives.

12

Case Studies:
What Can Other Organizations Teach Us?

There is much to be learned from the experience of other organizations about working with diversity. The case studies that follow provide an opportunity to view the initiatives of three companies, Hewlett-Packard, BDM International, and PRC. These real-life examples of integrated diversity initiatives demonstrate how differently the process manifests itself in organizations.

What This Chapter Does

This chapter provides a summary of the experiences of three companies as they actively worked with diversity. Readers can learn from the practices of these companies, identifying and emulating what worked and learning from what did not work and had to be redone.

Since Hewlett-Packard (HP) began working with diversity issues in 1985, its story provides encouragement to stay with a diversity initiative for the long haul, and HP's experiences give insight about ways to sustain commitment. The BDM case study is an example of how a grassroots effort can gain the sponsorship of the organization's leaders. The PRC case study shows how quickly a company can create fundamental change.

The diversity work in progress at PRC, BDM International, and Hewlett-Packard reveal the breadth and depth with which diversity issues can be approached through a wide variety of initiatives that permeate many layers of the organization. Each organization has shaped its initiative to reflect and be consistent with its own culture and has set the most appropriate priorities according to what the companies are and what they want to become.

Case Study: Hewlett-Packard

Hewlett-Packard designs, manufactures, and services electronic products and systems for measurement, computation, and communications. In part, HP's purpose is to create information products that increase effectiveness and speed the advancement of knowledge. Their products and services are used in industry, business, engineering, science, medicine, and education in approximately 110 countries.

Hewlett-Packard began to look closely at workforce diversity issues in 1985. This was prompted by the realization that although women and minorities were being recruited into the organization's workforce, their attrition rate was two to three times higher than the rate they were entering the organization. This information, coupled with feedback from an employee attitude survey, indicated to the HP leadership that people were not feeling valued or fully integrated into the organization in ways that developed job satisfaction or assured productivity. HP's long-standing affirmative action effort had not served to address the issues of retention and inclusion.

The organization appointed a diversity team made up of HP educational and diversity specialists from around the country. The team developed a training program on Managing Diversity that was integrated into the core curriculum for management training. Developing this program—which became Hewlett-Packard's first diversity education program—took a couple of years.

The Managing Diversity training program was designed to be adaptable to a one-to-three-day format, with modules that could be tailored to meet the needs of the participant group. The training program was supported by a statement from the CEO that communicated the organization's philosophy of valuing diversity. The program was supported throughout the company by a video that communicated HP executives' thoughts on diversity and a video of HP managers talking about diversity issues. First- and second-line managers in the organization were the first groups to receive this training.

After the implementation of the Managing Diversity workshops, the workforce diversity department began to implement several other initiatives. Additional educational courses were developed to build awareness of diversity issues, the college recruiting program for women and minorities was strengthened, and a formal development program that includes a mentoring component was established.

Despite having these worthwhile efforts in place, the diversity initiatives did not have the impact on the everyday life of people in the organization that everyone had intended. According to Emily Duncan, the manager of corporate workforce diversity at Hewlett-Packard, two critical events marked the significant turning point in the organization's actively valuing diversity.

First, the organization gained the support of upper-level leaders. The executive level of leadership (one layer below the CEO), which had been involved with the diversity initiative at the outset, appeared to lack the strength and consistency of leadership that was required to move the effort forward. One of the ways the diversity team approached this issue was to develop, with the aid of an external consultant, a one-day workshop called the Executive Diversity Education Program. This program consisted of three critical components:

1. Interviewing all executives who would attend the educational programs to hear their perceptions and ask their expectations about a daylong learning experience focusing on diversity.

2. Selecting individuals who could represent the perceptions, thoughts, and feelings of members of the diverse groups and inviting them to attend the workshop.

3. Using a training technique called fishbowl in the workshop. In this exercise, members of one group (in this case, women and minority employees) sit in the middle of the room and have an uninterrupted discussion in response to a set of questions about their work experience within the organization. Members of other groups (in this case, the white male executives) look on and listen to what is being said. This is a particularly effective method if the goal is to have people listen to the experiences of a group

of people without having the pressure to be directly involved in the dialogue. There is the opportunity to ask questions upon completion of the group discussion in order to promote clarity and understanding. The discussion reinforces the understanding and potential communication between the groups involved.

Upon the successful completion of the program, the senior executives decided to re-create it for the next level down in the organization, thereby getting the direct buy-in from the upper-level leaders in the organization.

The second major event was that the CEO elevated the issue of working effectively with diversity so that it became one of the three top business objectives for Hewlett-Packard worldwide, as part of reasserting HP's leadership as the best place to work for all people. (The other two business objectives were order fulfillment and financial performance.) The recognition of this issue by the CEO indicated that diversity would be approached as a critical business issue with worldwide implications. In addition, because diversity was one of the three top objectives, it became one of the cornerstones of the business plan. Therefore, at all levels, from vice president and general manager through the remainder of the organization, diversity objectives were addressed in the annual business plans.

These events had a major impact on bringing diversity into everyday life at HP. For example, managers began treating the issue of valuing diversity seriously in performance evaluations. More employee networking groups began to emerge. The organization added a diversity component to its employee attitude survey. These activities had the sponsorship and ongoing commitment of all levels in the organization.

The organization offers continuing courses on awareness of diversity issues. Further, there are several skill-building courses available, such as "Interviewing a Diverse Workforce" and "Managing a Diverse Workforce," that reinforce bringing diversity to a behavioral level in the organization.

Emily Duncan, the manager of corporate workforce diversity, sees her role as a change agent. She brings diversity into the strategic processes in all aspects of the organization. She describes looking at all of the practices and procedures that are in place to remove any existing or potential barriers and to see that HP is honoring its commitment to make the workplace work effectively for everyone. Her job is to ensure that diversity is part of the fabric of how HP conducts its business. Duncan's vision for diversity at HP is to create an environment that benefits from diversity at all levels, values individual differences, and enables all employees to develop and contribute to their full potential.

Full commitment to the diversity initiative is being tracked in a number of ways. Performance evaluations contain a component related to managing diversity effectively, and a diversity section has been added to the employee survey. Finally, the CEO receives quarterly reports on employment data.

HP has clearly recognized and made a commitment to diversity as a worldwide issue. Members of the corporate workforce diversity department are involved in visiting the organization's sites in other countries to help gather information and gain understanding of their specific and unique diversity issues, so HP can better address them in its overall strategic planning. Communicating continually the message of diversity, while working to integrate it into every aspect of organizational life, will ensure that Hewlett-Packard will remain one of the leading-edge companies in diversity work.

Case Study: BDM International, Inc.

BDM International, Inc., headquartered in McLean, Virginia, is an information technology company that has enjoyed rapid growth and successful diversification under the leadership of its president, Phil Odeen, who joined the company in 1992. The challenge at the time was to diversify BDM from being largely a defense contractor providing research, analysis, and other professional and technical services to the armed forces and military agencies into a broader-based company also serving civil government agencies, foreign governments, and commercial clients in the United States and abroad.

Odeen embarked on the changes he saw necessary, acknowledging BDM's highly successful past but convinced that "our world and our markets are changing, and we simply won't continue to be successful if we settle for business as usual." He stressed, however, that "in everything we do, there will be a blend of old and new, of retaining the best of BDM while trying to make it better."

In 1993, in the midst of significant organizational change, an ad hoc diversity task force was formed because its members recognized the need to more effectively manage diversity in order to be competitive in the changing marketplace. How this group came together and was officially sanctioned is interesting. Initially, a woman engineer went to a corporate vice president with concerns about her opportunities for advancement in the company. The vice president listened, and rather than assuming there was no problem because he had not experienced it personally, he decided to pursue the issue.

This vice president had had some recent experiences that demonstrated the existence of barriers to women and minorities. Several women with successful careers and promising futures had left the company. More and more working mothers had to make choices about work and family and then come to terms with their decisions. A large number of major clients were beginning to question the fact that the company's leadership and marketing force were predominantly white males.

The vice president suggested that the woman explore her concerns with another woman manager whose opinion he respected. This manager validated the experience of the first woman and added experiences of her own and of people who worked for her that had led her to conclude that the company needed to look at diversity issues. The diversity task force coalesced around these three people. They were joined by a general manager who was the highest-level woman in the company, the vice president of corporate human resources, the leader of corporate equal opportunity, a young African-American manager, and an Asian-American woman task leader. This was a diverse group of managers and nonmanagers, new and old employees, individuals from technical, administrative, and human resources disciplines.

The Task Force was formally sanctioned by the president, who recognized the link between diversification and capitalizing on diversity. He asked the task force to develop an implementation plan for capitalizing on diversity at BDM. The task force began by assessing employment data on workforce composition and attrition rates. It analyzed the current population by position, level, race, and gender. External consultants were brought in to assist with the development of the plan. They conducted thirty-six executive-level interviews with a threefold purpose: (1) to gather information about concerns of top executives related to capitalizing on diversity and their perception of the business imperative for doing so; (2) to acquire specific suggestions and ideas to be incorporated in the draft implementation plan; and (3) to build commitment from the top in support of a comprehensive organizational effort to capitalize on diversity.

Feedback from the interviews was included in a report and a rough draft diversity implementation plan was written. Each person on the senior management team was given the opportunity to read the report and offer input and advice to be integrated into the final report, "Capitalizing on Diversity at BDM." Two task force members presented the final report at the annual Vice Presidents' Conference. It was clear that a great deal of interest had been generated by the interviewing process and by the circulation of the report itself. "The report was a good vehicle, a thought-catalyst that is bringing forth a lot of positive comments," said one task force member.

The president moved quickly after the final report and implementation plan was delivered by the task force to address several issues he believed to be critical to the future success of the initiative. He appointed three vice presidents to be cochairs of the Diversity Implementation Group (DIG), which was to be an expanded version of the original task force. He requested that the business unit general managers develop diversity objectives that would be integrated into the overall business plan for their units, and he indicated that the managers would be held accountable for meeting the objectives. He requested quarterly meetings with the DIG, asked for strong leadership from the chairpersons, and requested that human resources be the focal point for action in order to make the plan a reality. He endorsed the following diversity goal statement: "BDM will recruit, retain, develop, and promote a highly qualified and diverse staff and management team, representing the cultural diversity in our business environment and community."

A campaign to communicate the corporate plan to capitalize on diversity and build awareness of the issue involved a video presentation by the president explaining the business imperative; a town meeting conducted by the president to explain the first steps in the initiative, to encourage participation in the survey and focus groups, and to respond to questions and receive suggestions; and articles published in the corporate publications. The DIG worked closely with the president and human resources to oversee and guide the implementation of the plan, to keep the momentum going, and to manage the communication strategy to ensure that people knew what was going on.

In the first month of the DIG's existence, a segment on diversity was included in a corporatewide employee survey, eleven focus groups on diversity were held, work groups developed plans for areas like recruiting and mentoring, and a new BDM Information Technology Minority Scholarship Program was developed and approved by the president.

According to DIG members, the diversity initiative was viewed hopefully but with some skepticism that it was "affirmative action revisited." People clearly have a show-me attitude and are looking for steady progress and demonstrable achievement for the effort. The greatest risk is of losing the momentum built into the first phase in the initiative. The DIG is fully aware that there must be continuous improvement.

As the company moves into the second year of the initiative, it is growing and successful. BDM recognizes that capitalizing on diversity is good business, and it knows that despite its commitment and enthusiasm, change will not occur overnight. It is committed to diversity for the long haul.

Case Study: PRC

Founded in 1954, PRC, a subsidiary of The Black and Decker Corporation, provides scientific and technology-based systems and services to government and commercial clients worldwide. PRC is headquartered in McLean, Virginia, and has more than 6,800 employees in 200 offices around the world. The company provides computer systems integration, systems engineering, software development, environmental engineering and consulting, and other professional and technology-based services.

PRC has experienced a fundamental change in the way the organization thinks about diversity and its business. It has shifted from focusing on compliance with laws and regulations to seeking a competitive advantage through hiring and re-taining people of all kinds and cultures, with a variety of work backgrounds.

One of PRC's most visible steps to be inclusive was the recruitment and hiring of a woman to the executive leadership team. Carole Spurrier was asked to join PRC from AT&T. She was hired initially as the senior vice president of business de-velopment and is now the senior vice president of corporate relations. In her present role she serves on the executive com-mittee, which is responsible for the direction and growth of PRC, and she manages the offices of internal and external com-munications, human relations, and congressional affairs. With respect to the diversity initiative, more important than any of these responsibilities is her presence as a role model for others in the business.

The changes at PRC go beyond the hiring of a talented woman for a top-level position. Real change means changing traditional business processes and practices that have uninten-tionally excluded a significant portion of the workforce. It has been said that the only significant competitive advantage left in business today is the talent and dedication of a company's employees. This is PRC's primary strength as a provider of sci-entific and technology-based systems and services.

Several years ago, PRC adopted total quality management (TQM) as its way of doing business. The principles of TQM—which include customer satisfaction, management by fact, re-spect for people, and continuous improvement—require a fact-based approach to the issue of diversity. The foundation for change was a cultural diversity assessment completed in De-cember 1992. With that in hand, change has accelerated.

PRC has placed an emphasis on diversity recruiting sources, including mandatory use of a search firm dedicated to providing diverse candidate slates to fill senior management openings. PRC has also developed a program that will provide up to twelve scholarships a year for promising minority stu-dents. The scholarships will be introduced in a staggered man-ner, with three offered the first year to college seniors, six offered the second year, nine the third year, and then twelve each year beyond that. This will be the start of PRC's strategic alliances with minority colleges and universities.

In 1994, PRC joined with INROADS, a minority student

intern program, to provide a four-year program for students throughout their college years. This program will ultimately provide PRC with a systematic process for developing a reservoir of talent for future needs as the company creates community partnerships.

PRC has actively implemented many other effective programs and policies to address diversity. Diversity awareness and sexual harassment prevention workshops are part of each manager's development. Valuing diversity is being included as a key performance assessment factor for all PRC employees. All employees annually review and sign a code of conduct, which includes standards for interpersonal communications, employee development, and creating an environment free from discrimination and harassment.

The compensation plan has been revised to clearly pay for performance, both team and individual. Team performance is measured by financial measures. Individual performance is measured equally by both what has been accomplished and how an employee has demonstrated PRC's values as measured by a 360 degree performance assessment. As part of the 360-degree assessment, employees rate themselves and are rated by their supervisor, coworkers, and subordinates. They receive feedback on their own performance based on these ratings. After an initial confidential feedback session for development purposes, the information is used to determine both pay and promotion opportunities.

The organizational improvements will make a difference as PRC competes for scarce talent in the years to come. Future plans include expanding the role and scope of the existing diversity councils, establishing a formal mentoring program, and improving the promotion system and succession planning.

Inclusion and the resulting benefits may prove to be PRC's single best strategic initiative to grow the value of the business.

Conclusion

The experiences of Hewlett-Packard, BDM, and PRC indicate the level of success that can be achieved through a thoughtful, comprehensive approach to working with diversity. The case studies demonstrate the appropriateness of customizing the process to meet the unique needs of one's organization, securing support from each layer of management, continually monitoring one's progress and changing direction when appropriate, and remaining committed for the long term.

The next section of the book, Part 3: Tools and Resources, provides readers with a range of assessment tools, outlines for training workshops, and recommended readings that enhance the ability to easily and effectively work with diversity.

Part 3
Tools and Resources

13

Focus Group Guide: Questions to Ask Focus Group Participants

This instrument is used by a focus group facilitator (described in Chapter 7) to guide the discussion within each focus group. The facilitator may ask questions in the order listed or follow the natural flow of the group discussion. It is important that all questions be asked to ensure that the same data are collected across all focus groups. One copy of the instrument should be duplicated for each focus group to be conducted. Before the meeting, the focus group facilitator fills out the top portion of the first page with the demographic information about the group. During the meeting, the facilitator records the responses to each question in the appropriate space in the focus group guide. The completed focus group guide is given to the project coordinator to be used in the analysis stage.

Focus Group Guide

Name of facilitator _____

Phone number _____

Description of the group the facilitator is meeting with (e.g., African-American men, people with disabilities):

_____

_____

_____

_____

Number of people in focus group_____

— — — — — — — — — — — — — — — —

1. Recruitment Practices
   A. What is your perception of current recruitment practices?

2. Entry and Hiring
   A. Do you perceive a difference in the entry level at which members of different ethnic/racial or gender groups are hired? If yes, please explain.

3. Rates of Advancement
    A. What is your perception of how the rate of advancement for men compares to the rate of advancement for women?

    B. Do you perceive a difference in the rate of advancement for people of different groups? If yes, please explain.

4. Role of Training
    A. Are there certain training courses that are essential to success in this organization? If yes, what are they?

    B. Who is eligible to take these courses? How are the participants selected?

5. Role of Assignments
    A. Are you aware of a job posting or vacancy notice system in this organization? If yes, is it readily accessible to you?

B. Are there certain assignments that are crucial to success? If yes, what are they?

C. How are assignments made? (How do you receive assignments?) Objectively, based on a set of known criteria? Subjectively?

D. How often do you think you or others have received a particular assignment for reasons other than your qualifications or experience (e.g., gender, ethnic/racial background, physical capability, or age)? Please explain.

E. How often do you think you or others have been passed over for a particular assignment at least in part because of your/their gender, ethnic/racial background, physical capability, or age?

6. Communication and Feedback
   A. How much useful feedback do you get?

   B. In what ways do you receive this feedback?

7. Performance Appraisal System
   A. Are you aware of any differences in the ways people from different groups are evaluated? Please explain.

8. Model for Success
   A. What do you see as the characteristics most critical to success in this organization?

9. Career Development
   A. How is career development currently conducted with employees in this organization?

B. Who has responsibility for career development?

C. To whom would employees most likely go for guidance in their career?

D. How much does your current supervisor assist you with your career development?

10. Barriers to Advancement/Inclusion
    A. Do you perceive any barriers to inclusion/advancement for women in this organization? If so, what are they?

    B. Do you perceive any barriers to inclusion/advancement for racial/ethnic minorities in this organization?

C. Do you perceive any barriers to inclusion/advancement for people with disabilities in this organization?

D. Do you perceive any barriers to inclusion/advancement because of age in this organization?

E. Do you perceive any barriers to inclusion/advancement for people of different sexual orientation in this organization?

11. Work/Family Issues
   A. In your perception, are there any policies or practices in this organization that are advantageous for people with family responsibilities? Disadvantageous?

   B. What decisions, policies, or practices have you seen the organization make regarding people who have responsibilities for children?

C. What decisions, policies, or practices have you seen the organization make regarding people who have responsibilities for elderly parents?

12. Attrition of Women and Members of Different Ethnic/ Racial Groups
   Do you perceive attrition to be high for any groups (e.g., women, members of ethnic/racial groups, people with disabilities)?

13. Role of Ethnic Characteristics
   Is there a "look" or "image" that helps a person advance at the organization? If yes, describe.

14. Mobility
   A. Is mobility a key to advancement?

   B. Is mobility a hindrance for certain groups? If yes, please explain.

15. Harassment

    A. Have you ever worked in a hostile work environment in this organization? If yes, please explain.

    B. Does harassment of any kind occur in the organization? If yes, please describe.

    C. Are you aware of any action someone in this organization has taken in response to harassment or a hostile work environment? If so, what was it and what were the results?

    D. Has harassment ever affected the career of anyone you know in this organization?
       If yes, how?

E. Has fear of harassment ever inhibited your behavior in any way?

16. Complaint System
    A. If you had a problem in relation to your career or working in the organization, whom would you go to for help?

    B. Do you trust the grievance and EEO system to handle complaints fairly and confidentially?

    C. If you had a complaint, would you use the internal EEO system to file it?

    D. If circumstances warranted, would you file a complaint externally or seek external assistance?

17. Multicultural Issues
    [*These questions are to be asked of all groups except white men. When facilitating a group of white men, proceed to Question 18.*]
    A. In your perception, what could be the effect of focusing on diversity issues?

    B. What feelings or concerns do you have about focusing on diversity issues?

    C. What feelings or concerns do you perceive other groups have about focusing on diversity issues?

    D. What is your readiness to address diversity issues?

    E. What do you perceive to be the readiness of the organization to address diversity?

18. Multicultural Issues

   [*These questions are to be asked of groups of white men.*]

   A. In your perception, what is the effect of focusing on diversity issues?

   B. How do you feel about the attention being given to women, members of different ethnic/racial groups, and people with disabilities?

   C. How do you and other white men handle your feelings and concerns about diversity?

   D. Have you observed white male backlash? If so, please explain.

E. How do you handle white male backlash?

19. Employer of Choice
    A. If you knew women, members of different ethnic/racial groups, or people with disabilities who were qualified and interested in an upper-management position, would you recommend this organization to them?

    B. Is the organization an employer of choice (a place where all people can fully contribute)? If yes, why? If no, why not?

20. Costs/Benefits
    A. In your perception, what are the potential costs and benefits of focusing on diversity? To you? To the organization?

21. Recommendations
    A. What recommendations do you have for improving the
       organization with respect to diversity?

14

Interview Guide:
Questions for Senior Managers

This instrument is used by interviewers (described in Chapter 7) as a guide to conducting interviews with senior managers. The interviewer may ask the questions in the order listed or follow the natural flow of the conversation. It is important that all questions be asked to ensure that the same data are collected across all interviews. One copy of the instrument should be duplicated for each interview to be conducted. Before the meeting, the interviewer fills out the top of the first page with the demographic information about the interviewee. During the meeting, the interviewer records the responses to each question in the appropriate space in the interview guide. The completed interview guide is given to the project coordinator to be used in the analysis stage.

Interview Guide

Name of interviewer _____

Name of person interviewed _____

Phone number of person interviewed _____

Description (gender, race, disability, job title, grade level, etc.) of person interviewed:

_____

_____

— — — — — — — — — — — — — — —

When you think about your career as a manager, certain events or episodes probably stand out in your mind, things that shaped your career as a professional. We want to discuss these items with you. Our purpose is to understand the profile of success within this organization, based on people's individual careers.

Please review these questions in preparation for our interview with you.

1. What are the qualities, skills, strengths, and characteristics critical for your success? Is knowledge of official guidelines for promotion, assignment, and training processes important? Did you have that knowledge?

2. What was your first managerial job? What did you learn from it?

3. Please describe the person who taught you the most during your career. What did that person do that made him/her so special? How did this relationship start? Do you consider this person a mentor/coach? If not, have you ever had a mentor/coach?

4. Have you ever been a mentor/coach to anyone? If so, to whom (race, gender, job function, grade level, age)?

5. What was your first important assignment? How was it obtained? What were subsequent important assignments? How were they obtained?

6. What training courses did you take? Were they important? Why?

7. How did you first become visible to people at higher levels in the organization? How did you benefit from this visibility?

8. What barriers did you face in your career path? How did you overcome them?

9. How did advancement into the senior management ranks affect the way you were seen or treated?

10. Did you ever do anything that put your advancement at risk (i.e., a mistake, an unsupported decision, etc.)? How did you recover from it?

11. Were you ever burned out and very frustrated and then managed to restart? How?

12. To what degree did your performance evaluations influence your career advancement? What influence did other feedback and evaluation have, if any?

13. Once you were considered a viable candidate for a high-level job, did you get any special attention, such as special assignments, challenges, or working for a powerful and visible boss?

14. What kinds of personal sacrifices have you had to make to get where you are today?

15. Have your career decisions been affected by the fact that you could be a role model for others who follow in your footsteps? How?

16. What has this organization done to help you succeed? Is there something the organization could have done but didn't?

17. Did the organization provide you with an opportunity to demonstrate all of your capabilities?

18. In this organization, do you think there is a difference in the rate of advancement for men, women, and members of different ethnic/racial groups? If so, to what do you attribute these differences?

19. In your perception, is there a consistent "fatal flaw" that causes high-potential employees not to make it into senior management? What derails women, members of different ethnic/racial groups, white men, and people with disabilities?

20. Do you think there is a glass ceiling in this company? If so, at what level does it exist?

21. Do you believe there are some positions that are more likely to produce senior management personnel than others? Which ones and why?

22. Does harassment of any kind (sexual, racial, etc.) affect careers in this organization?

23. Are there ways this work environment could appear hostile to any individuals or groups? If yes, please explain.

24. Do you know of any instances where people in this company failed to advance because of some type of discrimination?

25. What advice would you give to a younger manager about succeeding in this organization?

26. From your perspective, what would this organization be like if it were fully inclusive and supportive of all types of diversity? What would be different than it is now?

27. Do you have any additional comments you would like to make in regard to your own career or the career of others in this organization?

15

Diversity Assessment Survey

The diversity assessment survey is designed to collect data anonymously from employees at all levels of the organization. Guidelines about selecting employees to complete the survey and administering the survey are described in Chapter 7.

In order to tailor the survey to your organization, the task force can review and modify the questions and response options as appropriate. At a minimum, most organizations review the survey to determine if the terminology is appropriate for their organization.

Instructions

- This survey addresses barriers that may be affecting your career. It asks for your perceptions about your own career, rather than your perceptions about career advancement in general. Your responses will be completely confidential. We will examine the data only in the aggregate so we will not be able to identify any individuals separately. Thank you very much for taking the time to complete this questionnaire completely and thoughtfully.
- If you are using an opscan form, please mark your answers on the separate response form provided. Darken the bubble completely and avoid stray marks on the response form. Use a No. 2 pencil only. If you make a mistake or wish to change an answer, erase your old mark completely.
- There are 143 questions on the questionnaire. It should take you no more than one hour to complete it.

- Please answer *every question* on the survey. For some questions you may need to select "not applicable" or "I don't know."
- Please complete the survey within three working days and return both the questionnaire and the response form via courier mail in the enclosed envelope to:

_____

_____

_____

_____

Career Advancement

This section of the questionnaire is designed to obtain information and opinions regarding your advancement in this organization.

Please rate how satisfied you are with each aspect of working in this organization that appears below in items 1 through 25, using the following scale:

(A) Very satisfied
(B) Somewhat satisfied
(C) Neither satisfied nor dissatisfied
(D) Somewhat dissatisfied
(E) Very dissatisfied
(F) Not applicable or don't know

How satisfied are you with:

1. Your organization as a place for someone of your gender to work?
2. Your organization as a place for someone of your race/ethnic background to work?
3. Your organization as a place for someone of your physical capability to work?

   4. Your organization as a place for someone of your age to work?
   5. Your organization as a place for someone of your sexual orientation to work?
   6. Your organization as a place for someone of your gender to develop a career?
   7. Your organization as a place for someone of your race/ethnic background to develop a career?
   8. Your organization as a place for someone of your physical capability to develop a career?
   9. Your organization as a place for someone of your age to develop a career?
  10. Your organization as a place for someone of your sexual orientation to develop a career?
  11. Your ability to discuss work-related matters with your current supervisor?
  12. Your freedom to voice concerns/ideas to your current supervisor?
  13. Your freedom to voice concerns/ideas to management above your current supervisor?
  14. The appreciation you receive from your current supervisor for your contributions?
  15. Organizational policies regarding care for dependents (e.g., staying home with a sick child or taking time off to help an elderly parent)?
  16. Your promotion rate throughout your career?
  17. The amount of control you have over your career?
  18. The way you have been treated throughout your career because of your gender?
  19. The way you have been treated throughout your career because of your race/ethnic background?
  20. The way you have been treated throughout your career because of your physical capability?
  21. The way you have been treated throughout your career because of your age?
  22. The way you have been treated throughout your career because of your sexual orientation?
  23. The classroom training you have received?
  24. Opportunities throughout your career for developmental assignments?

25. The cultural diversity of your immediate work environment, e.g., the mix of people from different racial and ethnic groups?

Please rate how much influence you believe you have over the following aspects of your career that appear below in items 26 through 30, using the following scale:

(A) Total control
(B) High level of influence
(C) Moderate level of influence
(D) Low level of influence
(E) No control
(F) Don't know enough about this item to judge

How much influence do you believe you have over:

26. Your chances for promotion?
27. Your performance evaluation?
28. Your career development?
29. The training you receive?
30. Assignments?

31. Have you read the information in your employee handbook regarding the promotion process?

   (A) No
   (B) Yes, but I don't entirely understand it
   (C) Yes, and I understand it well

32. Are you satisfied with the promotion process described in the employee handbook?

   (A) I haven't read the information in the employee handbook regarding the promotion process
   (B) Yes
   (C) No
   (D) I don't know

There are several factors that may decrease your chances for promotion in this organization or derail your career. Please respond with regard to your own career in this organization and rate the factors that appear below in items 33 through 48, using the following scale:

(A) Does not affect chances for promotion
(B) Hindrance
(C) Barrier
(D) Don't know how factor affects chances for promotion
(E) Factor doesn't apply to me or my situation

If a particular factor does not apply to you as it is written, select choice E. For example, in responding to item 35, if you do work longer hours than normal, select choice E.

What effect has (does) each of the following had (have) on your chances for promotion?

33. Not getting key/developmental assignments?
34. Working part-time?
35. Not working long hours?
36. Not networking?
37. Your appearance?
38. Not having someone helping you and watching out for you?
39. Your level of assertiveness?
40. Your style of communication?
41. Your accent?
42. Taking maternity or paternity leave?
43. Taking a leave to care for dependents?
44. Having family responsibilities?
45. Your gender?
46. Your race/ethnic background?
47. Your physical capability?
48. Your age?
49. Your sexual orientation?
50. If there are any factors that you think have derailed your career in this organization that we have not addressed above, please describe them here.

Items 51 through 59 cover the degree to which the gender, race/ethnic background, physical capability, age, or sexual orientation of your supervisor affects or could affect your comfort level in interacting with him or her. Please use the following scale:

(A) Increases considerably
(B) Increases a little
(C) Neither increases nor decreases
(D) Decreases a little
(E) Decreases considerably
(F) Don't know

How much does it, or would it, affect your comfort level to have a supervisor/manager who is:

51. The same gender as you?
52. A different gender from you?
53. The same race/ethnic background as you?
54. A different race/ethnic background from you?
55. A person with a disability?
56. Younger than you?
57. Older than you?
58. The same sexual orientation as you?
59. A different sexual orientation from you?

Items 60 through 74 cover the degree to which the gender, race/ethnic background, physical capability, age, or sexual orientation of an employee affects or could affect the comfort level of his/her supervisor in interacting with him/her. Please use the following scale for items 59 through 67:

(A) I am not currently a supervisor
(B) Increases considerably
(C) Increases a little
(D) Neither increases nor decreases
(E) Decreases a little
(F) Decreases considerably
(G) Don't know

If you are currently a supervisor, how much does it, or would it, affect your comfort level to supervise someone who is:

60. The same gender as you?
61. A different gender from you?
62. The same race/ethnic background as you?
63. A different race/ethnic background from you?
64. A person with a disability?
65. Younger than you?
66. Older than you?
67. The same sexual orientation as you?
68. A different sexual orientation from you?

Please rate how much you think your career advancement has been affected by stereotypes held by others about the personal characteristics that appear below in items 69 through 73, using the following scale:

(A) Helped a lot
(B) Helped a little
(C) Neither helped nor hindered
(D) Hindered a little
(E) Hindered a lot
(F) Never perceived others to hold stereotypes about it

69. How much do you think your career advancement has been affected by stereotypes held by others about your gender?
70. How much do you think your career advancement has been affected by stereotypes held by others about your race/ethnic background?
71. How much do you think your career advancement has been affected by stereotypes held by others about your physical capability?
72. How much do you think your career advancement has been affected by stereotypes held by others about your age?
73. How much do you think your career advancement has been affected by stereotypes held by others about your sexual orientation?
74. If you think your career advancement has been hindered by stereotypes held by others, please describe those stereotypes here.

Communication and Feedback

The following questions address issues of communication and feedback of all types, although the focus is on supervisor-employee communication and feedback.

"Useful" feedback is both timely and related to specific job behavior. Given this definition, please describe the amount of useful feedback you receive in items 75 through 78, using the following scale:

(A) More than I want
(B) As much as I want
(C) Less than I want

How much useful feedback do you get:

75. From your current supervisor with your performance evaluation?
76. From your current supervisor on an ongoing basis (fairly frequently)?
77. When you voice concerns/ideas to your current supervisor?
78. When you voice concerns/ideas to management above your immediate supervisor?

In answering items 79 through 81, please rate how much support you receive using the following scale:

(A) More than I want
(B) As much as I want
(C) Less than I want

79. How much does your current supervisor assist you with your career development?
80. How much does your current supervisor help you obtain useful training?
81. If you currently have a mentor, e.g., someone who "shows you the ropes" regarding career advancement, how helpful is this person?

Family/Work Issues

This section is concerned with the relationship between work responsibilities and family responsibilities of all kinds.

82. What decisions have you made regarding your career because of your responsibilities for children living with you? (Choose all that apply.)

    (A) Never had children living with me
    (B) None
    (C) Have taken positions that were not advantageous
    (D) Have had breaks in service
    (E) Turned down the opportunity to take an important training course
    (F) Restricted the number of hours I could work
    (G) Other (please explain)

83. In what specific ways have your responsibilities for children living with you caused you to be treated differently in this organization? (Choose all that apply.)

    (A) Never had children living with me
    (B) None
    (C) Slowed my advancement as a result of conflicting demands on my time
    (D) Not given choice assignments
    (E) Been excluded from meetings scheduled at inconvenient times (e.g., before 9:00 A.M.)
    (F) Other (please explain)

84. In what specific ways have your responsibilities for elderly parents affected your career? (Choose all that apply.)

    (A) Never had to care for elderly parents
    (B) None
    (C) Slowed my advancement as a result of taking positions that were not advantageous
    (D) Slowed my advancement as a result of breaks in service

(E) Slowed my advancement as a result of conflicting demands on my time

(F) Made me more efficient at work

(G) Other (please explain)

85. In general, how have your responsibilities for children or elderly parents affected your career advancement in this organization?

(A) Helped a lot

(B) Helped a little

(C) Neither helped nor hindered

(D) Hindered a little

(E) Hindered a lot

(F) Never had children or elderly parents needing care

86. If you think there are policies at any level of this organization that are disadvantageous for people with family responsibilities, please describe them here.

_____

_____

87. If you would like to see policies implemented that would be more advantageous for people with family responsibilities, please describe them here.

_____

_____

Assignments

The following questions address your perceptions of the assignment process. In this case, an assignment is defined as a supervisory position, overseas or domestic; rotation to another department or to another office within your current department; rotation to another division; or a post on a task force or special project within your current office.

88. Are you aware of the vacancy notice system in this organization?

(A) I have never heard of it

(B) I have heard of it but I'm not sure what it is

(C) I know a little about it
(D) I know all about it

There are several factors that may increase your chances for receiving an assignment in this organization. Please use the following scale to rate the factors below in items 89 through 93:

(A) Necessary
(B) Helpful
(C) Does not affect chances
(D) Don't know

What effect does each of the following have on your chances for receiving an assignment?

89. Good job performance?
90. Perceived as having high potential?
91. Your career development needs?
92. Politics?
93. Developing networks?

Please rate how often you think the assignment process has been affected by the factors that appear below in items 94 through 104, using the following scale:

(A) Often
(B) Sometimes
(C) Rarely
(D) Never

94. How often have you received assignments that you thought were important for your career development?
95. How often do you think you have received a particular assignment at least in part because of your gender?
96. How often do you think you have been passed over for a particular assignment at least in part because of your gender?
97. How often do you think you have received a particular assignment at least in part because of your race/ethnic background?

98. How often do you think you have been passed over for a particular assignment at least in part because of your race/ethnic background?
99. How often do you think you have received a particular assignment at least in part because of your physical capability?
100. How often do you think you have been passed over for a particular assignment at least in part because of your physical capability?
101. How often do you think you have received a particular assignment at least in part because of your age?
102. How often do you think you have been passed over for a particular assignment at least in part because of your age?
103. How often do you think you have received a particular assignment at least in part because of your sexual orientation?
104. How often do you think you have been passed over for a particular assignment at least in part because of your sexual orientation?

Training Courses

The following questions ask your opinions about the process used for selecting people for training.

There are several factors that may affect your chances for being selected for a training course in this organization. Please use the following scale to rate the factors below in items 105 through 108:

(A) Necessary
(B) Helpful
(C) Does not affect chances
(D) Don't know

What effect does each of the following have on your chances for being selected for a training course?

105. Good job performance?
106. Perceived as having high potential?
107. Your career development needs?
108. Politics?

Please rate how you think the process for selecting people for training has been affected by the factors that appear below in items 108 through 118, using the following scale:

(A) Often
(B) Sometimes
(C) Rarely
(D) Never

109. How often have you taken training courses that you thought were important for your career development?
110. How often do you think you have been selected for a particular training course at least in part because of your gender?
111. How often do you think you have not been selected for a particular training course at least in part because of your gender?
112. How often do you think you have been selected for a particular training course at least in part because of your race/ethnic background?
113. How often do you think you have not been selected for a particular training course at least in part because of your race/ethnic background?
114. How often do you think you have been selected for a particular training course at least in part because of your physical capability?
115. How often do you think you have not been selected for a particular training course at least in part because of your physical capability?
116. How often do you think you have been selected for a particular training course at least in part because of your age?
117. How often do you think you have not been selected for a particular training course at least in part because of your age?

118. How often do you think you have been selected for a particular training course at least in part because of your sexual orientation?
119. How often do you think you have not been selected for a particular training course at least in part because of your sexual orientation?

Education

The following questions cover your educational background.

120. What is the highest level of education you have completed?

   (A) Elementary or junior high school
   (B) High school diploma or equivalent
   (C) Certificate from accredited institute or equivalent
   (D) Associate's degree or equivalent
   (E) Bachelor's degree or equivalent
   (F) Master's degree or equivalent
   (G) Doctoral or professional degree

121. Do you have more than one of any particular advanced degree?

   (A) No
   (B) Yes, two or more master's degrees
   (C) Yes, two or more doctoral or professional degrees

122. What subject(s) is (are) your degree(s) in?

   _____

123. How much do you think your educational level has affected your career advancement in this organization?

   (A) Helped a lot
   (B) Helped a little
   (C) Neither helped nor hindered
   (D) Hindered a little
   (E) Hindered a lot

124. How much do you think the subject area(s) in which you have earned degrees has affected your career advancement in this organization?

    (A) Helped a lot
    (B) Helped a little
    (C) Neither helped nor hindered
    (D) Hindered a little
    (E) Hindered a lot

Sexual Harassment and Related Issues

The following questions address issues of harassment and other forms of a hostile work environment, which are sometimes related to career progress. Sexual harassment is usually defined as deliberate, unwelcome, and repeated unsolicited verbal comments, gestures, or physical contact of a sexual nature. Harassment also includes working in an intimidating work environment caused by insensitive posters on the walls and overheard discussions that include derogatory or demeaning sexual references, and can involve the extreme act of sexual or physical assault. We are interested here in harassment only, not in discrimination (characterized as limited advancement opportunity based on race, sex, age, or national origin).

125. Have you ever been sexually harassed in this organization? (Choose all that apply.)

    (A) No
    (B) Yes, disparaging remarks or jokes
    (C) Yes, pressure for dates
    (D) Yes, deliberate touching
    (E) Yes, pressure for sexual favors
    (F) Yes, letters and/or telephone calls
    (G) Yes, physical assault

126. Has the sexual harassment affected your career and work performance? (Choose all that apply.)

    (A) I have never been sexually harassed
    (B) No effect on career or work performance

(C) Yes, I transferred to another office
(D) Yes, it made me feel too uncomfortable in my work environment to contribute and/or compete fully
(E) Yes, I was assigned to projects that were not career-enhancing
(F) Yes, I received a promotion, a good assignment, or other preferential treatment
(G) Yes, in some way not described above (please explain) _____

127. Have you ever harassed someone at work, possibly without even realizing it at the time?

(A) I definitely have not
(B) I don't think I have
(C) I don't know
(D) I may have
(E) I definitely have

128. Have you ever worked in a hostile work environment? (Choose all that apply.)

(A) No
(B) Yes, there were insensitive or derogatory jokes, remarks, or discussions
(C) Yes, there were inappropriate posters (or similar items)
(D) Yes, in some way not described above (please explain) _____

129. What action did you take in response to harassment or a hostile work environment? (Choose all that apply.)

(A) I have never been harassed or bothered by my work environment
(B) I made a complaint to my EEO officer
(C) I made a complaint to the EEO office

(D) I did nothing about it for fear of my career being hurt

(E) I did nothing about it because I thought that it would not help

(F) I did nothing about it because it did not bother me that much

Personal Information

The following information is necessary for analyzing the data by groups. No information will be released that could be used to identify any specific individual's responses, either directly or by inference.

130. Are you a staff or contract employee?

(A) Staff
(B) Contract

131. How long have you worked for this organization?

(A) Less than one year
(B) At least one year but less than three years
(C) At least three years but less than six years
(D) At least six years but less than ten years
(E) At least ten years but less than fifteen years
(F) At least fifteen years but less than twenty years
(G) Twenty years or longer

132. How long have you worked in this department?

(A) Less than one year
(B) At least one year but less than three years
(C) At least three years but less than six years
(D) At least six years but less than ten years
(E) At least ten years but less than fifteen years
(F) At least fifteen years but less than twenty years
(G) Twenty years or longer

133. What is your pay grade? Level? _____

134. Do you currently work full-time or part-time?

(A) Full-time
(B) Part-time

135. During your years with this organization, how often have you worked full-time as opposed to part-time?

(A) Always full-time
(B) Mostly full-time
(C) Mostly part-time
(D) Always part-time
(E) Other: _____

136. Which of the following best describes your job?

(A) Secretary/clerical
(B) Administrative support
(C) Supervisor/manager
(D) Facilities maintenance
(E) Labor/trades
(F) Transportation
(G) Other: _____

137. Do you have supervisory/management responsibilities?

(A) No
(B) Yes, at the first-line supervisory level
(C) Yes, at the first-line management level
(D) Yes, at the departmental level
(E) Yes, at or above the division level

138. What is your current marital status?

(A) Never been married
(B) Separated/divorced and not remarried
(C) Widowed and not remarried
(D) Married/Remarried

Items 139 through 141 cover your age. For example, if you are 25, mark the B box of item 139, the E box of item 140, and the E box of item 141.

139. Age Decade

    (A) 10
    (B) 20
    (C) 30
    (D) 40
    (E) 50
    (F) 60
    (G) 70

140. Second Digit of Age

    (A) 1
    (B) 2
    (C) 3
    (D) 4
    (E) 5
    (F) None of the above

141. Second Digit of Age

    (A) 6
    (B) 7
    (C) 8
    (D) 9
    (E) None of the above

142. What is your gender?

    (A) Male
    (B) Female

143. What is your race/ethnic background?

    (A) Native American
    (B) Asian American
    (C) Latino/Latina

(D) African American
(E) White
(F) Other: _____

144. Are you a person with a disability?

(A) Yes
(B) No

If there is anything else concerning career opportunity in this organization that is not covered by the survey, please describe it here.

Thank you very much for your help.

16

Outlines for
Training Workshops

The next section includes outlines for training workshops that promote working with diversity. These are suggestions of possible ways for organizations to address diversity through training. Each outline includes a general statement about the program, and the objectives, key topics, suggested audience, and suggested length.

The section is organized in five categories, which are broken down as follows:

I. Foundation Courses
- Facilitating Organizational Change
- Building a Diverse Workforce
- Prejudice and Conflict: Distant Cousins or Close Relatives?
- Valuing Diversity
- People with Disabilities: Our Untapped Resource
- Eliminating Sexual Harassment in the Workplace

II. Management and Supervisory Development
- Developing Your People
- Supervising in a Diverse Workplace
- Managing Men and Women
- Advanced Interview Techniques
- Job Descriptions: The Key to Legal Management of Employees
- Introduction to Task Force Management

III. Professional and Career Development
- Career Development
- Mentoring in a Diverse Workplace
- Strategies for Breaking the Glass Ceiling
- Image and Personal Power
- Personal/Professional Balance

IV. Professional Development for Women
- Women in the 1990s: Competition, Leadership, and Integrity
- Career Strategies for Women
  — Module I: Generations and Transitions—A Historical Perspective
  — Module II: Stages of Feminine Identity
  — Module III: Understanding and Appreciating Gender Differences
  — Module IV: Women as Leaders
  — Module V: Challenges to Women as Team Members
  — Module VI: Negotiating Differences
  — Module VII: The Internal and External Barriers to Women's Career Success
  — Module VIII: Political Awareness within Organizations
  — Module IX: Working with Integrity
  — Module X: Mentors—Finding One, Being One
  — Module XI: Networking
  — Module XII: Building Support Systems/Personal Nourishment

V. Interpersonal Effectiveness
- Building Intercultural Skills
- Building Cross-Gender Communication
- Conflict at a Crossroads: Resolving Conflict in a Diverse Environment

I. Foundation Courses

Facilitating Organizational Change

Program

Change is the number-one issue facing organizations today. Technological change, structural change, changes in management styles, and changes in personnel (downsizing, rightsizing, etc.) are common experiences in organizations and educational institutions across the country. Employees and managers alike are challenged to become agents of change. The purpose of this program is to provide change agents with skills to build the foundation for fluid change within an organization.

Objectives

- Explore ways to foster a positive climate for change.
- Learn to prepare the organization for upcoming change.
- Develop skills to initiate as well as effectively respond to change.
- Learn to recognize and respond to signs of resistance to facilitate change.
- Learn ways to acknowledge successful transitions.

Key Topics

- Understanding the dynamics of organizational change.
- The role of leadership in the change process.
- Celebrating change performance.

Suggested Audience

Managers and employees who are experiencing or managing the organizational change process.

Suggested Length

One day.

Building a Diverse Workforce

Program

This program enables an organization to remove barriers that prevent the inclusion of people from diverse groups. It focuses on developing an environment where no one sex, race, or culture has an advantage or disadvantage.

Objectives

- Examine current and projected demographic realities and the implications for labor, productivity, and profits.
- Identify the written and unwritten rules in the organization that prevent the inclusion and advancement of women and minorities.
- Develop recruitment strategies that facilitate the hiring of qualified minority and female employees.
- Help people become aware of the ways they discriminate against, judge, or isolate people who work for them or who apply for employment.
- Establish a personal action plan for full utilization within the organization's workforce.

Key Topics

- Workforce 2000.
- The benefit of working with diversity.
- How employees, managers, and the organization can promote diversity.
- The winning formula: Inclusion + Participation = Contribution

Suggested Audience

Supervisors, managers, and team leaders.

Suggested Length

Two days.

Prejudice and Conflict: Distant Cousins or Close Relatives?

Program

In many ways the organization is an extension of the larger society where prejudice is pervasive. Yet most of us do not want to be prejudiced nor do we know what to do when confronted with someone else's prejudice. This workshop will help you determine how much prejudice is causing conflict within your organization and what to do about it.

Objectives

- Identify personal prejudices and misinformation.
- Learn to recognize when prejudice is causing conflict.
- Develop strategies for resolving prejudice-based conflicts.
- Determine ways to create an organization that appreciates differences.

Key Topics

- Roots of prejudice; roots of pluralism.
- Prejudice and its role in causing conflict.
- Conflict within the team context.
- Interrupting prejudice: Constructive strategies for handling and preventing prejudice-based conflict.
- Communications skills necessary for positive conflict management.
- A welcome mat for all people: Building trust across cultures.

- Institutionalizing peace: The organizational role in causing or preventing prejudice-based conflict.

Suggested Audience

Managers, staff, intact work groups.

Suggested Length

Two to three days.

Valuing Diversity

Program

This workshop is designed to build awareness of the myriad ways in which people in organizations are diverse, and to increase appreciation of the value in this diversity. Participants broaden their definition of diversity by exploring cultural groups with whom they identify and examining the impact of stereotyping and discrimination on individuals and organizations.

Emphasis is placed upon building collaborative relationships as well as creating alliances and support between people in the workplace. This workshop will benefit employees and managers at all levels of the organization.

Objectives

- Expand awareness of the various categories of diversity.
- Heighten awareness of our own assumptions and feelings about difference.
- Build appreciation for all differences, especially race and gender.
- Begin to more effectively communicate cross-culturally.
- Gain insight into the organizational need for affirming and valuing a diverse workforce.

Key Topics

- Defining diversity.
- The impact of stereotyping.
- Raising diversity awareness.
- Celebrating and understanding differences.
- Alliance and community building.

Suggested Audience

All managers, supervisors, and employees.

Suggested Length

One to three days.

People with Disabilities: Our Untapped Resource

Program

This workshop is designed to develop awareness and sensitivity in participants by focusing on the skills and capabilities of people with disabilities.

Objectives

- Understand key points of the Americans with Disabilities Act (ADA).
- Recognize the importance of removing barriers that prevent Americans with disabilities from participating fully in the social and economic mainstream of our society.
- Explore attitudes and beliefs about people with disabilities that interfere with hiring and/or effectively managing these individuals.
- Identify ways to create a work environment that encourages full participation and opportunities for success.
- Learn specific skills related to interviewing, supervising, and evaluating the performance of people with disabilities.

- Reduce concerns about costs and complexities of reasonable accommodations.

Key Topics

- Facts, important definitions, and demographic information about people with disabilities.
- The experience of people within the organization who have disabilities.
- Myths and facts about people with disabilities.
- Removing obstacles to greater accessibility.
- Disability etiquette.
- Making your organization user-friendly for all potential workers.
- Interviewing and supervising tips and cautions.
- Employer programs and resources.
- Personal and organizational action plan.

Suggested Audience

All employees.

Suggested Length

One to two days.

Eliminating Sexual Harassment in the Workplace

Program

The purpose of this workshop is to give employees the tools to deal effectively with incidences of sexual harassment and to promote a harassment-free work environment.

Objectives

- Increase understanding of the parameters of sexual harassment and the legal implications under Title VII of the 1964 Civil Rights Act, as amended.

- Explore the impact of sexual harassment on the individual and on the organization.
- Clarify organizational policy and procedures for handling sexual harassment complaints.
- Delineate managerial responsibility to ensure that the policies and procedures are implemented in an effective and responsive manner.
- Increase understanding of how managers should respond to sexual harassment complaints.
- Identify proactive strategies for individuals who feel they have been harassed and for managers attempting to prevent sexual harassment.
- Recommend action steps to facilitate creating a sexual harassment–free work environment where employees feel free to express their concerns.

Key Topics

- Definition of sexual harassment.
- The legal imperative.
- Causes of sexual harassment.
- Coping with the "gray areas."
- Case studies: Is it sexual harassment? How should it be handled?
- The complaint procedure.
- Strategies for prevention or resolution.

Suggested Audience

All employees.

Suggested Length

One to two days.

II. Management and Supervisory Development

Developing Your People

Program

The purpose of this program is to help managers better facilitate the career development of their employees.

Objectives

- Construct a framework for facilitating the career development of employees.
- Identify other possible career directions and moves for employees in addition to up the career ladder.
- Explore the complexities of career development for a diverse workforce.
- Identify and select specific career empowering roles to play with diverse employees.
- Learn to facilitate a career discussion.
- Generate solutions to specific employee development problems.

Key Topics

- Career anchors and motivators: What drives your employees?
- Expanding career options: "Up" is not the only option.
- Empowering your employees.
- Job enrichment: Job loading and job enrichment strategies.
- Guidelines to managing a successful career discussion.

Suggested Audience

Managers and supervisors.

Suggested Length

Two days.

Supervising in a Diverse Workplace

Program

The challenge of the supervisory role is to function effectively in the areas of planning, organizing, directing, and controlling. This program is for newly appointed supervisors, individuals who have supervisory duties (team leaders, project leaders, etc.), workers who are preparing for promotion to the supervisory role, and supervisors who want to reexamine the role of supervision from the viewpoint of managing diversity.

Objectives

- Learn the steps involved in making the transition to first-line supervisor.
- Identify basic methods of planning, organizing, directing, and controlling work.
- Strategize methods to confront and prevent bias in the workplace.
- Explore the different styles of communication: informing, exploring, convincing, cooperating, controlling, complying, and coercing.
- Understand the nature of leading across cultures.
- Formulate guidelines for deciding what and when to delegate.
- Identify real and perceived challenges of giving corrective feedback to employees in a diverse environment and learn strategies to overcome those challenges.
- Prevent and manage conflicts effectively and efficiently.

Key Topics

- The transition from employee to supervisor.
- The supervisory role in working with and capitalizing on diversity.
- The task of representing both subordinates and upper management.
- Encouraging multicultural understanding.
- Communications styles and processes and leadership behaviors.

- Guidelines for delegating.
- Preventing misunderstanding by communicating clearly and giving ongoing feedback.

Suggested Audience

Supervisors, team leaders, and people considering becoming supervisors.

Suggested Length

Two to four days.

Managing Men and Women

Program

This workshop is designed to explore issues and develop strategies that will help leaders better manage and utilize gender differences on work teams. The workshop goes beyond a theoretical understanding of multicultural management and focuses specifically on facilitating gender differences in daily interactions.

Objectives

- Increase awareness of the differences between men and women.
- Learn how to capitalize on the strengths of each.
- Develop strategies to facilitate cross-gender understanding and communication.
- Facilitate greater cross-gender teamwork.
- Learn strategies to manage conflicts that arise because of gender differences.

Key Topics

- Historical context for gender issues in today's organization.

- Organizational issues and concerns of the 1990s regarding culture and gender dynamics.
- Managing work teams of men and women.
- Working with differences in the following areas: motivation, leadership, communication, conflict management, decision making, and giving and receiving feedback.

Suggested Audience

Managers and supervisors who want to better understand and facilitate gender issues.

Suggested Length

One to two days.

Advanced Interview Techniques

Program

Interviewing effectively is an art that must be practiced in order for supervisors and managers to be thoroughly skilled at getting high-quality legal information about an applicant, while at the same time ensuring that the applicant is left with a positive impression of the organization. This program is for supervisors and managers who are involved in interviewing, selecting, checking references, and/or hiring employees and who need a hands-on opportunity to brush up on their interview skills.

Objectives

- Explore the various types of selection interviews and when to use them effectively.
- Learn how to prepare and conduct a legal and effective interview.
- Increase awareness sensitivity to people of diverse groups.
- Learn to recognize and prevent bias in the interviewing process.

- Practice a variety of interview techniques in role-playing cases that are similar to interview situations that will be faced on the job.
- Identify individual interviewing strengths and weaknesses.
- Develop new, effective interview techniques while meeting the complex legal requirements of today's world.

Key Topics

- The key steps in effective and legal interviewing.
- Culture bias and cultural sensitivity.
- Questions you can and cannot ask.
- Practice, practice, practice! Opportunities to role-play in "real" interview situations and receive feedback on techniques, questions asked, and individual interview style.

Suggested Audience

Managers and supervisors responsible for hiring workers.

Suggested Length

One day.

Job Descriptions: The Key to Legal Management of Employees

Program

Starting with the Americans with Disabilities Act (ADA) of 1990, the job description has now become the single most important key to managing employees legally and effectively. This program is for supervisors and managers who have any responsibility in hiring, counseling, giving performance appraisals, dealing with employee problems, or disciplining employees.

Objective

- Understand the importance and multiple uses of a job description in legally managing your employees.
- Learn how to ensure that your job descriptions are accurate and valid.
- Identify how to use job descriptions and performance measures in hiring, counseling, giving performance appraisals, and dealing with employee discipline.
- Develop strategies for using job descriptions to enhance productivity and build teamwork.

Key Topics

- Why are job descriptions now so important to a supervisor/manager from both a legal and a management point of view?
- Tips for ensuring legal, valid, accurate, up-to-date job descriptions with workable performance measures.
- Using job descriptions to hire, counsel, appraise performance, discipline, and improve group performance and teamwork.

Suggested Audience

Managers and supervisors.

Suggested Length

One half-day to one day.

Introduction to Task Force Management

Program

Leading or serving on a task force is a responsibility that falls on managers and staff in organizations. Often, the task force flounders because the task force members and charge-givers are unaware of the necessary steps to get the job done effectively. What is required for effective task force management is an understanding of the key facilitation skills, roles, and group techniques that will drive the task force to accomplish its charge.

Objectives

- Define what a task force is and what it isn't.
- Identify key task force roles and responsibilities.
- Explore stages of group dynamics as they relate to the task force.
- Learn effective strategies and techniques for task force leadership.
- Understand the components and steps necessary to successful task completion.

Key Topics

- The goals of the task force.
- Development and presentation of the product.
- Overview of the task force process.
- Key task force roles: leader, task force member, facilitator, recorder, and support staff.

Suggested Audience

Any employee who intends to serve on or lead a task force.

Suggested Length

One day.

III. Professional and Career Development

Career Development

Program

This workshop helps participants explore their individual values, skills, and goals as well as their options in order to formulate the steps of a career plan. Participants complete selected self-assessment tools, written planning exercises, and role play interviews and participate in small-group problem solving.

Objectives

- Develop self-insight in order to manage career choices and moves.
- Formulate a framework for thinking about career satisfaction.
- Identify other definitions of success beyond upward mobility.
- Create ways to enrich current career positions.
- Take the next step in developing a career plan.
- Organize and practice career discussions.

Key Topics

- Creating a work lifeline.
- Prioritizing the values that drive and motivate your career.
- Enrichment: Possible directions a career can move.
- Wishcraft: Changing wishes to realities.
- Dispelling the myth of luck and choosing proactive behavior.
- Clarifying a career plan.
- Guidelines to a successful career discussion.

Suggested Audience

Employees, supervisors, and managers.

Suggested Length

One to two days.

Mentoring in a Diverse Workplace

Program

The purpose of this workshop is to enable employees to better offer and receive career development support from one another. The workshop serves to help employees redefine mentoring, coaching, sponsoring, and networking in an organizational climate where advancement is slower and where working with diversity is emphasized.

Objectives

- Explore the nature and characteristics of developmental relationships.
- Define networking and mentoring as different kinds of career-building help.
- Describe the range of functions provided in a mentoring relationship.
- Identify responsibilities in building a mutually enhancing relationship.
- Clarify the complexities of cross-gender and cross-cultural mentoring.
- Identify potential pitfalls in a developmental relationship and how to avoid them.

Note: The workshop is greatly enhanced by a panel of four employees who will share their insights into developmental relationships from their experience as mentors and mentees.

Key Topics

- Traditional versus new mentoring.
- The keys to empowerment.
- The benefits of mentoring.
- What do you have to give and receive?
- What to look for in a mentor or mentee.
- Initiating, maintaining, and terminating the relationship.
- The limits of mentoring.
- Strategies to handle cross-gender and cross-cultural mentoring.

Suggested Audience

Any employee interested in giving or receiving career development support.

Suggested Length

One half-day to one day.

Strategies for Breaking the Glass Ceiling

Program

This workshop is designed to help women, minorities, and people with disabilities explore the most critical issues affecting their career success in the 1990s. The focus will be on defining the glass ceiling and its effect on organizational and individual performance. Barriers to career advancement, job satisfaction, and full productivity will be identified. The goal is to equip women, minorities, and people with disabilities with the necessary awareness and skills to determine a future course of career action consistent with personal goals and organizational expectations.

Objectives

- Define the glass ceiling and outline invisible barriers to career success.
- Identify the five specific barriers that impede the advancement of women and minorities in organizations.
- Understand how these barriers apply to women and individuals from different minority groups.
- Explore strategies to increase organizational awareness of the invisible barriers and ways to eliminate them.
- Learn specific skills and techniques to overcome these barriers.

Key Topics

- Workforce 2000 and its impact on the glass ceiling.
- Five significant invisible barriers: assignments, lack of feedback and communication, stereotyping, adverse work environment, and work/family policies.
- Strategies for breaking the glass ceiling.

- Understanding the culture and politics of the organization.
- Gathering opportunity and advancement information.
- Opportunities for visibility.
- Negotiating tough interpersonal situations that create a hostile work environment.
- Clarifying values and priorities.

Suggested Audience

Women, minorities, people with disabilities, and all people interested in empowering people to break the glass ceiling.

Suggested Length

One to two days.

Image and Personal Power

Program

This seminar enables participants to enhance the image they project to others by communicating with confidence and personal power. The focus on specific self-projection techniques and concrete interpersonal skills helps participants to increase their professional impact, influence, and visibility.

Objectives

- Project a stronger image with coworkers, superiors, and customers.
- Use verbal and nonverbal techniques to effectively communicate your ideas.
- Build and project confidence.
- Handle criticism (both fair and unfair).
- Maintain self-control in difficult situations.
- Increase visibility and credibility, especially in groups and meetings.

Key Topics

- Essential elements of personal power.
- Credibility builders versus credibility robbers.
- Impression management through nonverbal effectiveness.
- Your personal style (strengths and weaknesses).
- Winning support and cooperation for your ideas.
- Three kinds of criticism and how to handle each.
- How to keep confrontations from flaring up.

Suggested Audience

All employees.

Suggested Length

One day.

Personal/Professional Balance

Program

The purpose of this workshop is to help individuals learn the skills of balancing their personal and professional lives by learning to balance their internal and external experience. Participants will learn specific how-to techniques to reduce the internal and external conflict and stress of their multicommitted lives.

Objectives

- Understand the four stages of burnout.
- Clarify the values that drive your career and personal life.
- Identify your own personal style and its strengths and weaknesses in coping with multiple demands.
- Examine needs for perfectionism and "superhuman" behavior.
- Align priorities with high payoffs.

- Learn how to set limits and say no.
- Develop strategies to create and maintain balance in your life.

Key Topics

- The dimensions of stress for the multicommitted worker.
- The cost of the superperson syndrome.
- How integrity and values shape the quality of one's life.
- Living our multiple commitments or being lived by them.
- The holistic guide to a balanced lifestyle.
- Four steps to setting limits and saying no.
- Individual, organizational, and societal responsibility in preventing the superperson syndrome.

Suggested Audience

If you are a partner in a dual career marriage, a working parent (or are deciding to be one), or anyone struggling to balance individual, family, and career goals, you would benefit greatly from this workshop.

Suggested Length

One to two days.

IV. Professional Development for Women

Women in the 1990s: Competition, Leadership, and Integrity

Program

This workshop is designed to help women explore the most critical issues and answers affecting women's career success in the 1990s. The goal is to equip women with the necessary awareness and skills to determine a future course of career action that is consistent with personal values, strengths, and ambitions. The uniqueness of this workshop is its focus on the most current issues for women as well as its commitment to strike a balance between tough skills necessary for success and the need for integrity and support.

Objectives

- Define hurdles facing women in the 1990s.
- Identify feminine leadership differences.
- Broaden the range of leadership behaviors.
- Align knowledge, values, and action.
- Formulate guidelines for empowering strategies women can offer each other.

Key Topics

- Organizational issues and challenges.
- Feminine leadership.
- Competitive power versus collaborative power.
- Working with integrity.
- Women-to-women empowerment and support.

Suggested Audience

Women at all levels.

Suggested Length

One to two days.

Career Strategies for Women

Program Overview

The attached series of twelve modules is designed to help women explore critical issues and develop skills central to career success in today's workplace.

Objectives

- Develop awareness of the link between individual aspirations and organizational goals.
- Heighten gender awareness and identify specific differences based on male and female perceptions as they affect the work environment.
- Explore how gender differences relate to organizational needs, managerial theory, and cross-gender communication.
- Recognize internal and external barriers to women's career development and ways to overcome them.
- Develop strategies and skills to determine a future course of career action consistent with personal values, strengths, and ambitions.

Suggested Audience

Women at different levels in the organization, depending upon the module.

Suggested Length

One half-day to three days. The entire series of modules composes a three-day program. However, individual modules may be selected as stand-alone offerings or in combination with other modules to form shorter programs. The modules build on one another but also stand alone so that participants may attend as many modules as they like. The benefits of this approach are the flexibility it allows, the time to digest and apply the information, and the minimum disruption to a workweek.

Module I: Generations and Transitions—A Historical Perspective

Purpose To track the impact of the last few decades on women in the workplace and how one's own transition greatly affects self-perception and the perception of others.

Exercise Participants are grouped according to age: women in their twenties, thirties, forties, fifties, and sixties. Members of each age group are asked to recall their developmental years by answering the question: "What experiences and messages influenced your professional self-image and expectations?" Each age group records participant responses and reports to the whole group.

Learning Points

- The last few decades have had a changing impact on women.
- Women have different perceptions unique to their background and age and also share common experiences.

Module II: Stages of Feminine Identity

Purpose To heighten awareness of the developmental process any nondominant group goes through to acquire a sense of its own identity.

Minilecture Four stages of feminine identity: acceptance, resistance, redefinition, and incorporation.

Exercise In small groups, participants will discuss the following questions:

- What are the critical incidents that have occurred in your life that have enhanced or inhibited your developmental process through these four stages?
- What stage are you currently in?
- What are the determining factors that impact your future development?
- What are the effects of women's relationships with one another based on these four stages?

Learning Points

- Women have experienced these stages of acceptance, resistance, redefinition, and incorporation.
- The stages are not absolute but are revisited at different times in a woman's life.
- Each stage provides challenges to learn that move us into the next stage.

- How a woman experiences her own feminine identity defines how she works with others to affect organizational change, how she performs on teams, and how she mentors other women.

Module III: Understanding and Appreciating Gender Differences

Purpose In this module, participants explore the newest research on gender differences and how these differences play out in everyday work situations. The focus is on fostering cross-gender appreciation and understanding the unique qualities men and women bring to the workplace. Participants gain a new perspective on the behavior of each gender and insights into the value of each. Specifically highlighted will be gender differences in communication, decision making, problem solving, and team behavior.

Exercise The facilitator will lead the discussion of gender diversity focusing on: the world of play of boys and girls, communications and decision-making styles of men and women, and male and female cultural models for teamwork (based on the work of Deborah Tannen). Participants are encouraged to share their personal experiences and insights.

Learning Points

- Men and women are socialized very differently in our culture.
- The feminine style has been undervalued and underutilized in most organizations.
- Both masculine and feminine styles are necessary to success and add value to accomplishing organizational goals.

Module IV: Women as Leaders

Purpose To highlight differences in the ways men and women lead.

Exercise Participants will form small groups and generate examples of case situations where they have noted differences in the ways men and women lead. In addition, they will describe the characteristics of an effective leader, regardless of gender. Small groups will report back to the large group. The facilitator will guide the large-group discussion.

Learning Points

- Leadership style has an impact on and implications for women's organizational effectiveness.
- To be effective leaders, one must balance between male/ female leadership styles.

Module V: Challenges to Women as Team Members

Purpose To develop strategies to successfully contribute and be fully included on mixed gender teams.

Exercise Participants in small groups will be asked to discuss and generate a list of what they perceive to be the greatest challenges to women in their efforts to be fully contributing and effective team members. Each group will report back to the large group, and the facilitator will highlight the common themes that emerge.

Each small group will then design a case study featuring one of the major challenges identified and pass the case to another small group to analyze, problem-solve, and generate strategies. Each group will report on their strategies for confronting the challenging situation. The facilitator will conduct a group discussion to deepen understanding and underscore significant strategies helpful to women as team members.

Learning Points

- Women often experience unique challenges to their inclusion on a team.
- Those challenges are frequently recognized by women but not always clearly seen by men.
- Challenges can include: having contributions ignored, being interrupted, having ideas attributed to someone

else, being stereotyped to play support roles, having leadership challenged, finding it difficult to claim "airtime," and being reluctant to assert ideas, preferences, disagreements, etc.
- Women can identify supportive strategies when given the opportunity to problem-solve together.

Module VI: Negotiating Differences

Purpose To identify and explore one's natural negotiating style and learn alternative methods of negotiating.

Minilecture The Integrative Negotiation Model recognizes and supports the notion that women are natural negotiators and that insight into their own negotiating style will enhance their interaction with coworkers, supervisors, and subordinates. The negotiating styles that will be examined include: dominating/defeat, collaborating, compromising, avoiding/withdrawing, and accommodating.

By revisiting the workshop section on gender differences, participants will see that men and women may have certain tendencies in negotiating. Furthermore, the most effective negotiating approach is likely to integrate the strengths of both the male and female model.

Exercise In triads, participants will assess their negotiating style as it relates to the Integrative Negotiating Model and role play a challenging interpersonal situation. Each partner will describe a situation in which she has had (or will have) to utilize negotiation skills. Participants will use a personal situation as the basis for a role-play with a partner. Group members will coach each other on applying the concepts taught to strengthen one's negotiating behaviors and approach.

Learning Points

- Each person is likely to have a preferred style of negotiating that has its own strengths and weaknesses.
- Identifying needed behavior changes and practicing those changes can prepare you for real-life negotiations.

Module VII: The Internal and External Barriers to Women's Career Success

Purpose To explore the subtle barriers to their own career success that women sometimes create and the barriers to women's career success that are imposed by the external environment.

Minilecture Five internal barriers to success: waiting, dependence on positive feedback, vulnerability to criticism, reluctance to take risks, and distorted definition of competence. Five external barriers to success: stereotyping, fear of taking a risk on women, lack of commitment to development strategies, promoting according to comfort and conformity, and lack of support for work/family balance.

Exercise In small groups, participants will discuss:

- How have you experienced the internal barriers to women's success?
- What have you learned about internal barriers?
- How have you experienced the impact of external barriers?
- What have you learned about strategies to minimize the impact of external barriers?

Groups will report out learnings, and the facilitator will highlight important strategies.

Learning Points

- Many women have real experience with internal and external barriers to career success.
- Women can share creative and successful ways to overcome barriers.

Module VIII: Political Awareness within Organizations

Purpose To clarify the effect of politics and power on people within organizations and to increase political savvy.

Minilecture The exercise is introduced with a brief lecture regarding the relationship between politics and power that operates in every organization.

Exercise Participants will independently complete a questionnaire to assess the political environment of their workplace. In small groups, participants will share their responses and insights regarding their individual experiences in this political environment. This is followed by a report to the large group.

Learning Points

- The political environment impacts individuals' effectiveness within that organization.
- An organization's political environment can be described and understood by identifying certain key factors.
- There are costs and benefits to any organization's politics.

Exercise Participants will return to small groups and generate strategies and techniques for utilizing political savvy to their benefit. Small groups will again report back to the large group.

Learning Points

- Power within an organization can be enhanced by utilizing political astuteness.
- Political astuteness stems from an understanding of the political environment.

Module IX: Working with Integrity

Purpose To explore the power of integrity and acting in alignment with one's values.

Minilecture and Discussion This exercise is introduced with a short lecture and discussion regarding having the courage to act in accordance with one's knowledge and values.

Exercise First alone and then in small groups, participants will address the following questions:

- From whom did you learn that living with integrity matters?
- What does integrity mean to you?
- Describe a recent experience/situation that challenged your integrity.

Small groups will report their insights to the large group.

Learning Points

- Integrity is present when values and actions are aligned.
- Courageous action is required when one's integrity is challenged.

Module X: Mentors—Finding One, Being One

Purpose To clarify the functions and benefits of mentoring, the responsibilities of mentors and those they instruct in building and maintaining a relationship, how to find a mentor, and the challenges of cross-gender mentoring.

Minilecture and Discussion This discussion provides information on how to find a mentor, the functions of a mentor, traditional versus new mentoring, and the roles and responsibilities of mentors and those they instruct. Special emphasis will be placed on the challenges of cross-gender mentoring and what to do about them.

Learning Points

- Mentors can provide a variety of ways that are helpful to career success.
- Mentoring has become more episodic and empowerment-focused rather than long-term and advancement-focused.
- There are specific steps that can be taken to find a mentor.

- Mentors and those they set examples for have different responsibilities to seeing that the relationship succeeds.
- Cross-gender mentoring presents unique benefits as well as unique challenges to be overcome.

Module XI: Networking

Purpose To recognize the importance of networking as an opportunity to find resources for career growth and satisfaction.

Minilecture The one-minute résumé exercise (described in the next paragraph) is introduced with a brief lecture on how to develop networking skills. It emphasizes how to create and support developmental relationships to meet a variety of career needs.

Exercise One-minute résumé: Participants will learn to network effectively by creating a one-minute résumé to communicate clearly and concisely to others about their skills and needs. Participants will practice using their résumé with each other to gain understanding of how networking works as a process of mutual exchange.

Learning Points

- Effective networking is a skill that can be developed.
- Clarity of one's personal talents and strengths as well as one's needs is required.
- Most group gatherings can provide valuable opportunities to gain new information, to make contacts, and to practice the principle of mutual exchange.

Module XII: Building Support Systems/Personal Nourishment

Purpose Assess how the participants nourish themselves mentally, emotionally, physically, socially, and spiritually, and determine ways to better handle the demands of a multifaceted personal and professional life.

Exercise Participants will complete a self-assessment profile of their current position on the Personal Nourishment
Model. Participants will determine where they want to be
based on a set of guided questions designed to facilitate growth
and self-exploration in this area.

Learning Points

- Individuals must nourish their personal development to
  achieve balance between their personal and professional lives.

V. Interpersonal Effectiveness

Building Intercultural Skills

Program

This workshop is designed to raise awareness and heighten
sensitivity that will enable participants to function produc-
tively in a multicultural environment.

Objectives

- Examine mainstream American cultural assumptions
  and values.
- Examine selected other cultures' assumptions and values (including nonmainstream American).
- Develop sensitivity to significant differences and similarities.
- Learn strategies for intercultural communication and interaction.

Key Topics

- Communicating across cultures.
- Culture bias and cultural self-awareness.
- The role of cultural assumptions and values.
- Culture shock and cultural adaptation.

- Values and the workplace.
- Motivating the multicultural workforce.
- Problem solving and team building across cultures.

Suggested Audience

Employees who travel or conduct business with customers outside the United States.

Suggested Length

One day.

Building Cross-Gender Communication

Program

From as early as preschool years, men and women are raised in cultures that emphasize different sets of values and skills. In adults, those differences result in ways of working, relating, and communicating that are not usually fully understood or appreciated by the other gender. This workshop aims at exploring gender differences and how they play out in everyday work situations. The program focuses on fostering cross-gender appreciation and an understanding of the unique qualities men and women bring to the workplace as a result of their socialization. Participants can expect to gain a new perspective on the behavior of the opposite sex and insights into improving everyday interaction between men and women.

Objectives

- Increase understanding of gender differences to help view them as strengths.
- Develop methods and tools to help manage the tensions inherent in gender relations.
- Develop strategies to foster inclusion and enhance cross-gender collaboration.
- Practice a model for cross-gender communication in the workplace.

Key Topics

- The impact of a changing workplace on both men and women.
- Gender differences in leadership, communication, decision making, and team behavior.
- Giving and receiving feedback.
- Recurring tensions in male/female work relations and what to do about them.
- Looking at the world through the eyes of the other gender.
- Factors facilitating cross-gender collaboration.
- Strategies to eliminate the gender communications gap.

Suggested Audience

Managers, staff, intact work groups.

Suggested Length

One to three days.

Conflict at a Crossroads: Resolving Conflict in a Diverse Environment

Program

Do all people handle conflict the same way? What do you do when cultures collide? This workshop will cover key elements as a means of understanding the role culture plays in constructively resolving conflicts.

Objectives

- Understand your own conflict style and how it may be different from that of others.
- Explore how culture influences conflict resolution.

- Develop strategies for resolving conflict in diverse work environments.
- Determine your organization's conflict "personality."

Key Topics

- The roots of conflict.
- Different ways of handling conflict.
- Culture clash or fit: The role of culture in managing conflicts constructively.
- Attitudes and skills necessary for building trust.
- My way or no way: Biases and assumptions.
- Beyond Band-Aids: Preventive strategies for managing conflict.
- Erecting bridges: Team building across cultures.
- The organizational conflict culture, or understanding "the way things are done around here."

Suggested Audience

Managers, staff, intact work groups.

Suggested Length

One to three days.

Selected Bibliography

Publications

Anderson, Margaret L., and Patricia Hill Collins. *Race, Class and Gender: An Anthology.* Belmont, Calif.: Wadsworth, 1992.

Block, Peter. *Flawless Consulting: A Guide to Getting Your Expertise Used.* San Diego: University Associates, 1981.

Byham, William C., and Jeff Cox. *Zapp! The Lightning of Empowerment: How to Improve Quality, Productivity, and Employee Satisfaction.* New York: Harmony, 1988.

Carew, Irene. "Women's Emerging Identity and Implications for Leadership Management." Paper delivered at the University of Massachusetts, Amherst, Mass., 1984.

Carney, Clarke, and Sarah McMahon, eds. *Exploring Contemporary Male/Female Roles: A Facilitator's Guide.* San Diego: University Association, 1977.

Cross, William. *Shades of Black: Diversity in African American Identity.* Philadelphia: Temple University Press, 1992.

Elgin, Suzette Haden. *Genderspeak: Men, Women, and the Gentle Art of Verbal Self-Defense.* New York: Wiley, 1993.

Faludi, Susan. *Backlash: The Undeclared War Against American Women.* New York: Crown, 1991.

Farley, Christopher John. "The Art of Diversity." *Time,* Fall 1993, 20–24.

Fernandez, John P., and Mary Barr. *The Diversity Advantage: How American Business Can Out-Perform Japanese and European Companies in the Global Marketplace.* New York: Lexington, 1993.

Filipczak, Bob. "Is It Getting Chilly in Here?" *Training,* February 1994, 25–30.

Galer, Michele, and Ann Therese Palmer. "White, Male and Worried." *Business Week,* January 31, 1994, 50–55.

Gilligan, Carol. *In a Different Voice: Psychological Theory and*

Women's Development. Cambridge, Mass.: Harvard University Press, 1982.

Gutek, Barbara. *Sex and the Workplace.* San Francisco: Jossey-Bass, 1985.

Hacker, Andrew. *Two Nations: Black and White, Separate, Hostile, Unequal.* New York: Ballantine, 1992.

Hardiman, Rita. "White Identity Development Theory." Paper delivered at the University of Massachusetts, Amherst, Mass., 1982.

Helgesen, Sally. *The Female Advantage: Women's Ways of Leadership.* New York: Doubleday, 1991.

Jackson, Bailey W. "Black Identity Development." Paper delivered at the University of Massachusetts, Amherst, Mass., 1982.

Johnston, William B., and Arnold H. Packer. *Workforce 2000: Work and Workers for the Twenty-First Century.* Indianapolis: Hudson Institute, 1987.

Katz, Judith H. *White Awareness: Handbook for Anti-Racism Training.* Norman, Okla.: University of Oklahoma Press, 1978.

Kim, Jean. "Process of Asian American Identity Development: A Study of Japanese American Women's Perceptions of Their Struggle to Achieve Positive Identities as Americans of Asian Ancestry." Paper delivered at the University of Massachusetts, Amherst, Mass., 1981.

Kram, Kathy E. *Mentoring at Work: Developmental Relationships in Organizational Life.* Lanham, Md.: University Press of America, 1988.

Lakoff, Robin. *Language and Women's Place.* New York: Harper Colophon, 1975.

Lewin, Kurt. *Field Theory in Social Science: Selected Theoretical Papers.* Edited by D. Cartwright. New York: Harper & Row, 1951.

Loden, Marilyn. *Feminine Leadership or How to Succeed in Business Without Being One of the Boys.* New York: Times Books, 1985.

Mior, Anne, and David Jessel. *Brain Sex: The Real Difference Between Men & Women.* New York: Dell, 1989.

Morrison, Ann M., et al. *Breaking the Glass Ceiling: Can Women Reach the Top of America's Largest Corporations?* Reading, Mass.: Addison-Wesley, 1987.

Murray, Margo, and Marna A. Owen. *Beyond the Myths and*

Magic of Mentoring: How to Facilitate an Effective Mentoring Program. San Francisco: Jossey-Bass, 1991.

National Capital Area Chapter, American Society for Public Administration. *Breaking Through the Glass Ceiling: A Career Guide for Women in Government.* Washington, D.C.: American Society for Public Administration, 1992.

Schwartz, Felice N. *Breaking with Tradition: Women and Work, The New Facts of Life.* New York: Warner, 1992.

Storti, Craig. *The Art of Crossing Cultures.* Yarmouth, Maine: Intercultural Press, 1990.

Tannen, Deborah. *You Just Don't Understand: Women and Men in Conversation.* New York: Morrow, 1990.

Tatum, Beverly Daniel. "Talking About Race: The Application of Racial Identity Development Theory in the Classroom." *Harvard Educational Review* 62 (Spring 1992): 1–24.

Terkel, Studs. *Race: How Blacks & Whites Think & Feel About the American Obsession.* New York: New Press, 1992.

Thomas, R. Roosevelt, Jr. *Beyond Race and Gender: Unleashing the Power of Your Total Work Force by Managing Diversity.* New York: AMACOM, 1991.

Vogt, Judith F., and Kenneth L. Murrell. *Empowerment in Organizations: How to Spark Exceptional Performance.* San Diego: University Associates, 1990.

Weaver, Gary, ed. *Readings in Cross-Cultural Communication.* 2d ed. Heights, Mass.: Ginn, 1987.

Weisbord, Marvin R. *Productive Workplaces: Organizing and Managing for Dignity, Meaning, and Community.* San Francisco: Jossey-Bass, 1990.

Audiotapes

Stevens, Robert Tennyson. *Imagination Activation.* Asheville, N.C. Audiocassette series.

Stevens, Robert Tennyson. *Outcome Facilitation.* Asheville, N.C. Audiocassette series.

Index

HF 5549.5
. M5 L43
1995

1 AKY 6632   4/24/95   Hill

MFM